starts slow gets really good !

FIELD NOTES
ON THE
COMPASSIONATE
LIFE

FIELD NOTES ON THE COMPASSIONATE LIFE

A SEARCH FOR THE SOUL OF KINDNESS

MARC IAN BARASCH

"Love Sonnet XVII" by Pablo Neruda, used with permission from University of
Texas Press, from *100 Love Sonnets/Cien Sonetos De Amor*, reissue edition,
June 1, 1986 (Texas Pan American Series), translated by Stephen Tapscott.
All rights reserved.

"Cry Out in Your Weakness" by Mohammad Jelaluddin Rumi, used with permission
from Maypop Books, from *Jelaluddin Rumi in Mathnawi II*, first edition, February
1, 1990, translated by Coleman Barks. All rights reserved.

Book design by Carol Angstadt

Library of Congress Cataloging-in-Publication Data

Barasch, Marc.
    Field notes on the compassionate life : a search for the soul of kindness / Marc
Ian Barasch.
        p.   cm.
    Includes bibliographical references and index.
    ISBN-13 978–1–57954–711–0 hardcover
    ISBN-10 1–57954–711–7 hardcover
    1. Conduct of life.   2. Compassion.   3. Kindness.   4. Happiness.   I. Title.
BJ1531.B27   2005
177'.7—dc22   2004029376

Distributed to the trade by Holtzbrinck Publishers

2   4   6   8   10   9   7   5   3   1   hardcover

To the Givers

The heart sees, the heart hears, the heart speaks,

the heart walks, the heart falls, the heart rejoices,

the heart cries out, the heart comforts, the heart suffers,

the heart surrenders, the heart errs, the heart trembles,

the heart awakens...

—*The Midrash*

CONTENTS

ACKNOWLEDGMENTS

A book like this, on a subject like this, can only be the product of many helping hands and steadfast hearts. To thank them properly would take an epoch. Still, I must try:

Richard Pine, the compleat agent, understood immediately why the project would be a good thing and, thank God, stayed with it. Rodale's Tami Booth took a heroically hands-off approach, giving me the latitude to discover my subject's vast treasures. My editor, Mariska van Aalst, figured out just how to read between the lines, displaying natural talents as a muleteer. Annie Gottlieb provided gentle, cogent critique and made sparks fly with hammer-and-tong smithing on moonless nights. Dana McDowell, intrepid research assistant, showed a supernal diligence in helping me find things I didn't know I was looking for. Claudia Robinson helped me stockpile the extensive library that proved vital to the task.

Ginny Jordan's early belief and unswerving, demonstrable faith in this book were its genesis and exodus. Neva Newman, tried-and-true, thick-and-thin companion—though lifetimes, I'm certain—took one look at a certain shapeless mess (the book; the author) and dove right in.

Hector Black, Harold Mintz, Steve Aman, Pete Dobrovitz, Aimee Morgana, and Joseph Sebarenzi welcomed me into their homes, opening their lives with unstinting honesty. They were among the many who offered me their stories, holding nothing back, asking nothing in return. I wish I could have included them all.

There were those who shared with me the bounty of their life's work: Courtney Cowart of Nine-Twelve; Bill Fields of the University of Georgia's Language Research Lab; Doug Vakoch of SETI; Dean Radin of IONS; Doc Childre and Rollin McCraty of HeartMath; Linda Silverman of the Gifted Development Center; Fleet Maull of the Zen

Peacemaker Order; Toni Henderson of the British Columbia Transplant Society; Melodye Feldman of Seeking Common Ground; Robin Casarjian of the Lionheart Foundation; Frans de Waal of Yerkes Primate Center; Susan Hepburn of the University of Colorado Health Sciences Center; and many others who provided me with generous access and crucial insights.

Most essential were those who gave friendship new meaning (actually, its oldest one, selfless affection): Michele Correy, whose deep caring was never in doubt. Maryse Elias, whose doting friendship more than once kept this vessel from capsizing in high seas. The Buckley family, who taught me about "making relatives," and gave me warm shelter from the storm. John and Margo Steiner, who were never less than all there. Tano Maida, ever available to share his lucid Tea Mind and infallible sense of direction. Jill Satterfield, who provided unflagging good cheer and a sun-drenched perch in New York. Lynne and Bill Twist, who offered their unassuming friendship and the insight that those who set out to save the world can belt out show tunes *and* be incontestably effective.

And my family: Leah, who has for every day of her life brought me more joy; her mother, Latha, who showed up for some truly timely interventions; my brother, Doug, who was stalwart, kind, and true; my parents, who taught me how love is infinitely renewed.

There were those who were bearers of special gifts: Mark Gerzon, Sharon Salzberg, and Rabbi Zalman Schachter gave me crucial early encouragement. Angeles Arrien, Georgia Kelley, and David and Lila Tresemer provided the means to attend a pivotal conference that helped set this work on its course. Dr. Mark Renneker offered the sustenance of his kindness and his craft, along with instructions in how to surf absolutely anything. Dr. Keith Block and Dr. Jeremy Geffen urged me to just get on with it. Robin Temple, who kept healing front and center. Jamie Pendell gave me lessons in *metta* forever engraved within. Donna Zerner furnished advice and counsel. Larry Laszlo looked at me, as he looks at life, through a compassionate lens. Nyoman and his family in Ubud, Bali allowed me to work on my galleys in paradise. Khenpo Tsultrim Gyamtso pulled me out of tailspin with eight words of pith-instruction ("Scared mind comes from nowhere, and goes nowhere"). Chogyam Trungpa, Rinpoche wound me up (not too tight) and placed me squarely on the path.

Then there were those who showed me their love at times when I couldn't see why they'd bother. This book would not exist—nor could I—without the Givers in my life. You know who you are; you have my heart.

PREFACE

I am thankful that thorns have roses.
—*Alphonse Karr*

E very now and then, I'll meet an escapee; someone who has broken free of self-centeredness and lit out for the territory of compassion. You've met them, too, those people who seem to emit a steady stream of, for want of a better word, love-vibes. As soon as you come within range, you feel embraced, accepted for who you are. For those of us who suspect that you rarely get something for nothing, such geniality can be discomfiting: *They don't even know me. It's just generic cornflakes.* But it feels so good to be around them. They stand there, radiating photons of goodwill, and despite yourself you beam back, and the world, in a twinkling, changes.

I appreciate these compassion-mongers, even marvel at them. I rarely think that I could *be* like them. Sure, I've tried to live a benign life, putting my shoulder to the wheel for peace, justice, and Mother Earth (mostly churning out words on a page, bouncing signals off the satellites). I doubt that it's made me much less egotistical (maybe a bit more so). I still have that too-cool objectivity that can suck away my sympathies like an outgoing tide.

But I want to be good. Not that cramped, chiding Moral Majority good (I'll keep my minority status, thanks). Not sticky-sweet, watch-your-insulin-level good. Just deep-down, unfailingly kind. The fact that I'm not, when the world could use so much more kindness, frankly vexes my spirit.

Oh, I'm a nice enough guy. Like most people, I adore my offspring, even when they drive me crazy; love my parents, despite the corkscrew of childhood; dote on my siblings (though there *is* that scrapbook of old slights); treasure my friends (even if they sometimes let me down). Conventional wisdom wouldn't fault me for saving the

1

best stuff for my nearest and dearest and giving the rest of humanity the leftovers.

Thus it is, say the sages, that the harvest of kindness—of kindredness—is winnowed down to a precious few grains. For at the center of all spiritual traditions is the beacon of a truly radical proposal: Open your heart to everybody. *Every*body.

Is this even possible? These days, I feel a pressing need to try. I began writing this book in a hard season, a fall that felt like the Fall from grace itself. The airwaves were saturated with saber-rattling, and soon enough, the lockstep march to war. I was living alone, mostly content, but sometimes, in what Brits call the hour of the black dog, a little desolately. There were times I'd find myself replaying old phone messages to reassure myself love wasn't just a fond illusion. A free-floating angst had crept in the back door, sniffed around the premises, and liking the amenities, decided to settle in.

I wasn't the only one playing host. A surprising number of friends were feeling similarly bereft. All that paranoia, circulating through the troposphere, a taste of ashes on the wind; each of us a little skittish, teeth set on edge. Compassion seemed in short supply, while the politicians publicly mouthing the word only debased its currency. It felt urgent, in a world turned colder, to find a life more centered in the heart.

But how? What *is* compassion, that x-factor that every faith (the founders, if not the followers) exalts as a supreme virtue? When the Dalai Lama says, "My only religion is kindness," and the Pope calls for a "civilization of love," it can't be just mealy-mouthed piety. Kindness and love are powers unto themselves, able to transmute even the most relentless enmity. Nelson Mandela once remarked he befriended his jailers, those grim, khaki-clad overseers of his decades of hard labor in a limestone quarry, by "exploiting their good qualities." Asked if he believed all people were kind at their core, he responded, "There is no doubt whatsoever, provided you are able to arouse their inherent goodness." If that sounds like wishful thinking, well, he actually *did* it.

*N*ot that he, or anyone in their right mind, would claim it was easy. Compassion isn't simply opening a spigot and coating everything in a treacly, all-purpose goo. It requires a gut hunch that whatever I do unto others, I do unto myself. It calls for appreciating not only what comforts us, but what pierces us. (Compassion comes from the Latin *cum patior*, "to suffer with," while apathy—literally, "not to suffer"—connotes a heart benumbed). It's why the sweetest people are often those who have been most wounded by life. They know what it feels like and almost can't help but care.

Still, even among those in the caring professions, I've seen a creed posted on office doors and bulletin boards:

> **People are unreasonable, illogical, and self-centered.**
> **Love them anyway.**
> **If you do good, people will accuse you of selfish, ulterior motives.**
> **Do good anyway.**
> **The kindness you show today will be forgotten tomorrow.**
> **Be kind anyway.**

Why bother? Sure, it's better to reach out than to turn a blind eye. And yes, if you're trying to get to heaven, it's probably the route with the fewest traffic delays. But there's another reason: A compassionate life is more fulfilling. If happy people can be believed—not my-fabulous-life-is-going-great happy, or new-age-Happy-Face happy, but those who emanate true contentment—it's only when the ego bows

3

out that the curtain rises on real life. That it's more blessed to give than to receive is not just a moral nostrum, they say, but a prescription for authentic joy.

*D*id I really believe that? I'm ever on guard against disillusion; I don't want to be shocked if even my better angels turn out to have size twelve clay feet. When a South Asian *tsunami* snuffed out uncounted lives, the world responded with a great torrent of charity. But we still live on a planet where thirty thousand kids starve each day while we obsess over our calories. We go to work in the morning with every good intention even as our diligence stokes an iron giant that is grinding up the earth. There are days compassion seems as notional as a dusting of powdered sugar on a devil's food cake.

The world has long been divided among those who think human beings are essentially kindly creatures who only need love to flourish and those who say we're fundamentally selfish. Though I usually vote the love column, there are times, browsing the morning paper, I feel I'm reading dispatches from some anti-matter universe that could annihilate on contact all belief in human virtue.

This book began as an experiment, an investigation; as some attempt to persuade myself once and for all. I wanted to know what it takes to overcome that I-me-mine I'm convinced ruins everything; to sweeten my tongue, change my jealous mind, think of other people first, just to see what happens. Spiritual teachers throughout history have insisted we each possess the requisite piece of equipment: one standard-issue human heart. It is not, they say, a case of being born with the right disposition, but of cultivating, like diligent, sweat-stained gardeners, the kernel of benevolence that is our birthright.

I want to believe it, God knows, but I had to inspect the thing from top to bottom. I longed to break bread with the saints (or with some reasonable facsimile). But I also needed to sit down with a man of violence because once, in a bitter argument with my ex-wife, I pounded the wall and was appalled to see I'd put my fist through plaster. Compassion is easy enough in a vacuum; but what happens when what's hardest to bear is right up in your face?

My strategy was somewhat Jesuitical: to develop that persuasion of mind that paves the way for a conviction of the heart. I found myself being convinced—maybe more than I'd expected—by examples and exemplars; by theology and neurobiology; by my own forays into the deep (and sometimes dark) backcountry of human kindness. Conviction crept up on me, almost without me noticing. It went from a nice fairy tale, a just-so story, to what-if, to maybe so, to a tentative but persistent yes. I felt, after a while, I'd been given a pair of magic glasses with special lenses that only see the good in people—if I could only remember to put them on.

1

THE CIRCLE OF COMPASSION

If one completes the journey to one's own heart,
one will find oneself in the heart of everyone else.
—*Father Thomas Keating*

When I was in my twenties, my Buddhist teacher tricked me into taking a vow of universal compassion. Using some spiritual sleight-of-hand I've yet to unravel, he made it seem I could aspire to a tender concern for everybody, even putting their welfare before my own.

Fat chance, I'd thought. But in his wily way, he had framed this vow—the *bodhisattva's* promise to live for others—as a case of enlightened self-interest. It was not, he told me, a matter of wearing a one-size-fits-all hair shirt. I was taking the vow for my own good. It would give me some leverage to pry loose, finger by finger, the claustrophobic monkey-grip of ego; give the heart a little breathing room. By treating others generously, I might find them responding in kind. I felt I was being made privy to an ancient secret: *To attain your own human potential, be mindful of everyone else's.*

At some point in my vow ceremony, a deceptively casual affair

7

held in a rocky field, it *had* seemed as if my vision suddenly cleared. I'd glimpsed, like a sky swept clean of clouds, everyone's innate okayness. Years later, I still marveled at the spiritual chutzpah of the liturgy: *However innumerable are beings, I vow to save them all.* It was vintage Buddhist bravado—a pledge to empty all the world's oceans using only an eyedropper. Hardly knowing what I was doing, I'd planted myself in a millenia-old tradition that claims you can love all without preconditions, exclusionary clauses, or bottom lines; that says life isn't *quid pro quo*, but *quid pro bono*.

To my surprise, the vow hadn't made me feel obligated, but liberated from my own suffocating strictures, from the narrowness of my concerns. It was as if I'd been waiting for a signal, a green light to step onto the crosswalk to the opposite curb; some goad to be compassionate not out of blind craving for virtue, but because it seemed the only genuinely interesting thing to do with my life.

Just forming the intention to make myself useful felt salutary, like some fast-acting antivenin to my snakebit business-as-usual. I had assumed life was about magnifying myself (for the greater good, of course), but now that seemed like the wrong end of the telescope: It made everyone else look small. I soon took a job running a residential therapeutic community in exchange for room and board, surprised at my ability to care for the walking wounded. I stopped thinking so much about how others had let me down, broken my heart, failed to anticipate my needs or take my oh-so-unique sensitivities into account. I began striving to see—and even nourish—other people's possibilities, receiving in return those surprise concoctions that the human spirit dishes out when it feels accepted and at its ease.

But there came a point on my journey when I'd stumbled badly and fell far: a dire illness, an interminable recovery, penury, loneliness, full-on despair. Friends clucked in sympathy but stepped gingerly over the body. Family didn't do much better. I had a soul-curdling realization: The people you love (and who ostensibly love you) may not be there when you need them most. I got through it—the kindness of strangers and all—but I was soon back to squinting at people through my cool fisheye, seeing their preening vanity, their intellectual shortfalls, their ethical squishiness. It took time to realize such shortsightedness takes a toll—let alone that there was anything I could do about it.

Finding my way back to meditation helped. Nothing like getting a good, long look at myself (and funny how much I looked like everyone else). I noticed how often my social trade-offs were more about getting than giving; how many of *my* thoughts revolved in geosynchronous orbit around Planet Numero Uno. Inner work is a warts-and-all proposition; it gets harder to kid yourself. Still, my teacher had insisted one thing was certain: Despite seeing all the ego's pitfalls and pratfalls, real *bodhisattva*s make friends with themselves. Everyone, he said, possessed some worth past quantifying or qualifying, some value beyond judgment or fine-tuning—and that included oneself.

To love our neighbor *as ourselves*, after all, is the great injunction of every religion. But what does loving yourself *mean*? It's one thing to say it; another to know it in your bones. Do I talk to the mirror, whispering sweet nothings? tenderly imagine a little homunculus inside and pet it, tickle it, scratch it behind the ears? The spiritual consensus seems to be it's like learning to love anyone: You start by getting to know them. The side-benefit to this, compassionwise, is that to know yourself is also to know the person sitting next to you, and the one halfway around the world. "Read thyself," wrote philosopher Thomas Hobbes. "Whosoever looketh into himself . . . shall know what are the thoughts and passions of all other men."

Still, having looketh'd into myself, I can't say I loveth all I see. I *have* read myself, and there in oversize type it says: petty, suspicious, greedy, vain, jealous, lazy, stingy, dull (and that's just on the page; there's more between the lines). That I also reckon myself to be magnanimous, conscientious, loyal, thrifty, brave, and intermittently humble is beside the point. It's not enough to offset scourging self-judgment with a roll-call of compensatory pluses. We have to take ourselves (and each other) whole. The Dalai Lama points out that the Tibetan term for compassion, *tsewa*, generally means love of others, but "one can have that feeling toward oneself as well. It is a state of mind where you extend how you relate to yourself toward others." If it's true that what goes around comes around, compassion is about nothing if not love's tendency to circulate.

And radiate. Alexander Pope (poet of the "eternal sunshine of the spotless mind") envisioned compassion as a series of concentric circles rippling outward:

> " . . . Self-love but serves the virtuous mind to wake,
> As the small pebble stirs the peaceful lake;
> . . . Friend, parent, neighbor, first it will embrace;
> His country next; and next all human race."

It sounds great. It *is* great. But for many of us, there's a nagging doubt that this whole compassion routine could edge into self-effacement—into loving others *instead* of ourselves, giving away the store until the shelves are bare. The usual formula is first to stockpile some extra self-esteem—*then* you can afford to be generous. That isn't quite how the nineteenth-century religious philosopher Søren Kierkegaard saw it. The command to love thy neighbor, he wrote, had but one purpose: "as with a pick, [to] wrench open the lock of self-love and wrest it away from a person." (He said it approvingly, but . . . oh, great, now compassion will *burglarize* us.) What about looking out for number one? Isn't it prudent to follow that flight attendant's advisory: *First place the mask over your own nose and mouth, tightening the straps to begin the flow of oxygen*? We're of no use to anyone if we're passed out in our seat from hypoxia.

It's a hard balance to strike. If I am not for myself, who will be? But if I am only for myself, what am I? There is a growing sense in our society, left, right, and center, that the balance has woozily tipped; that our obsession with seamless self-contentment ("What I love about Subway is it's all about *me!*") has occluded our ability to love each other. Our cultural default setting has become "get your own needs met." Our psychosocial mean temperature, suggested one recent article, is "people-friendly narcissism." Our therapeutic model focuses so much on strengthening the ego-self that it omits what some dissident psychologists call the self-in-relation. One group of mostly female psychologists has proposed "openness to mutual influence" as a more reliable barometer of mental health than self-esteem.

But self-esteem remains our all-purpose buzzword, a stock phrase in therapists' offices, corporate training modules, even elementary school curricula. This is fine on the face of it: After all, what's the alternative—self-loathing? Psychologist Abraham Maslow coined the term itself in 1940 after observing a monkey colony in a Madison, Wisconsin zoo. He was fascinated by the cockiness of the troupe's dominant alphas and the social benefits they accrued, so reminiscent of socially successful people. His concept of self-esteem had its origin, then, not as simple self-affirmation, but as the alpha's great cry of triumphal self-love: I *Am* Somebody—and You're Not. (Maslow's first stab at terminology was "dominance-feeling.") This self-esteem was more akin to that sense of self that made Sinatra sing how swell it was to be king of the hill.

What Maslow failed to stress was the social dimension. Even in a primate colony—especially so—no ape is an island: Modern primatologists point out that an alpha animal, contrary to its reputation as solitary lord of all it surveys, is thickly enmeshed in a social webbing, dependent on the reciprocities of group life. Maslow's paragon of the "self-actualized" person ("authentic, individuated, productive," with "a surprising amount of detachment from people in general") begins to sound less like a social creature than a self-pollinating flower.

Taking potshots at Maslow may be a little unfair. At a time when psychology was obsessed with what goes wrong in the psyche,

Maslow championed the things that go right. He was an exuberant advocate of human potential when most shrinks spent their fifty-minute hours chronicling pathology. And he did posit that self-actualization would inevitably lead to responsibility for others. But his emphasis on personal growth as the be-all helped spawn a national cottage industry devoted to building a better me, some enhanced self-to-the-tenth-power with its full entitlement of psychospiritual fabulousness. Not such an awful idea, I suppose, but as the song goes, Is that all there is?

I dropped in on a human potential workshop recently. Plenty of talk about self-empowerment and self-realization, self-efficacy and peak performance, but compassion didn't rate a second billing on the marquee. It made me wonder what sort of selfhood we're seeking: the self that "gets its needs met" but is never fufilled? or the self that abundantly gives yet is never emptied? Instead of self-discovery, what about *other*-discovery, our real terra incognita?

I wonder, too (as a pragmatic question, not a moral one), if this pedal-to-the-metal pursuit of happiness really does make us any happier, or if we have the whole thing backwards. "The American way is to first feel good about yourself, and then feel good about others," notes the Benedictine monk Thomas Keating. "But spiritual traditions say it's the other way around—that you develop a sense of goodness by giving of yourself."

I've been an Audrey Hepburn fan since I was a boy with my first major movie-star crush, all the more when I discovered that the adorable, to-die-for gamine of *Breakfast at Tiffany's* was also a great humanitarian. I once came across a lost nugget of her philosophy while waiting in the dentist's office. A fashion magazine had asked her for her beauty tips, and she'd written back:

"For attractive lips, speak words of kindness.
For lovely eyes, seek out the good in people.
For a slim figure, share your food with the hungry.
For poise, walk with the knowledge you never walk alone.
If you ever need a helping hand, you'll find one
at the end of each of your arms."

This homily, a sort of St. Francis Prayer for the Maybelline Set, is a graceful rebuttal to the fetish of self-improvement. Instead of being all about me, it's about us; instead of getting and having, it's about giving and then giving some more. St. Francis himself went beyond mere charity. The son of a rich clothier, he gave up wealth and privilege to dress in rags and hang out with lepers. This was taking kindness to an extreme few of us would find attainable, let alone remotely appealing. But compassion has a certain down-and-dirty quality and a more than casual familiarity with the soul's darker, draftier labyrinths.

At its root meaning of "to suffer with," compassion challenges our tendency to flinch away from life's too-tender parts. I know this much: When I acknowledge my own pain, I am much less squeamish about drawing nearer to yours. I seem to acquire my compassion piecemeal, hurt by hurt. After a bad sprain and time spent on crutches, I became more sympathetic to the locomotion-impaired—the lame and the wheelchair-bound, those who hobbled on canes and walkers.

Perhaps Thomas Aquinas was not so far off when he claimed, "No one becomes compassionate unless he suffers." I take this less as a mandate for medieval masochism than an indecorous call to embrace our own authentic experience. If we're not at home with the depth of our feelings, we're likely to skirt the deep feelings of others. Do we love ourselves/others only when we/they are feeling fine? (Or as a rural proverb has it, "Do you only care about your cow when it's giving you milk?") I've become suspicious of the unblemished life. Maybe the heart must be broken, like a child's prize honeycomb, for the real sweetness to come out. Although something inside us yearns to walk on air, never touching the ground, compassion brings us down to earth. It has been likened to the lotus, whose exquisite, fragrant blossom grows out of the muck and mire.

The Buddha, the jewel in the lotus himself, didn't start out in the mud. He was raised like a hothouse flower, living the cosseted life of a pampered young prince. His royal parents, fearing a prophecy that he would grow up to become a spiritual teacher instead of a king, confined him within high castle walls, surrounded by every luxury in a kind of Hindu 90210. The lame, the sick, and the down-and-out were banished from sight. It wasn't that his parents were afraid their son would be shocked by the sight of suffering (after all, he was to be a battle-hardened feudal monarch), but that he would *respond* to it. They were afraid, in other words, that their son might become compassionate.

One day the prince secretly ventured outside. He stumbled first upon a diseased beggar, then a dead man. The walls that had separated him from the world-as-it-is crumbled. Indeed, the castle might be thought of as a sort of metaphorical ego-structure: Don't we often try to secure happiness by fortifying ourselves against imperfection? When the Buddha proclaimed his First Noble Truth, *dukha* ("dissatisfactoriness"), he was pointing to the dissatisfaction of this ego-driven existence. A traditional image from the Sanskrit is an oxcart wheel that wobbles because its axle is out of kilter: To be self-centered is to be off center from life itself. In the end, the Buddha's enlightenment was to accept everything and everyone as they are; to sit down, as it were, for the full meal, and stop trying to eat around the broccoli.

Though his teachings acquired an aura of detachment in the Western mind (my own included), the image of some solitary quest for higher consciousness misses the point. When I first took my vows and embarked on the Path, I assumed that after X years of diligent meditation, I'd be a wise man with a small secret smile, wafting clear and calm through my own inner space, in some permanent altered state. Lovingkindness would be a spin-off technology from my private moon shot, like Tang or Teflon. But after some time spent trying to attain escape velocity, I noticed that most spiritual teachings regard compassion as the main event—*the* path to enlightenment, the way to slice through self-deception, the means and the motive to relinquish small thoughts for Big Mind. "Spiritual practice is not just about feeling peaceful and happy," a Buddhist lama once told me, "but being willing to give up your own comfort to help someone else. Unless there's some sacrifice for others, it's just meditation by remote control!"

*W*hat *do* we mean by compassion? The word itself is one among many used to describe the profundity of human connection; but it's the only one, I'd submit, which implies kindness without condition. Empathy, for example, refers to our ability to feel and perceive from another's viewpoint. But acutely sensing someone's feelings can also be disturbing (the plight of the "oversensitive"), leading as easily to drawing back as to reaching out. Sympathy is famously tender-hearted, but can also remain at arm's-length (think "sympathy card," or "I sympathize with your concerns, but . . ."). Even when it comes to altruism, the noblest self-sacrifice can be merely parochial, reserved for one's family or the insiders of one's religion or nation, too often at outsiders' expense.

Then, of course, there's the heart's miracle-potion of love. "All, everything that I understand," exclaimed Tolstoy, "I understand only because I love." Love to him was not just romance's quickened pulse, but the plangency of some universal heartbeat—a distinction that, in our eagerness, we often brush right past. We crave love's fierce attachment, its irresistible force of gravity. Next to the possessive throb of desire (*yo quiero* in Spanish means "I love" *and* "I want"), kindness can sound like weak tea indeed (*just a tad to wet the whistle,* ever *so kind of you*). We give lip service to compassion; we give lip-lock to love.

But with great love often comes great exclusivity. In the chivalric love story of Tristan and Isolde, Tristan's heart is said to be "sealed and locked from all the world save her alone." Kierkegaard referred to erotic love as "the very peak of self-esteem, the *I* intoxicated in the *other I* . . . [T]his united *I* selfishly cuts itself off from everyone else." Yet just as self-love can lead either to self-absorption or the discovery of common humanity, so can romantic love spiral inward or blossom out; make us hoarders of private happiness or philanthropists of the heart. To talk of love as a singular phenomenon reflects more the parsimonious limits of language than the complex facts on the ground.

I once fell in love with a beautiful, brilliant young woman who came into my life like Cupid's sledgehammer, right between the eyes. I was like a dazed cartoon character with twittering bluebirds circling my head. Amazingly, she fell in love with me, too, or so it seemed. The only problem was . . . I'd apparently made it all up. As she later explained with remarkable patience, what I'd taken for the romantic real deal was to her just budding friendly affection. When I'd gotten over my embarrassment, I had to laugh. I'd misinterpreted her every gesture, word, and look, seizing on parts to construct a whole picture more to my liking.

This kind of love is a long day's journey from compassion (I certainly hadn't taken *her* feelings into account), or from those emotional commitments I share with those I love and who, thankfully, love me back. But I am amazed, reflecting on it, at the complex palette of emotions that had so vividly painted this non-affair. It wasn't just lust-at-first-sight. I'd felt a profound sense of cherishing toward someone I hardly knew. I'd seen in pristine focus a perfect (and I mean *perfect*) stranger's unique goodness. William Blake's observation, "Love to faults is always blind/Always is to a joy inclined," was on full display. (In one British study, when a person in a brain-scanner was shown a

photo of their beloved, the neocortical regions associated with judgment shut down, going dark as a Broadway theater on a Monday.)

This bestowal of value on another, seeing them in their supernally
best light, is a strong component not only of romance but compassion.
Faced with love's many nuances, the Greeks wisely concocted a whole
spectrum of terms to describe it, from *storge* (tenderness) to *erotike*
(sexual desire) to such fortunate grace notes as *eunoia* (benevolence). Science is bearing out the distinctions. A study of college students in the grip of a hot new romance showed unique activity deep
in the limbic system—activity that differed markedly from the neural
signatures of long-term relationship and friendship. (In other studies,
lust, passion, and long-term attachment have been shown to have differing brain chemistries.)

When I was in the throes of my big crush, I'd also noted a yearning
to care for, to do for—that sense of almost maternal nurturing that
lovers, male and female alike, feel toward each other when they call
each other baby. Indeed, the type of love most often cited as an
analogy for compassion is mother-love itself. The Hebrew word for
compassion, *rachamim*, is the plural of the word for womb. Christianity's most tender image of compassion is the Pieta. Said the
Buddha: "Like a mother who protects her child, her only child, with
her own life, one should cultivate a heart of unlimited love and compassion toward all living beings." Science has recently shown how the
interactions between mother and child—all the soft stroking, gazing,
vocalizations, and nurturance of infancy—become the basis for all
subsequent relatedness. (Says Allan N. Schore of the UCLA School of
Medicine: "[O]ur brains are physically wired to develop in tandem
with another's through emotional communication, beginning before
words are spoken.")

Researchers who study maternal attachment have been zeroing in
on oxytocin, a master hormone in mother-infant bonding. Intriguingly,
oxytocin is also implicated in the experience of falling in love. Released when we touch, it also functions as a sex hormone in both

females and males. (One recent newsletter spotlighting new directions in pharmacology has pegged it as a sure bet for erectile dysfunction.) Oxytocin has even acquired a certain coolness factor. A casual Web surf reveals everything from a Christian marriage site extolling it as proof of the virtues of conjugal cuddling to a sex fetishist site pondering whether a tight-laced corset causes it to be released into the bloodstream.

Does oxytocin make the world go round (or at least lubricate it as it spins on its axis)? A friend of mine, a specialist in international conflict resolution, described an incident that made me wonder. He'd been summoned to a meeting of political opponents whose bitterness was virtually paralyzing a government. Communication had broken down completely, along with all trust. The high tension in the room, he said, was enough to electrocute you. But in the midst of one angry exchange, a baby who had eluded the child-care services crawled out onto the floor between them.

"Suddenly these men who were on the verge of throttling each other got this *awww* look in their eyes," he recalls. "I've never seen a situation turn around faster. Hardened positions seemed to melt. People made concessions. It was like someone had slipped them a drug."

Which in effect might have been the case. "In the presence of a baby," notes neuroscientist Sue Carter of Chicago's Psychiatric Institute, "both males and females will produce oxytocin, leading to tender, maternal-like feelings.* How might this translate into other sorts of social attachment?" Given that, as Carter points out, "A single exposure to oxytocin can make a lifelong change in the brain," it's not a trivial question. Some suspect that oxytocin is the culprit in "helper's high," those glowing feelings of warmth and well-being described by almost everyone who does volunteer work. A group of

---

* Interestingly, it has been reported that when male chimps are on the verge of mutual aggression, one will sometimes snatch a baby from its mother's arms and brandish it before his rival, which seems to abruptly defuse the conflict. Is it a form of hostage-taking or an instinctual gesture that catalyzes a sort of hormonal truce?

UCLA researchers is studying the link between oxytocin and the emotion they call "love of humanity," wondering if the hormone might be the actual milk of human kindness.

Here science approaches the view of love proclaimed in the mystical traditions. According to the Sufis, for example, the feelings we have for family, friends, and lovers are all aspects of divine love. The narrowest affection can lead to compassion for all, even to the universal mystery they call the Beloved. In an essay entitled "My Heart Can Take On Any Appearance," the Islamic sage Ibn El-Arabi proclaimed the highest love to be "like the love of lovers, except that instead of loving the phenomenon, I love the Essential. A purpose of human love is to demonstrate ultimate, real love." High romance or doing-the-laundry love, simple affection or mad crushes, maybe all are prismatic beams of one transforming light.

I recently saw a film about a morose, beaten-down man whose job in a Las Vegas casino was to bring gamblers calamitous bad luck. Known in the trade as a "cooler," when he drew near, the dice became frigid, the cards grew a layer of hoarfrost, and the queen of hearts wept icy tears. But then he fell in love, and the world turned topsy-turvy. Everywhere he went, slot machines that had spit lemons now pealed with ecstatic jackpots, the dice were too red-hot to handle, and baccarat tables practically sprouted crocuses. Even murderous goons and heartless goombahs were stirred to noble deeds. It was a wonderful evocation of that love which flouts the law of averages, beats the house odds, and finally breaks the bank.

I have a few friends who embody this brand of beneficent love some researchers refer to as "generativity." I'd first gotten to know Alicia and Paul (not their real names) when I was teetering at the edge of a private cliffhanger. They'd heard I was hurting, and though they barely knew me, they'd shown up one day with a check that pulled me back from the brink. No strings, they'd assured me as I stammered my thanks. I didn't have to do good with it, reciprocate in any way tangible or intangible, or even, they joked, have dinner with them. Just *be*, they said. It wasn't just the sum, several months' food and rent, that startled me, but the clear sense I got of the givers' unencumbered hearts.

Over the years, we've become close friends. Alicia and Paul live on a hilltop bordered by redwood forest with their three kids, a cockatoo, an ancient desert tortoise, a once-feral cat, a snake, and a pet white rat, all of whom gather around their large breakfast table each morning and seem to get along famously. The family is both well-off and deeply well-intentioned. They save swatches of rainforest; they build schools and teach in them; they take political refugees into their home; they plant community gardens, digging in the dirt. The last time I saw her, Alicia had just received her massage certification so she could give dying hospice patients the tenderness of her touch.

I sat in their kitchen one recent morning, looking out on a vista that was almost absurdly breathtaking: clement, mist-shrouded valleys undulating like bumps in a green carpet, rolling up to the edge of a silvery sea. Paul wandered in for breakfast. Soon, so did a pet rooster, its spurs clicking regally over the ochre tiles until, abandoning all dignity, it leaped onto his lap. "It's spooky," he said. "Even our animals are nice." He wasn't bragging, just bemused. With his straw-blond hair and ruddy, open face, Paul's surfer-dude placidity yields only occasional glimpses of the shrewd businessman who secured the family's fortunes. He clearly adores his kids, who are all stalwart, funny, and for tweeners preternaturally considerate. He doesn't see himself as particularly compassionate, he tells me, just lucky—lucky to have made enough money to be able to give some away; lucky to have met his wife.

He credits Alicia for giving him the compassion 411. "Philanthropy's not that hard. Learning how to be really kind to people— that's more elusive. Alicia's sort of a genius in that department."

I can attest to it. She makes you feel so favored—as if you'd done something extraordinary by simply existing—that you can't help but osmose a little of whatever she has and try to pass it along. Alicia, I'd always assumed, was one of those from-the-cradle love-bugs, born with some extra endowment of solar warmth.

"You've got to be kidding," she says. If anything, she insists, she was "born sad, not sweet"; an anxious, self-enclosed kid. It was her mother, a "kind of saintly" woman with an eighth-grade education, who got through her shell. "She flat-out taught me compassion. She said that life's greatest joy was to 'pull the beauty out of people,' because that makes your life beautiful, too. She was rock-solid in her devotion to other people. She'd be there for that super-annoying person no one else wanted to be around, take care of the one who'd landed in the biggest mess. She adopted every single fuck-up in my family, and a fair number of passing strangers." At age eighty-five, her mother still corresponds weekly with dozens of people in varying degrees of muddle and distress; people who, Alicia says, "count on her letters to help them hold on."

"I'm not at all like her," Alicia claims. "I'm much more critical of people. Mom kept saying the secret was just to take a genuine interest in others—just ask them questions, want to know how they are, really. I'd try that and it would feel good, so I'd do it some more. Step by step, I got to see how wonderful that sensation is of serving others." Alicia also credits her kids ("they taught me how to nurture—but that's nothing unusual, right?"), a few books, and sundry gurus. But she says it wasn't until she met Tommy that it all came together.

He had dropped by one day to visit a friend who was doing construction on their house. Tommy had been told he had less than a year to live: AIDS. He had no money. No place to stay. "Well, it seemed so obvious," says Alicia. "Not just to say, Gee, I'm so sorry, good luck; but *duh!* you can stay *here.*" Alicia and her family and a group of friends agreed to divide up the tasks. "I assigned myself to care for him physically, give him massages, that kind of thing. I found I just loved it. When you see the suffering a person's enduring, there's no way you can't respond. It takes you beyond yourself. Suddenly all those judgments you'd make if you just met them at a party evaporate. You're stripped down to two people doing their best to partake of this mystery."

Tommy had been walking with a cane when they first met him. Six months later, he was a quadriplegic. "But God, was he fun! He had this sparkly, devilish, bad-boy quality. Even when he was really sick, he'd want to go down to Baha and throw some big soiree, so we'd organize this whole elaborate caravan of his friends and our friends and IVs and wheelchairs and just *do* it. You think you've loved before, but this kind of thing opens your heart a thousand times. Tommy seemed to get more and more transparent the closer he got to death, and it enfolded you. I was with him when he died, when that transparency just turned into light."

Her weekly hospice work grew out of that experience. Alicia at fifty still has that lean, blonde, freckled California-girl look, her shoulders tan and muscular from paddling in the surf. It's easy to imagine her large, strong hands kneading the failing flesh and comforting the moribund. But aren't there times, I press her, when you wonder why you're putting yourself through this; when you think of other things you could be doing—times you feel repulsed?

"I would have thought so," she says. "But the worse it got, somehow the more I felt attracted. After all the surgeries, the bodies look like battlefields. You feel the loneliness of that person whose skin is falling off, who has tubes coming in and out of everywhere. And still, behind this war-torn shell, you feel the incredible strength of humanity. It may sound strange or corny, but there's nothing more heavenly than connecting with that."

Alicia's no sentimental pushover. She says she has a "fierce" side. She describes one of her charges who was "frankly an asshole, and the fact that he was dying hardly softened that one bit. He ticked me off something terrible. I had to draw the line: I'm not just a rug to be walked on, and I'm not doing you a favor if I let you." But she's learned to do something when she feels cornered: to "clear away evaluation and just rest someplace that doesn't have all those opinionated *voices* in it. When you do that, then out comes this love that melts people— not melts who they are, but who they *aren't*. Finding that is just like finding yourself. It makes you feel great." She laughs. "I swear, it's a totally *selfish* thing."

While we've been talking, the phone has been ringing. And ringing. Somebody wants something. Alicia gets up to answer. "If we can't help each other, what's the point?" she says. "Everything else gets kinda old after a while."

Now I'm not trying to sell you on Alicia and Paul as Mother Teresa and Mahatma Gandhi. They've had rough patches like any couple; they're spiritually unfancy folk. They enjoy their bounty with a contagious *joie de vivre*. You could quibble that, sure, it's easy to open your heart in the lap of luxury; but I've met insanely wealthy people who are more miserable than Midas.

Besides which, I know another family that's just like Alicia and Paul's, except they're living a gritty existence barely above the poverty line. If 90 percent of life is showing up, they go the other 20. Their door is always open, even if the weathered porch is sagging in. There's always a pot of chili on the stove. If you drop by, their easy affection embraces you (and you, and you, too). Their small living room feels crowded with conviviality. You can stay a few nights on the fraying couch if cat dander and dog hair don't bother you too much. They take care of jobs and kids and ailing grandparents and friends' troubles and community causes, and when I ask them how they do it, they say, "Do what?"

Folks like these have basically eliminated any option of pretending that I don't know what we can be for each other. I know I could stand to be kinder, more generous, fiercer in cleaving to the good, true, and beautiful. I've been pondering something John of the Cross wrote: "Where you find no love, put love, and you will find love." Maybe it could be worth a shot.

*O*ne evening, I gathered a random assemblage of people to chew the fat about love. Heady types mostly, some with sharp elbows, so they were a little cautious at first. "There's no remedy for love," said a poet, lamenting its "misconception and intrigue." But after they'd proved to each other they weren't just soppy romantics, they admitted there was more to the story.

"Love dismantles the whole judgment thing," said one, a lawyer. "The sluice gates open, and more water flows over the dam. When that happens, love's a verb—you can love anything."

"When we're in love, we're a love *factory*," a woman said. "We're churning out so much, we have tons extra to give away."

"Whenever you love," opined a political activist, "you're undermining consumer culture. Who needs all that *stuff* when you have other people?" He gave a little smirk. "Like they say: Accept no substitutes!"

"Love is like the great pulsating orb in old sci-fi movies," someone effused toward the end of our increasingly well-oiled evening. "The one where no matter how many missiles you fire at it, it just absorbs them all and keeps getting bigger and bigger!"

After they tumbled out into the night, noticeably buoyed, I thought about that last one. *Doesn't* love encompass everything you can throw at it? Doesn't the whole human repertoire spiral out of and circle back to love? Even justice, Martin Luther King once said, is "love correcting that which revolts against love." It may have been the evening's wine talking, but suddenly everything seemed to have *something* to do with love. The same love-molecule, like water, everywhere, in every form: boiling into steam as passion, or freezing into glistening hate, or just flowing, upstream and downstream, into every crack and crevice, irreducible.

Don't know how to handle your husband, wife, boyfriend, girlfriend, boss, employee, parent, child, friend, enemy? Love! Everything else is just a finger in the dike, holding back an ocean that, ironically, you could happily drown in. Sometimes I think, trying to get it through my own thick seawall of a skull, that compassion means only this: When in doubt, *just love.*

By the next morning, the effects of the evening's mild bacchanal had worn off; but I still half-believed it.

2

ROOTS, BRANCHES, AND THE CLEAR BLUE SKY

> Therefore I say, grant reason to any animal with
> social and sexual instincts, and yet
> with passion, he must have conscience.
> —*Charles Darwin*

Sometimes when the world seems a lovelorn place, I contemplate a snapshot over my desk of two bonobo apes hugging and kissing with lush abandon, and I perk right up. I'm inspired by these fellow primates whose social life is, in the words of one zoologist, "ruled by compassion" and whose method of solving conflict is said to be make love, not war. They are, I like to think, not only a reminder of where we come from, but of what sort of creature we are at heart.

This image—peaceable, gregarious hominoids with hardly a mean bone in their bodies—isn't the usual picture of our evolutionary heritage. The official family portrait hanging over the mantelpiece of science depicts us as an aggression-prone, brainy ape driven by selfish instincts and constrained (at best) by a thin thread of culture. It's only lately that some scientists are stressing traits we share with higher primates that reflect on us more kindly—conciliation, nurturance, our flair for alliance. And especially empathy. More than superior smarts and a talent for predation, it may be our ability to sense what others are feeling that has put us on evolution's fast track—and will be the saving grace that keeps our stock rolling.

At least that's the hope, as we career around the latest hairpin turn. The quest to understand our creaturely makeup in an era of suitcase nukes and feckless ecocide is hardly a trivial pursuit. We seem to bring to the table a certain appetite for destruction—though we can't be entirely faulted for eating with our hands. We grew up in a rough neighborhood, Brute Nature, a place notoriously red in tooth and claw.

But Charles Darwin himself, great chronicler of the "struggle for existence," found in animals the ancient taproot of our goodness. In their instinct for "mutual aid," he saw the moral lineaments of human society. His writings are filled with admiring accounts of animal reciprocity, cooperation, and even love—a word, shunned by most evolutionary biologists, that appears some ninety-five times in the *Descent of Man* (against only two entries for "survival of the fittest"). Darwin beheld in even the humblest mammal the origins of the Golden Rule: Their "strong sexual, parental, and social instincts," he suggested, "give rise to 'do unto others as yourself' and 'love thy neighbor as thyself.'" Our ancestral line, contrary to its selfish-gene reputation, has given us a startling capacity to care deeply what happens to each other.

*M*y father agrees that evolution is a marvelous thing; he's still hoping our species will try it sometime. "Look at the world," he'll exclaim over one of our episodic brunches, pointing to some fresh geopolitical outbreak of primate xenophobia or the latest greedy corporate monkey-grab. "Obviously, human beings have a design flaw." He handicaps our odds of making it through our current bottleneck at fifty-fifty.

Time was when veering down this road with him would end in a serious bagel-slinging contest. Our fate is not in our double helix, I'd argue heatedly. It's families that nurture love or hate, societies that cultivate kindness or cruelty, culture that massages the kinks from our instincts. By now we both know it's a ritual debate. He'll propose, for a tiebreaker, our nearest kin, the chimps; smart and sociable, sure, but incessant political intriguers, sometime rapists and murderers— *just like us*, he'll say, Q.E.D. I'll put forth the bonobos, just as close a kin (more, some would say), with their nonbelligerent, cooperative, matriarchal ways. He is ever unpersuaded. "Our genes have got us primed for conflict, not compassion; someday a smart DNA engineer is going to figure out how to fix us."

Call it the Loose Screw School of popular anthropology. Our selfish genes, it's said, make a monkey of our highfalutin conscience. We remain too well suited to the ancestral environment: We're just hominids in top hats and tails, dragging our knuckles to the fancy-dress ball.

It *does* often feel like we're a misconfigured product of the same Darwinian novelty company that brought us the platypus and the dodo, long overdue for a factory recall. We're not so much designed as jerry-rigged, using spare parts from earlier models. Our state-of-the-art neocortex is set atop an old mammalian limbic system brimming with volatile emotion, wrapped around a hissing, fight-or-flight, reptilian walnut-brain. Slapdashedly solder it all together (the lingo of modern neuroscience is "wiring," "circuits," and "modules"), and you get a species at once sublime and scurrilous, generous and genocidal, kindly and concupiscent. We *want* to be loving to each other, share our breadfruit, put down our big sticks, but we're just a brainpan simmering on an instinctual hotplate.

To understand the mysteries of our making, science has looked to the creatures closest to the original prototype. On that branch of the tree upon which we perch (and will for hundreds of thousands more years, barring self-extinction or some truly imprudent gene-splice), there's nobody here but us anthropoids—you and me, gorillas and orangutans, chimps and bonobos—aka the great apes.

The family resemblance has always been unmistakable, but genomics has confirmed the patrimony: We're not just similar to chimps—we share with them a downright cousinish 99.4 percent of our DNA. We're *thisclose*. A 2003 report to the National Academy of Sciences, issued some 130 years after the publication of the *Descent of Man*, argued that since we are "only slightly remodeled chimpanzee-like apes," we should expand *Le Club Humaine* to include some more low-brow members. If the Victorians of Darwin's day grew faint at a glimpse of the monkey in the mirror, they'd swoon dead away to see the hirsute Chimp and Bonobo parties led to the corner table long reserved for Genus Homo.

If that happened—and taxonomically, it just might—it would be a big boost for animal advocates who regard apes as cognizing, feeling beings who deserve some designation of personhood ("extending the circle of compassion," as Jane Goodall puts it, "to our closest living relatives"). Others find the genomic hoopla overblown. "A banana's got 30 percent of human DNA," huffed one biologist, "but I find it hard to believe a banana is 30 percent as conscious as I am." Others still—and not just fundamentalists slapping Evolution's Just a Theory stickers on Alabama schoolbooks—find the kinship unsettling, seeing in chimps' proclivity for mayhem dim omens for the human prospect.

The world has always been divided between those who believe we're basically kind and those who say we're basically cutthroat. Is compassion a fundamental human instinct, or does it depend on putting a lid on our inner chimp? Is it our birthright or just a filigreed artifact of culture? I decided I'd best go to the source on that one.

*T*he Georgia woods, majestic and miasmic, suggest the primeval forest of our origins. The racket emanating from the cloister of white and ochre Quonsets clumped in its midst only adds to the impression. Faint hoots, shrieks, grunts, and an occasional piercing scream punctuate the humid air as I near the barbed wire–topped enclosure of the Yerkes National Primate Research Center. The place exudes a primordial musk, a pervasive smell of fur and dung and Cretaceous vegetation.

I'm met by Frans de Waal, a lanky, quizzical zoologist in blue jeans and wire-rims who directs the center's Living Links program. In books like *Chimpanzee Politics* and *The Ape and the Sushi Master*, de Waal has taken a witty and penetrating look at the evolutionary bases of human behavior, from the loftiest altruism to the most lowdown maneuvering. De Waal has found in chimps, who peeled off from a shared common ancestor a few million years ago, clues to the interplay between selfishness and kindliness that keeps our own species scratching its head.

We clamber up to his mission control center, a makeshift-looking yellow tower whose bird's-eye view of the chimp colony reminds me of the adopt-a-family computer game "The Sims" (or more to the point, the Simians). The creatures below, formally known as *Pan troglodytes*, go about their daily business amid spare furnishings done in Late NeoPrimate: a few plastic barrels to climb and perch upon, some big rubber tires for swinging, a free-standing eight-foot wall for privacy (especially for secret trysts between subordinate males and wandering prize females).

At first, it seems like not much is really happening, but it's only my naive eye. De Waal, as attuned to the chimp social whirl as a gossip columnist for the *Troglodyte Times*, knows all, sees all, reporting every interaction in a complex code of numbers and letters on his Palm Pilot. He points out some females off in one corner picking through each other's fur, as essential a chimp social grace as a kaffeeklatsch. "And look, over there," he says, gesturing at two roistering juveniles, "they're laughing." Sure enough, their wide-open mouths, upturned lips, and soft chuckling as they tickle and tumble are so recognizable it would be impossible to call it anything else.

I've never been so close before to large primates without a distracting contingent of screaming kids and parents clasping melting Mr. Frostees. When a female chimp climbs up on a barrel for a better look at me, it's just the two of us. Receiving the full attention of an intelligent nonhuman is an unanticipated shock to the system, a thrill along the nerves. No casual passerby on a city street would regard me with such frank and unwavering curiosity. De Waal says that chimp empathy is more an expression of instinct than intellect ("Chim*pun*-zees," he says with a trace of his native Dutch accent, "don't *neet* to have an *idee*"), but I imagine I see wheels turning behind those brown eyes, a cogitation however rudimentary.

Suddenly she scampers down with a *waaa*! as the alpha male makes a stagey entrance, his fur bristling as if charged by a static field. As if sheer charisma's not enough, he's set one of the orange canisters on its side and rolls it before him like an engine of war, pounding it loudly. It has the desired effect: shock and awe.

"Can you hear? They're all making submissive sounds," de Waal says, and indeed, there's a din of high-pitched hooting reminiscent of Cheetah in the old Tarzan movies, followed by subservient "pant-grunts": *yesboss, yesboss, yesboss.*

Boisterous just doesn't describe this guy ("Björn," says de Waal helpfully). Every gesture is outsized and histrionic; he's part panjum-drum, part Tasmanian devil. He galumphs through the enclave, noising off, seizing the topmost perch (an alpha must be His Highness), filling every inch of social space with his Songs of Myself while his subjects howl his praise. He rolls his juggernaut through the compound with speed, beating it as rhythmically as a tom-tom. *Thump-thump, thump! Thump-de-thump, thump, thump!*

"Maybe says something about the origins of drumming," de Waal suggests mildly. He clues me in to an ongoing struggle for dominance between Björn and the number two male, Socrates (aka Socko), each courting the allegiance of a third male whose loyalty's up for grabs. Socko, cunning and ever politic, grooms Björn, occasionally ducking his head—the ape equivalent of genuflecting to kiss the ring—even as he covets the throne. If Björn were overthrown by some act of *lèse majesté*, Socko would grab the same reins of rank, declaring himself Supreme Orange Plastic Barrel Roller and incumbent Dearest Breeder. It's a bit depressing and all too human to contemplate. These guys are as likely to live in egalitarian, compassionate harmony as to randomly type out *The Tempest* (or more to the point, *Richard III*).

While Jane Goodall has emphasized chimps' more charming side, other researchers have stressed their talent for deceit (especially sexual sneakiness), violence (up to serial killing), theft, battering, infanticide, cannibalism, and intergroup warfare. But chimps also exhibit what we think of as human virtues: aid to the weak, sharing of resources, social rules that reward good citizens with extra grooming and punish bad guys with ostracism. De Waal has eloquently described how the toughest rivals will reconcile after a fight; stretching out their hands to each other, smiling, kissing, and hugging; or how a bystander to a battle will sling a comforting arm around the shoulder of a victim (he calls this "consolation behavior"), all suggesting that empathy is a thirty-million-year-old habit unbroken since the hominoid dawn-time.

*B*ut if there are Ghandis ambling around the primate world, they'd turn up among the bonobos. Regarded until the 1930s as "pygmy chimps," bonobos are now recognized as *Pan paniscus*, a species of strikingly different character. Robert Yerkes, the center's founder, had in the 1920s unwittingly kept among his chimp population a bonobo he'd dubbed Prince Chim, whose gentle, thoughtful temperament so enraptured him that he hailed him as an "intellectual genius." (While the colony's chimps tended to shred books for amusement, Prince Chim would sit delicately paging through one as if trying to understand what humans saw in it, an egghead reading Emerson in the locker room.)

Many decades later, de Waal, dubbing bonobos "the forgotten ape," meticulously chronicled not only their high intelligence but their conciliatory customs. His own disposition is so amiable, his speech so measured and considered, it's easy to forget what a relentless infighter he's been for his theories. He tells me he has made his largely male colleagues deeply uncomfortable by pointing out that this decidedly non-macho species can claim just as much kinship to us as the chest-beating chimps. But unlike the bellicose trogs, when bonobos meet a potential rival group, it's less like a battle than a tea party (often a rather erotic one, a simian *Picnic Sur L'Herbe*). As the bonobo males hang back standoffishly, females will approach the opposing tribe's bravos to do the peacemaking—usually some variant of sleeping with the enemy.* Conflicts inside bonobo groups often end through the efforts of females, who will interpose themselves between rivalrous males like so many U.N. blue helmets. No wonder feminists have made bonobos an animal-world icon: Sisterhood is powerful.

De Waal says he feels a little responsible for "bonobos being idealized as peacenik hippies next to the bad-guy chimps." But he expresses more regret that the bonobo wasn't studied earlier for clues to the origins of human behavior. If bonobos instead of chimps had

---

* To say nothing of sleeping with their friends, bonobos of both genders are, in a word, rather sweetly slutty. They'll do it with Lyle and they'll do it with Lola. They'll do it solo or in a cluster of contorted limbs and happy hoots and grimaces. (The original swingers, they've been observed *in flagrante delicto* hanging from a branch.) Unlike all other primates except for you-know-who, they French-kiss with osculating abandon and have sex face-to-face. Much of it isn't exactly sex as we understand it, though, but quick, erotically tinged assurances of affiliation, affection, and conciliation—one scientist compares it to "full-body hugging." De Waal has a standard shibboleth: "The chimpanzee resolves sexual issues with power, and the bonobos resolve power issues with sex."

been taken as the prehuman model, the killer-ape crowd would never have gotten such traction. The scientific premises about our primate inheritance—and hence our modern assumptions about our basic nature—might have stressed equality of the sexes, familial bonds, and peacemaking rather than male dominance hierarchies and naked aggression.

Primatologists are finding in the bonobos evidence that it is not tooth-and-nail competition but conciliation, cuddling, and cooperation that may be the central organizing principle of human evolution. "Survival of the kindest," de Waal calls it. "Could it be," he wonders, "that the bonobo is cognitively specialized to read emotions and to take the point of view of others? In short, is the bonobo the most empathic ape?"

It is a heretical position, not only in singling out bonobos for such a distinction, but for attributing empathy to an animal in the first place. Empathy has often been considered a uniquely human capacity, requiring a human level of intellect. T. H. Huxley, known as Darwin's Bulldog for his ferocious early championing of natural selection ("ruthless self-assertion," he wrote, by which "the stronger tread down the weaker"), maintained that our ability to feel compassion and to act for the benefit of others depended on the unique powers of human rationality to "curb the instincts of savagery."

But clearly, not all animal instincts are savage; many are rather tender. Should we assume we're so much more empathetic than, say, a bonobo just because we have more cognitive firepower? (Indeed, we often behave as if we've *lost* touch with our innate kindness. Our very ability to govern our feelings enables us to overrule our natural sympathies.) Empathy may be less a top-down *pronunciamento* from sweet reason on high than a bottom-up instinct from the "biological substrates" we share with lower creatures.

At its most basic level, though, empathy is a form of largely mindless automatic resonance. Its likely origins can be found in the evolutionary biology of parenthood. The animal-mother who proved most sensitive to the needs of her offspring was most likely to assure their survival, a capacity marked in natural selection's double-plus column—and reinforced by strong emotion. A human mother's gut-level response to her baby's four-alarm cry is an experience likely shared by a cat anxious to get to her squeaking kittens, or a father bird rushing to stuff a fledgling's mouth.

Infant animals, from their side, survive by *evoking* empathy, signaling their vital needs with dependent, "adorable" helplessness to which parents are hardwired to succumb. Adults of many species mimic infantile behavior when they want to elicit sympathy from others. Even a formidable male chimp defeated in a dominance struggle will sit in the dust pouting, emitting the occasional sorrowing yelp, reaching out so pitiably that eventually another chimp can't bear it and comes to comfort him.

Signals of distress are powerful stimuli for the empathic response, suggestive of compassion's primal meaning of "to suffer with." This can lead to animal behavior that appears startlingly *sympatico.* In a study conducted in 1964, a group of psychiatrists at Northwestern University trained rhesus monkeys to pull a chain to get a reward of their favored food. But when the same chain was rigged not only to deliver food but a nasty shock to a monkey in an adjacent cage, the others soon refused to yank it. The desire to avoid seeing, hearing, and feeling the distress of a companion overrode the desire to eat. One particular rhesus went without food for twelve days rather than pull the chain. It's hard to interpret this monkey hunger-strike in any other way than he was willing to starve rather than endure what was apparently an unbearable "aversive stimulus" of hurting one of his fellows.

In the early 1990s, Italian neuroscientists pinpointed a mechanism in the primate brain that might form the primitive basis for the empathic response. They discovered specialized neurons in macaque monkeys' premotor cortex (the brain area that plans and executes physical tasks), which had a unique property: These cells would activate not only when the animal performed a specific movement, but when it watched the *experimenter* perform the same action.

For example, if a monkey had previously plucked a raisin from a tray and then watched the experimenter's hand pick up a raisin, the same neuron would fire in its brain in both cases. These "mirror neurons," as they were quickly dubbed, seemed to act as an internal reflection—a kind of Simon Says—of another creature's experience. Primates appear to have a brain mechanism dedicated to empathy's basic motto: I feel *you* in *me*.

Mirror neurons have now been found in the human brain, a largely unheralded discovery whose implications are sparking a quiet scientific revolution. "Mirror neurons will do for psychology what DNA did for biology," asserts neurobiologist Vilayanur Ramachandran, director of the University of California's Center for Brain and Cognition. "They will provide a unifying framework for a host of mental abilities that have hitherto remained mysterious."

One of these abilities is surely empathy. One study showed that the same cells that light up when a person's finger is jabbed with a pin also light up when someone *else's* finger is pricked. We've all experienced this effect. We wince when we see someone stub her toe and hop painfully on one foot. We know how it feels. A parent takes her child to the pediatrician for a vaccination, then involuntarily flinches when the needle jabs. She "can't stand to see him hurt." (She's also had her own close encounters with hypodermics.)

Mirror neurons, writes one scientist, "suggest that an archaic kind of sociality, one which does not distinguish between self and other, is woven into the primate brain." Just as our brain is said to have a primitive "grammar nugget" that enables us to acquire the hallowed complexities of language, perhaps we have a "Golden Rule nugget" containing the neurological ground-rules for compassion itself. Mirror neurons may help produce the most primitive form of empathic response, which researchers call "emotional contagion." You've heard it loud and clear if you've ever gone to a G-rated matinee. Someone's child starts to cry, and all toddlers within siren range promptly join in the wailing. It's not that they consciously worry about the other child. The other kid's distress simply triggers a similar distress in them, just as we burst out laughing when others laugh or one person's fear can flare suddenly through a crowd.

Is emotional contagion the reason that animals respond in ways that seem to be empathic? My friend's new puppy, sitting in her lap as we chat one afternoon, suddenly gives her a hard nip. "Ow!" she yells, raising her finger sternly. "No!" The dog jerks his head back for a minute in surprise, then lunges at her again with his needle-sharp teeth, clearly having a great time.

"Okay, here, watch this," she tells me. "Something they taught us in dog-training class."

She mimes crying. *"Boo-hoo,"* she weeps softly, piteously, putting her hands over her eyes and peeking out from between her fingers. *"Boo-hoo-hoo."* I am incredulous when the dog instantly stops biting, looks quizzically into her eyes, then clambers toward her face to lick it, whining in what sounds like sympathy and performing what certainly looks like an attempt to comfort her. What *is* puppy love?

Whatever it is, it may not be so far from ape-empathy. In *The Ape and the Sushi Master*, Frans de Waal tells the story of a researcher in early-twentieth-century Moscow who raised a mischievous chimp named Yoni whom she could never lure from the roof with any system of rewards, even his favorite foods. Finally she hit on a foolproof technique:

> "If I pretend to be crying, close my eyes and weep, Yoni immediately stops his play or any other activities, quickly runs over to me . . . from where I could not drive him down despite my persistent calls and entreaties. He hastily runs around me, as if looking for the offender; looking at my face, he tenderly takes my chin in his palm, lightly touches my face with this finger . . ."

In this account, the chimp does not respond to her "distress signal" only by becoming distressed itself, but acting to protect and comfort her. Though it could be argued this, too, is simply a way to remove an

38

aversive stimulus, it does look suspiciously close to actual empathy, compassion's cornerstone.

Thomas Aquinas could have been describing the empathic instincts of, say, a rhesus when he wrote: "From the very fact that a person takes pity on anyone, it follows that another's distress grieves him . . ." But he added a critical coda: "[O]ne grieves or sorrows for another's distress, in so far as one looks upon another's distress as one's own . . . *because it makes them realize the same may happen to themselves* [my italics]." Here empathy jumps the track to include cognition—an ability to mentally walk a mile in someone else's moccasins.

Moral theorists from Aristotle onward have argued this is why compassion is a singularly human characteristic. Alone among creatures, our unprecedentedly large, complex brains give us the logical skills for moral reasoning and the imagination to place ourselves in another's circumstances (psychologists call this latter "perspective-taking," or "cognitive empathy"). We are moved to care about others because we can put ourselves in their predicament, viewing their situation from, as it were, the inside out.

Researcher Carolyn Zahn-Waxler, a psychologist at the National Institutes of Mental Health, has identified the first stirrings of true empathic behavior in children between one and two years old. Here, for example, is how a twenty-one-month-old child responded when his mother pretended to be sad: peering into her face to determine what was wrong; looking concerned; giving her a hug while making "consoling sounds." Intriguingly, in some of the sessions that took place in peoples' homes, Zahn-Waxler also found that the family dog responded as quickly and effusively as the child to the "distressed" parent, whining and licking and looking distressed. So what, if anything, was the difference between the dog's response and the child's?

Zahn-Waxler thinks a child at this age begins to realize that others are similar to *but distinct from* himself. At that momentous juncture, she writes, "indiscriminate emotional contagion is superseded by cognitive empathy, a willed and knowing stepping into the role of the other."

Now the heart's blind, automatic resonance (that "archaic sociality which does not distinguish between self and other") is augmented by the insight that, in the words of philosopher Paul Ricoeur, "the other is also a self."* Mother is not just an extension of me. A two-year-old may ask an upset parent, "What's wrong, Mommy? Why are you crying? Can I help?" True, he may try to soothe away the upset because it is disturbing *him*, but now he will also try to *understand*. It is the beginning of moral reasoning: the capability to see past oneself and into the heart of another.

The word *empathy* is a translation of the German *Einfuhlung*, a term coined in 1903 by a student of aesthetics named Theodore Lipps. He was searching for a way to express the strangely intimate emotional connection that arises between a viewer and an onstage performer. He used the example of watching an acrobat stepping across a high wire, that moment of breathless suspension when audience members gasp as if they themselves were teetering on a tightrope; the sense of, as Lipps described it, "I feel myself inside of him."

Lipps defined empathy as an "inner participation . . . in foreign experiences." Cognitive scientists refer to this ability to read another's feelings, thoughts, or intentions as a "theory of mind" (or just by the shorthand "mind-reading"). When a friend tells us her sister has fallen seriously ill, we feel heartstricken. We can imagine the anxiety she must feel in the pit of our own stomach; we can sense her helplessness at being unable to take a loved one's pain away. When she announces that the doctors have told her that her sister will be well again, we rejoice with her at the news. It is generally held that an animal, even a higher primate, cannot feel such "true" empathy, let alone compassion, because they are unable to *think* themselves into another's situation.

---

* Interestingly, the only creatures capable of so-called "cognitive empathy" seem to be those which are also able to recognize their own image in the mirror: humans, possibly dolphins, and the great apes. (Bonobos will even drape themselves in banana-leaf shawls and strut back and forth preening: the original fashion victim. A macaque monkey, however, will attack its own image as if it were a rival.) Does it take a "self" to fully imagine an "other"?

*W*hat, then, are we to make of Kanzi the bonobo? Raised from infancy by psychobiologist Sue Savage-Rumbaugh, who literally coparented him with an adoptive bonobo mother, he has on occasion shown what might be interpreted as cognitive empathy. Once, for example, attempting to open a jar of cherries by throwing it on the ground, Kanzi accidentally bounced the jar off the leg of his keeper, who screamed in pain and grabbed her knee. Kanzi, seeming to assume that she had hurt her hand, grasped her palm and gently turned it over, inspecting the skin. Noticing an old scar, he moved her hand in the direction of a water canteen. When the woman verbally asked what he wanted (Kanzi has shown a remarkable level of language comprehension), he pointed to the canteen and then to her old injury, as if urging her to douse her hand with water. As she did so, Kanzi tried to wash her wound.

Can an ape get inside your head? It could be argued that Kanzi didn't have a full-blown understanding of his keeper's needs: Cooling water was what *he* would have wanted if *he'd* had a painful scrape. (Apes have been observed cleaning wounds in the wild with water, though usually with their own saliva.) But his behavior seemed consistent with a central human moral tenet: Do unto others as you would have them do unto you. He was at least standing on the threshold of "perspective-taking," the ability to see the world through another's eyes, a hallmark of human compassion.

Kanzi is thought by some to be standing at humanity's very doorstep and knocking with a rather smart rap (in more ways than one). When Darwin, speaking of the dawning of the human moral sense, proclaimed that "we also differ from the lower animals in the power of expressing our desires by words, which thus become a guide to the aid required and bestowed," he hadn't reckoned with an ape who seems not only to have the rudiments of morality, but also speech—albeit an artificial visual language known as Yerkish. Kanzi began learning Yerkish's hundreds of abstract colored symbols (called lexigrams) when he was a baby clambering around his mother during researchers' fruitless attempts to teach her. Shocked scientists soon realized that Kanzi was acquiring language exactly the way a human infant does, simply by being exposed to it. The bonobo brain, they've since concluded, has an innate, downright freaky capacity for language.

Kanzi (Swahili for "buried treasure") has been adjudged in tests to have the linguistic competence of a human child. He is bilingual (trilingual, if you count Ape). He understands two to three thousand English words. He has even jammed on keyboards with rock legend Peter Gabriel. Here, I thought, is an ape worth talking to: I needed some questions answered.

After several months of negotiation ("Barbara *Walters* asked and we said no," an official informed me), my interview request was unexpectedly granted. I was instructed to take a certain highway to the far outskirts of Atlanta, turn off at an anonymous black mailbox, and drive through a series of electrically controlled gates. My host, a researcher named Bill Fields, pulls up to meet me in one of the special little jeeps they use to tool around the fifty wooded acres of the Language Research Center (LRC). It's all very Jurassic Park.

Bill, a cognitive scientist in his early fifties with broad shoulders and a thinning shock of blond hair, spends a lot of his waking hours palling around with a posse of bonobos, mostly Kanzi's clan-mates. We head straight to the language room, where Bill shows me a panel of hundreds of one-inch squares embossed with colored symbols. When he presses one lexigram symbol and then another, the images flash up on a nearby plasma screen and their pronunciation issues forth. I expect neutered, Stephen Hawking–like electronic diction, but Bill's own recorded voice booms out in a cheerful southern drawl, "Me! . . . Want! . . . More! . . . Grapes!"

The chart of Yerkish signs is as totemic as a Rosetta stone among the center's researchers: They've made it into wall posters, silk-screened it onto staff T-shirts, and laminated it onto portable fold-up boards (to "talk" to apes in the field). Some of the symbols are relatively straightforward. "Grapes" is a red G with stylized bunches hanging from it; the outline of a house stands for a log cabin on the property. But the overall impression is of a hieroglyphic frieze from the Klingon home-world.

The sign for "squirrel," for example, is a purple circle with an X and a squiggle. "Visitor" is a triangle topped with a round circle. A few images stand for purely abstract concepts: "Yesterday" is a shadowed white moon over a dark pyramid, and other equally recondite symbols mean "now" or "later" (bonobos apparently have a sense of past, present, and future). It's taken research assistants as long as a year to attain the measure of Yerkish fluency that for some bonobos is now second nature.

Bill lets a few of Kanzi's relations into the lab and plants me by a Plexiglas window to observe. Bonobos' appearance is often described as "gracile": long legs, narrow shoulders, high foreheads. Unlike the beetlebrowed chimps with their alternately adorable, ribald, or saturnine look, bonobo features seem, well . . . *sincere*. Each has a mat of black hair with a natural part running neatly down the middle, like some lost tribe of Borscht Belt comedians. They spend a surprising amount of time walking upright, arms swinging at their sides in a gait that eerily resembles computer animations of the skeleton of Lucy, our 3.5-million-year-old *Australopithecus* ancestor.

Watching them, I immediately sense how like us these creatures are. The young ones begin showing off for the stranger. One juvenile puts a black plastic garbage bag over his head and scuttles about comically. Then he drapes it over himself like a cloak, climbs up the mesh of his cage, and jumps down, looking for all the world like a kid playing Batman. A bonobo baby named Nyota peers up at me and executes a few perfect little standing backflips, then clambers up to a ledge and sits in a fair imitation of Rodin's *Thinker*, one hand parked pensively under his chin (and the other grasping his crotch).

I watch as Kanzi's grown-up sister, Panbanisha, swipes a brush through her hair, then runs it down her fur (there seems to be a difference—at least to her). She ambles over to her attendant, Liz, a strong-looking blonde with a stoic, forbearing expression, then pulls off the young woman's sneakers and begins gently scraping under her toenails with a tiny stick, as intent as any manicurist. Any doubt that hair salons and nail parlor franchises are attributable to primate grooming instincts vanishes.

Panbanisha glances at me occasionally, poking a few desultory lexigrams on her electronic panel. I'm hoping she'll say Do Unto Others, or maybe just Two Legs Good, Four Legs Bad, but she seems to regard me as room service, requesting repeatedly that I bring her more grapes and peanuts and her favorite, lemon ice.

Unlike de Waal's Chimpville, I can see that the Land of Bonobia is more of a let's-all-hang-out-together place. It seems as much interspecies commune as animal research colony. Bill walks in, effusive with praise. "Panbanisha, you are so beautiful!" he exclaims, though I only see a large hairy creature with sagging dugs and a genital swelling. She grins from ear to ear. Her son, catching her mood, does a little capering dance.

"Each bonobo shares the feeling of the group," Bill tells me. "Bonobos are only happy when *everybody*'s happy." He describes an orangutan named Mari who had lost her arms and preferred to spend most of her time outdoors. "All the bonobos would refuse to eat a bite until we put Mari's meal together and served it to her out there. Then Panbanisha would insist we bring a blanket out to Mari at night."

Bill thinks we can learn a thing or two about social mores from the bonobos. "They always want conflict resolved—immediately, if possible," he notes. Studying bonobo conciliation—the "biology of forgiveness in nonhuman primates," as he puts it—might yield clues about "why we desire to forgive or be forgiven, and how to encourage it." The bonobos' remarkably sensitive responses to each other—what Bill terms "empathic elaboration"—could answer fundamental questions, he says, about "the universality of empathy: How much is innate, how much determined by cultural filters?"

When I ask him if the apes might be learning empathy from being

44

around people, he rejoinders, "I learn it from them. Or maybe we're just kindred spirits." He makes no bones about it: The bonobos are his soul mates. Bill was always the sensitive one in his family, the misfit. When he was a kid, he refused to eat meat (his father, a Baptist minister, finally forced him to drink Geritol for iron). He fretted incessantly about a neighbor-lady's problems. When a cousin was scandalously sent off to prison, Bill devotedly stayed in touch when the other relatives shunned him.

Bill's real family, as near as I can tell, is here. It's more than a study. He's living his life in tandem with these hairy fellow hominoids. When I mention a bonobo has just bared its fangs at me, he's mildly put out. "Fangs? They're incisors," he snorts. *"Fangs? Then we have fangs, too!"* When he describes how he used to carry the infant Nyota facing outward so the curious primate could gaze at the world, I tell him I carried my infant daughter the same way, then realize with a laugh we're swapping Dad stories.

"I *do* think of Nyota as my son," says Bill. "It's hard for me to see him as just some animal. He's like the smartest and the handsomest, the sweetest child." He confesses to sometimes gently nibbling Nyota's toes when the ape-toddler is drifting into Slumberland.

Finally, Bill takes me to meet Kanzi in his outdoor cage. I take a seat a few feet away, while Bill "talks" with a portable Yerkish chart—making introductions, he says—supplementing his symbol-pointing with inaudible words. It's a private conversation: Bill whispers, Kanzi cocks his ear carefully. Bill whispers again; Kanzi indicates some lexigrams. After a while, watching Kanzi's gestures, his expressions, his casual facility with symbols, he *does* begin to look like a man fitted in an ape suit by some B-movie props department. (For that matter, Bill, with his pale blue eyes, pale white skin, and large soft face, starts to resemble a lost species of albino ape.) Kanzi points to a few more symbols, shooting me an impenetrable glance. Bill tells me that Kanzi has indicated he wants to watch Bill and I "chase."

"He wants to see who's dominant," he says. "He wants me to jump on you and play-bite you, to chase and tickle. But it's too hot and buggy for *that*." I feign a look of bitter disappointment. In truth, the thought of being chased, bitten, and tickled by a hulking if genteel Finnish man before an audience of approving (or worse, *disap*-proving) ape-people, well . . . it's just not how I was raised.

*L*ater, Bill and I sit in his cramped office, which is lined from floor to twelve-foot ceiling with tapes and CDs of thousands of hours of bonobo observation, a fraction of twenty-five years of data collection. Bill enumerates some of Kanzi's other cognitive feats. With a little training, Kanzi has proven nearly as adept as our early ancestors at toolmaking. He can knap stone "knives" by knocking two rocks together, choosing the sharpest flake by testing the edge with his tongue and lips, then using the crude blade to saw through a piece of tough hide covering a box of goodies. Bill shows me some footage on his PowerBook. Sure enough, there's Kanzi, flaking one of his flint shivs. Then Bill fast-forwards to show me footage of another ape named P-Suke, who was "wild-caught" and never taught language.

"Now watch," Bill says. The same rocks are placed in P-Suke's hands. He lets them fall from his grasp. The ape's hands are then manually guided to knock the stones together. He stares down, blank and uncomprehending, letting them roll from his fingers. And so it goes. P-Suke just holds the two rocks and does . . . nothing. It's dark at the head of the stairs: He hasn't got a clue. No amount of coaxing or training makes the light go on. For five *years*, they have been trying to teach P-Suke to do what Kanzi managed to learn in a matter of hours.

"Why is that?" I ask Bill, baffled. He silently reaches over, takes a pen from his desk, lifts it in the air, and plops it on top of a notebook.

Then he glances at me. I realize I'm supposed to understand, but I feel a bit like P-Suke. The point eludes me.

"How is tool manipulation different from the manipulation of symbols in language?" Bill asks rhetorically. "The answer is, not much. Language, culture, and tools are like the father, the son, and the holy ghost: They're aspects of the same thing."

Suddenly a realization dawns, and it feels a little stunning. Kanzi, due to his facility with one system of symbols—language—can catch onto the skill and perhaps even the *concept* of toolmaking that characterized early man. Kanzi has a different *mind* than P-Suke, a symbol-using mind; and that has brought him a new way of—for want of a more cautious term—thinking about the world.

Kanzi wasn't the brilliant offspring of a famous ape doctor and a leading ape lawyer. He was just a regular Joe Bonobo until he was handed (or seized for himself) the tools of symbolic thinking. "The primate brain is the hardware. Culture is the operating system," Bill says. "I can run a simple system on my computer hardware, like DOS 1.0, or I can run Windows, or I can run Linux. Kanzi's operating system has become different from P-Suke's; Kanzi's brain can now run the genera of culture."

*B*ill's approach is, it's safe to say, unconventional. His take on the bonobo world is that of an ethnographer, he says, a student of culture; and the notion that animals can have culture has been one of anthropology's great divides. Animals are said to have only "species-specific behaviors": genetically fixed, instinctual, nearly as preprogrammed as robots. Sure, chimps can be trained to mimic culture—to dress in street clothes or grimace in mock-garrulity on the Chimp Channel. But to say apes are affected by culture beyond minor ways observed in the wild—differences in the way one group uses a twig to filch red ants, say, or slight variations in handclasps during grooming—remains somewhat heretical.*

Unlike de Waal, Jane Goodall, Diane Fossey, Birute Galdikas, and other primate researchers, the scientists at the Language Research Center are not even trying to observe apes' "natural" behavior. They have shifted their focus from what an ape brain does to what an ape brain *can* do. Bill describes the center as a "Pan-Homo Culture" where two types of primates with large vocabularies and the capacity for symbolic thought can share an uncommon meeting ground.

It has even the animal rights activists muttering darkly on their Web sites: What are they *doing* in there? Is it the Island of Dr. Moreau? They've heard Kanzi's ballooned to twice the normal weight of a bonobo in the wild (too many M&Ms). But Bill and his colleagues are focused on pushing the envelope—on seeing how fast and how far a prehuman brain souped up on symbols can go.

"When it comes to big-brained primates," Bill tells me, harping on a favored theme, "whether us or them, there almost *is* no

---

* This truism may be about to change. In 2004, a landmark paper appeared chronicling the social modification of what are usually considered hardwired traits among baboons. The male baboon is normally highly aggressive, harassing and attacking females and low-ranking males in order to climb the social ladder. But one troupe of baboons in Kenya suffered a unique catastrophe: Its most aggressive males—dominant alphas who had, with typical belligerence, claimed the exclusive right to forage for easy pickings in a nearby garbage dump—had eaten some discarded meat tainted with bovine tuberculosis and promptly died off. The remaining group members, consisting of subordinate males who'd lost out on the brawls over garbage goodies, together with all the females and their children, had undergone, in the words of *New York Times* science journalist Natalie Angier, "a cultural swing toward pacifism, a relaxing of the usually parlous baboon hierarchy, and a willingness to use affection and mutual grooming rather than threats, swipes and bites . . ." This shift toward distinctly more bonobian-sounding social relations has now persisted for two decades, even though the original kinder-and-gentler male survivors have either died or drifted away. New males who join the group still adhere to the unusual, unbaboonlike norms. One scientist expressed amazement that it was not merely a change in a rote behavior—in, say, a way of cracking nuts—that was being transmitted, but "an attitude . . . the social ethos of the group." The implications for human culture can scarcely be overstated. "If baboons can do it," as Frans de Waal put it, "why not us?"

species-specific behavior. A large, complex brain is not much re-strained by the genome. What feedback from the environment—from culture—can do to the neurological substrates is almost limitless."

He's conjuring a radical view of evolution, of the remarkable po-tential of primate brains to, in effect, shape themselves. We're talking late at night, our conversation more like a seance lit by the phosphor glow of his computer. Sitting in the dark, too absorbed in wild speculation to turn on the light, I feel a surge of hope; I also get the willies. I think of us at *our* evolutionary juncture, trying not to fall behind our own learning curve, looking for the sweet spot be-tween smarts and heart, extending our right hand to each other while the left is still at each other's throats. That our collective push-me-pull-you sorely needs to evolve toward a better game is a no-brainer.

Back at the cages, it's time for dinner. Kanzi has directed Bill to tell me to sit on a stool. Kanzi tells Bill that he's not comfortable with me standing over him. Dominance hierarchy. *It's an ape thing: You wouldn't understand.* I sit looking at Kanzi; he looks back probingly into my eyes.

"Kanzi," I say, "let's be friends. Can we be friends?"

He sits, not seeming to hear or caring to respond, but after a minute drags his portable lexigram-board closer and casually taps on it a few times. *Chase*, Bill translates. *Tickle.* I take note of Kanzi's hir-sute arms, thick as fenceposts, with their massive, arboreal triceps. This is not just the Peaceable Kingdom; bonobos are astoundingly strong, and they *can* be aggressive on occasion. Bill himself has only half a middle finger, the outcome of a rare Pan-Homo dispute; some outburst, he says, over lines of authority. "Another time, Kanzi," I say. *Another time.* Two baby bonobos settle in at the far end of their cage by the video monitor. Tonight they get to watch *The Lion King*, and then it's off to bed.

*O*n the way home, I can't help seeing the world in Primatevision. The airport is a captive colony, perfect for observing hominoid behavior. There's a pair-bonded couple keeping a tolerant, protective eye on their playful juveniles. In front of me, on a long, slow line, is an irritable middle-aged alpha. When his mate says, "Put the ticket in your jacket pocket, Sid," the old silverback rears up and growls loudly, "It *is* in my jacket pocket. You *saw* me put it in. *Quit* your damn nagging!" The female hangs her head, speaks softly, soothingly, grooming some lint from his rumpled sportscoat pelt.

This effect lasts for weeks. Humanity's shenanigans do suddenly look an awful lot like the *Planet of the Apes* (and come to think of it, isn't the typical Hollywood blockbuster just a variation on beloved primate themes: *chase, run, fight, eat, hug, tickle?*). It was hard not to think as I clipped my toenails, *claws;* as I bit into an apple, *fangs* (or rather, *incisors*); as I acted extra-gregarious at a party, *display behavior*, impressing some and leaving others cold (*social hierarchy*); as I got into a political argument, pushing way too hard to win (*dominance conflict*); then apologizing (*conciliation*) for any boorishness; caught myself deferentially ducking my head (*submission, ugh!*) to someone I thought of as a better writer; provided a soft shoulder (*consolation*) to a friend with marital problems. My social finesse seemed disconcertingly undergirded with apely agendas. How many of my little daily transactions are tainted by trying to maximize rank, secure a better food supply, and maneuver for breeding privileges? How many are out of pure human generosity, compassion, and sensitivity to others?

But in the weeks and months that followed, I found myself most haunted by the memory of P-Suke—a by no means stupid, just typical *Pan paniscus* with an unstretched mind—and Kanzi, who through some culture-induced mental alchemy has become a sort of *Pan sapiens.* In what ways am I, are we all, like P-Suke, the stones of full cognizance just rolling from our grip? In what ways are we like Kanzi, tweaking our operating system to new levels of understanding?

Kanzi is said to have more brain than he needs to succeed in his environmental niche. So do we—though I wonder if we have enough heart? When de Waal says that the bonobo's "greatest intellectual achievement is not tool use but sensitivity to others," I wish I could feel with full certainty the same applies to us.

Asked about what sometimes looks like a distinct lack of compassion in human society, the Dalai Lama has said: "Perhaps we just pay less attention to compassion and caring; we reinforce it less. Whereas in some sense, we fully embrace hostility and anger as an emotional state, fueling and reinforcing it. If we were to give the same amount of energy, attention, and reinforcement to compassion and caring, they would definitely be stronger."

If our spiritual traditions are any clue, we have been trying since forever to reroute or suppress our aggressive circuits and reinforce our caring ones. All those variants of the Golden Rule, software patches to modify our HomSap 1.1 operating system, building squarely on a kernel of code, *you in me, me in you,* the mirror neuron mantra.

We assume that our course of development runs from childhood to adulthood; but spiritual teachers have always claimed there is a superseding path, if we choose to take it, which leads to higher consciousness. What else is the extraordinary compassion of the saints but proof-of-concept that we can bootstrap our primate inheritance to its optimum capacity for kindness? That heritage has already endowed us with more compassionate traits than selfish ones: nurturance of family, emotional commitment to friends, sympathy, affection, a sense of fairness and empathy, forgiveness, maybe even altruism. Whether you believe your Maker to be the Good Lord or Darwin's Blind Watchmaker, they've been working from a similar schematic— one with built-in capacities for modification and much room for improvement.

It may sound silly to say, but my short time with the bonobos has made me more trusting of the instinctual foundations of my own unruly emotional life; has given me a certain confidence in our good nature. (Liberate the Substrates?) Sure, maybe the good stuff is alloyed with chimply cunning, and my impulses are more often fight-or-flight than unconditional love. But hey, I'm riding on a vintage primate chasis here: I'm just glad to know that a responsive heart comes standard and pre-installed. Maybe I don't need to furrow my high brow so hard to be noble. The precursor to all nobility has been beating for uncountable millenia right in my still-hairy chest.

A famous chimp named Washoe, the first to use American Sign Language, once leaped over a dangerous high-voltage fence to pull a newly arrived chimp from the water, risking her life for an individual she'd known only a few hours. And chimps fear and *despise* water. Here, surely, are clues to the roots of compassion, if not—who knows?—its o'er-spreading branches, and the clear blue sky. Researcher Roger Fouts describes how Washoe, who had lost both her offspring as infants, reacted when a keeper told her that her own newborn had just died. Looking deep into the grieving woman's eyes, Washoe signed, "Cry," tracing on her own cheek the path a tear would take down a human's (chimps don't shed tears). Then Washoe signed, "Please Person Hug."

We've come so very far from Washoe in our astonishing, lonely odyssey of two million years. But who's to say we're not just an eyeblink from our most distant yesterday compared to where we will arrive some distant tomorrow? Our journey to realizing full humanity may have just begun. But meanwhile, if I had my druthers, I'd engrave Please Person Hug on the Great Seal, put the lexigram for Grapes in one eagle talon and Chase-Tickle in the other. Just as an experiment, to see where we might go from there. Just to see how far we could take it.

3

EMPATHY: YOU IN ME, ME IN YOU

See yourself in others
Then whom can you hurt?
What harm can you do?
—*The Buddha*

I once spent a day shadowing the Dalai Lama. It was during his first visit to America (Middle America, at that), and I was covering him for the local paper, but that was just my alibi. I wanted to take his measure, to see for myself what this incarnation of Avalokitesvara, the deity of compassion, was really like when the rubber sandals met the road.

He struck me as bright and curious—an exceptionally *nice* man—but a living Buddha? Yet as the day wore on, it crept up on me: His caring never seemed to waver. He emanated a steady warmth without gaps, moods, or slipups. I watched him meet with the clueless mayor of Denver, a stogie-chomping old pol whose small talk inched dutifully over the official terrain of tourism and molybdenum mining. The Dalai Lama stood listening, duck-footed, hands folded, eyebrows cocked, his trademark smile hovering somewhere near delight. Hizzoner presented His Holiness with a picture book of the state's Rocky Mountain wonders, the sort you'd pick up at an airport gift shop. The Dalai Lama accepted happily, sitting down to leaf through it with what appeared to be genuine interest. When he came upon a color plate of a bighorn sheep, its clear ruminant's eyes caught in mid-graze, he told the mayor warmly, "We have this kind in *our* mountains, too!"

They chatted awhile, and before long, the doughty old pol had cracked a smile, was heard to chortle; he *liked* this golden-skinned man in the maroon robes. He looked crestfallen when an aide whispered to him about a waiting appointment and a city to run.

As the Dalai Lama made his way from the reception area, a news cameraman abruptly leaned forward. "Your Holiness, can I ask you something?" he blurted, then lowered his voice. "About my wife—" The Dalai Lama halted in his tracks, his retinue bumping into each other like a vaudeville troupe. He inclined his head toward the other man's until they nearly touched, placed a hand on his shoulder, and then, eyes brimming with sympathy, spoke softly with him for a while, his voice like the soughing of wind. The other man's voice rose and fell in agitation, but I couldn't make out the words—was his wife ill? about to divorce him? As they talked, the Dalai Lama's face seemed to subtly mirror his expression, as if taking on a share of his burden. And slowly, the man's own face softened, resolving into a look of gratitude.

And so it went, throughout the day and into the evening. Mayors or Teamsters, cabbies or kings, each person received the same keen, heartfelt regard. The Dalai Lama seemed to enter intimately into each person's world while remaining firmly grounded in his own. His quality of empathy, at once indiscriminate and specific, began to overwhelm me, not least because he made it seem so ordinary: ordinary kindness, ordinary consideration, taken to an extraordinary degree.

The Dalai Lama has often claimed he is a simple person. Though some find this a little coy, on one level it rings true. Isn't our image of holiness just a placeholder for what we all might be, if our best moments were multiplied to an nth degree of constancy? The religious icons of compassion reach out to us in an apotheosis of recognizably human caring. The Chinese goddess Kwan Yin weeps as she extends her thousand-armed embrace to those who need succor. The Hindu deity Hanuman, depicted as half-ape, half-god (sound familiar?), cleaves open his chest to reveal his naked, undefended heart. The sacred heart of Jesus, Son of Man, is pierced with thorns, bleeds real blood. Vulnerability, these images say, is holy. It is our capacity to be moved by each other that makes us whole.

*I*n one study of empathy, a psychologist asked a precocious eight-year-old named Adam: "If you knew how someone else felt, would you be more likely to help them than if you didn't?"

"Oh, yes," Adam answered. "What you do is, you forget everything else that's in your head, and then you make your mind into their mind. Then you know how they're feeling, so you know how to help them."

"Some kids can't do that," he added, "because they think everybody's always thinking the same things."

I doubt many adults could articulate it as well. First, Adam says, you have to forget yourself, set aside your own storyline. Then you need to pay a special form of attention to another person, intuiting their thoughts and feelings as if from the inside out. (Adam stipulates that some people can't do this because they assume the other's viewpoint is exactly like their own.) Only then can you know how to ease their heart.

Adam describes the kind of empathy that advances through the gates of compassion. In its most basic form, though, empathy is just our biologically based propensity to get under each other's skin. When

I perceive your mood, a neuronal circuit flashes on. Your sadness or happiness evokes a corresponding feeling in me before I'm quite aware that it's happened. Studies have shown that just seeing another person's expression triggers, below the threshold of consciousness, the same facial muscles in the observer, which in turn stimulates the same inner feeling. A 2003 UCLA study revealed that when one person *deliberately* imitated another's smile, the emotional centers in his own brain lit up with happiness.

We are designed to be emotionally entangled. If you live in a bustling city, this sort of resonance occurs a dozen times a day. You hear a child lost in a crowd of shoppers crying for her mommy, and your heart instantly goes out to her (along with a half dozen other people who are already dashing toward her to help). When a laughing couple passes by, their arms around each other's waists, you feel a scintilla of their joy. When a heated argument erupts on the street corner, your own adrenaline fractionally redlines.

Responses may vary, of course. One person may stride by a beggar with stony contempt, while another, stricken, puts a dollar in his Styrofoam cup. Someone might look at a pair of lovers and feel jealous or sorrow over a joy long departed, or annoyance at their lovey-dovey giddiness (*give it a rest, kids*). But these are afterthoughts to a primal identification that has already occurred, as viscerally and immediately as stepping on a tack. Somewhere below the threshold of awareness, the mirror neurons have already launched into their oddly nondual theme song, *you in me, me in you.*

Of course, simply catching someone else's emotion doesn't necessarily lead to *caring* about them. In a series of remarkably subtle observations, Mengzi, a Confucian philosopher of the fourth century B.C.E., told of a king who looked out from his balcony and saw a man leading a piteously bellowing ox to be sacrificed. "Let it go!" the king shouted down. "I cannot bear its frightened appearance, like an innocent going to the place of death!" The man responded by asking to get a Band-Aid?" Young children often cry to see someone in pain and seek to be consoled. But Nicholas was as calm and collected as an emergency medical tech, somehow right there with me, only wanting to help.

His precocious response (so says his doting uncle) was an example of that other-directed empathy that goes beyond mere contagion or resonance. Studies have shown that it even has a different physiology: It is associated with a decreased heart rate, while contagious distress causes an increase. It may literally be a healthier response. The two states also have differing facial expressions and varying degrees of skin conductance. Unlike contagious distress, other-directed empathy shows "somatic quieting . . . which often accompanies an individual's focusing attention on the external environment"—suggesting that it is a form of attention that reaches out to another's plight rather than inward, toward one's own reactions to it.

Being able to feel our way into another's soul, to sense what is going on behind their social mask, is the passkey to kindness. A friend gave me a quote a few months ago, a one-liner from the Jewish sage Philo of Alexandria, that I haven't been able to get out of my head: "Be kind, for everyone you meet is fighting a great battle." I've found, with a little practice, I can at least get this far.

"Sorry about the wait," the cashier apologizes. It *has* been a long time. She's been moving like molasses; the line at her register creeps forward by millimeters. According to the unwritten laws of retail, I'm entitled to a small display of petulance. Instead, I try to take her point of view. She's been on her feet all day. She's harried and underpaid. The job is repetitive, and impatient customers treat her like an appliance. "Hey, it's okay," I tell her, looking back at the line. "There's only one of you and ten of us; we've got you surrounded." She smiles, shooting me a relieved look, and I feel good to have made someone's day easier. I've been lately trying to do this, a compassion miniaturist, as much as I can. It's a trick of sorts—I feel like a kid with a new magic kit; the multiplying rabbits, or more, the disappearing thumb—but amazingly, it works almost every time.

I wouldn't say it's just a cheap trick, but I know it's not a very costly one, especially when compared to what some refer to as *radical empathy*. Adam Smith, godfather of capitalism, a man whose name is forever linked to narrow self-interest, might seem an unlikely source of insight into the nobler regions of the human heart. But he came up with one of the better working definitions I've seen of, as it were, the emotional mechanics of high-level empathy. In *The Theory of Moral Sentiments*, he observed that true compassion is based on "an imaginary change of situations," describing it thusly:

> When I condole with you for the loss of your only son,
> in order to enter into your grief I do not consider what I,
> a person of such a character and profession, should suffer,
> if I had a son, and if that son was unfortunately to die:
> but I consider what I should suffer if I was really you,
> and I not only change circumstances with you, but I
> change persons and characters. My grief, therefore, is
> entirely upon your account, and not in the least upon
> my own.

This swift jackknife dive into another's pool of experience—some theorists refer to it as "alterity"—is an imaginative leap. Your tragedy may remind me of one of my own and make me weep; or your happy occasion may call to mind my similar one. But it is only when I become utterly alert to you *on your own terms*, open fully to your experience, that you know you are being seen, heard, and felt. This sort of empathy is enigmatic; it almost teleports us into another person's frame of reference. Or perhaps it could be thought of as a form of bilocation: Centered in my own heart, I'm also, through some spiritual legerdemain, centered in yours.

The notion of a reversal of place lies deep within the DNA of all spiritual traditions. The ninth-century Buddhist sage Shantideva urged all who wished to follow the path of compassion to partake in "this sacred mystery: to take the place of others, giving them his own." The saints wash the feet of the sinners, knowing themselves to be no greater than the least. The apocryphal tale of the Danish king who, in response to Nazi orders that all Jews wear a yellow star, donned one himself is emblematic of many Danes who were moved to risk (and sometimes lose) their own lives for their persecuted countrymen. In a more homely example, former senator Bob Graham of Florida used to take what he called a "workday" once a month, performing an ordinary job like bagging groceries or showing up incognito as a flight attendant to serve passengers their meals. It was good political theater, but also a method of feeling his way into his constituents' hearts, minds, and lives.

Still, it is one thing to feel *for* someone else; it is another to, in some sense, *become* them. Is it possible to take this exchange too far—merging with another at the expense of your own authentic selfhood, or even the possibility of genuine relationship? Martin Buber refused to use the word empathy because he objected to any connotation that the self could—or should—become lost in the experience of another. "A *great* relation exists only between real persons," he wrote. "One must be truly able to say *I* in order to know the mystery of the *Thou* in its whole truth."

Psychologists are particularly nervous about any social bond that smudges the ego's boundaries. After all, how many unhealthy relationships are based on a person with a fragile ego overidentifying with his or her partner's needs? How many givers are sucked dry by takers when they become confused where they leave off and the other begins? People in the helping professions have an expression for times they feel they're sacrificing themselves on the altar of their clients' needs: *over-caring*. Some clinicians view what they term *affective resonance,* when one person's heartstrings twang too closely in tune with another's, as an outright pathology.

Writer Alfie Kohn sums up the prevailing guideline among psychologists as to when deep empathy is even practicable: "One must feel sufficiently unthreatened and free, psychologically speaking, to relax a vigilant watch over (and attachment to) the self and to risk adopting someone else's perspective." He adds, as an afterthought, that it may also require "a certain generosity of spirit." Just so. But isn't generosity of spirit the jumping-off point for a meaningful life, not just a cliff's edge fraught with psychic peril?

It's an imprecise science, if science at all. If a person's ego-boundaries are too thick, he or she may appear callous, obtuse, tone-deaf to others' feelings. On the other hand, there are those whose antennae are so sensitive they can't help being receptive to everyone else's broadcast; they may lose their own signal in the din, becoming gullible, suggestible, all too permeable.

The insensitive are a common enough social archetype—those folks who know just who they are and exactly what they want, bulling their way through life's china shops with little concern for incidental breakage. They're as often as not valorized as self-assertive go-getters with robustly healthy self-esteem. It's the hyperempathic who are viewed as weirder and, in a strange way, less trustworthy. It's not only that their sensitivity may cause them to be invaded by *our* feelings; with their boundary-transgressing acuity, they may also invade *us.*

It's not so surprising that the Empath has become a standard sci-fi character, though usually more a figure of pathos than threat. In a famous Ray Bradbury story, a Martian wanders into a human colony on the Red Planet. One of the last survivors of a superempathic race, he is a shape-shifter. For one grieving family, he becomes the spitting image of their lost son; for another, their dead daughter resurrected; to a lonely woman, he is her runaway husband, returned home at last.

The Martian says he is "imprisoned" by others' thoughts, captured by their strongest needs. When he tries to leave, he is surrounded by a crowd of clamoring Earthlings whose selfish desires for unqualified empathy turn him finally into a chimera, "melting wax shaping to their minds . . . his face dissolving to each demand . . . his face all faces, one eye blue, the other golden . . ." The story speaks volumes about our cultural anxiety that we will lose ourselves by simply being too open to others.

It seems surpassing strange to take on another person's pain as if it were your own. In an early *Star Trek* episode titled, fittingly, "The Empath," the crew of the *Enterprise* visits a distant stellar research station and discovers a young woman without vocal cords (and so only able to listen) who has an eerie power. When she touches a wound on Captain Kirk's forehead, it miraculously appears on *her* forehead, then disappears. "Her nervous system is so sensitive, so highly responsive," says the somber sawbones Dr. McCoy, "that she can actually feel our emotional and physical reactions. They become part of her."

Here the Empath is a healer, albeit at a price to herself. Some might call it a bad case of over-caring. But she is also like the traditional shaman, who purports to suck the illness from another's body into her own in order to heal it. I've interviewed medical doctors— those who are not just good technicians but, in a way that's hard to quantify, genuine healers—who describe this sensation of taking another's suffering into themselves. "It does hurt," one told me, "but I can't explain it; it's a good hurt—a *giving* hurt."

The figure of the Empath, at once healer and freak, stirs unease in our autonomy-obsessed culture. We long for deep connection and unconditional caring. Yet the contempt one hears for "bleeding hearts" reflects an ambivalence, even an outright prejudice, toward the highly empathetic. Their attunement to us makes *us* vulnerable to *them*. They could get inside our heads, violate our right of mental privacy. Besides, they must have a chink in their character armor as big as a barn door.* We get an impression of watery mutability; of quicksilver, slipping in through the cracks in our facades, taking on the shape of whatever container they flow into. They seem, in a word, like chameleons.

The joke is on us, though: Researchers have documented what they have dubbed the Chameleon Effect in just about everybody. Whether we know it or not, we're all a little like Bradbury's Martian, unconsciously mimicking each other's inflections, facial expressions, and gestures. (Not surprisingly, those who do this most readily also rate highest on the empathy scale.) Most of us, for example, feel an urge to yawn upon seeing another person do so. Psychologists have found that people who are particularly susceptible to this "contagious yawning" are also significantly better at drawing inferences about others' mental states—in other words, they are more empathic. (If reading about this just made you yawn, then *bingo*.)

Is acute empathy neurotic or healthy? The ultimate spirituality or excessive "codependency"? Don't we *need* to resist others' gravitational fields, lest we be pulled from our orbit by every passerby? All through the day, the mirror neurons sound their siren song—*you in me, me in you*—but in a single, near-autonomic flicker, we overrule them. We can't afford to respond to everyone, gushing compassion like a hydrant without any shutoff valve of judgment. Each of us tends to strike our own balance—partly from upbringing, or conscious decision, or life experience, but also from differences in tem-

---

* Empathy *can* be used to gain power over others, an ability that shows up even in apes. Two chimps named Austin and Sherman were once kept together at the University of Georgia's Language Research Center. Austin, the subordinate male, figured out a key psychological truth about the dominant Sherman: Sherman was afraid of the dark. Austin used this insight to manipulate him: "[Austin] would go outside and make unusual noises to frighten Sherman, then rush in, looking back outside as if someone was out there. Sherman would become fearful and allow himself to be comforted by Austin." Austin, in other words, was a bit of a con man. Con men, too, are notoriously empathetic, using their ability to see into you to mold themselves to your fondest expectation or suss out your secret fear—and then use it to clean out your bank account.

perament. We are not all made the same. Our empathic style may have something to do with where we naturally fall on that sliding scale between head and heart—a scale that turns out to be very wide, indeed.

I've just met someone who is *all* heart. Cassie has to be one of the friendliest eight-year-olds ever. We've only known each other for ten minutes, and this elfin-looking child has already taken my hand, gazed up at me with her wide-spaced eyes, and exclaimed affectionately, "My *good* friend!" Her playmate Laurel, a dark-haired little girl dressed in purple and pink, is just the same, as outgoing and sympatico as can be. So is her friend Regina, as well as young Josh. They even *look* the same, with their narrow faces, broad foreheads, pointed chins, and quick, wide smiles.

"Like brothers and sisters," Cassie's mom marvels, and as it turns out, these children *are* genetic relations in a sense: Each one is missing a few crucial genes on their seventh chromosome, producing the rare disorder known as Williams' syndrome. It includes distinctive facial features (hence the misnomer, "elfin-face syndrome"), short stature, learning disabilities, and a slew of health problems (especially in the heart's aorta). But strangely, despite typically mild retardation, Williams' kids often show pronounced musical abilities, deft verbal facility, and an extraordinary level of empathy. Laurel has easily memorized songs sung in Gaelic and Arabic. She can play exquisite Indian flute, executing all the subtle flutters of timbre without knowing how to read a note. She's sociable, quick, voluble. When I say, "See you later, alligator," she chimes in without hesitation, "After a while, crocodile." Yet I'd seen her minutes before unable to distinguish her right hand from her left.

What especially intrigues researchers is how these kids, deficient in so many ways, routinely score much higher than their peers in so-cial skills—not only in remembering names and faces, but in their pro-nounced empathic responses. All the parents tell me their kids are unusually sensitive to others' pain. When I put on my eyeglasses and accidentally pinch my finger in the metal hinge, Cassie's face is flooded with concern. She seems drawn to my injury like an iron filing to a magnet. "Are you okay?" she asks with great sympathy as she peers at the red welt. "Does it hurt?" Her mother, a hospice nurse, tells me of the time Cassie met one of her patients, an elderly dying man who "looked really scary—emaciated, jaundiced, tubes coming out of his nose. Cassie went right up to him, gave him a big hug, put her head on his shoulder, and said, 'Grandpa!' They became instant best friends. She insisted on visiting him every day until he passed away. 'My little sweetie,' he'd say, and light up like a Christmas tree."

To Williams' syndrome children, *everyone*'s a friend, a trait re-searchers call "hypersociability." As one mother puts it, not without exasperation, "No stranger-awareness whatsoever. I try to teach her what a stranger is, but the farthest I've gotten is she'll go up to someone and ask, 'Are you a stranger?' and then say, '*Now* we're friends!'"

We tell the kids that today we're going on a treasure hunt. *Trea-sure!* They all look at each other, disbelieving their luck. "Treasure!" they say, their eyes wide, their mouths little O's of delight, sunny little optimists on an impossibly sunny day. "Oh, *thank* you, Mommy!" says Laurel, and it comes from the bottom of her heart. They clearly are treasures to their parents. One parent contrasted her own chronic reticence with her daughter's social confidence. "Here I had this little girl with all these problems, and she'd walk into a room full of people, never shy, never self-conscious, and say, 'Hi, my name's Katey. What's your name?' I would think, How did she do that? She makes it look so easy. She taught me how to forget about myself."

I get the impression of little people with translucent membranes instead of skin—you can *see* their hearts pulsing. They exude affection. I watch Cassie march right up to a woman inching along on a walker and say with profound conviction, "I *love* your earrings." The woman basks in the glow of the best compliment she's heard all day. They chat, though Cassie's conversation is limited. She's fascinated by all things crystalline, and the diamonds in the woman's earrings are what she most wants to talk about.

Cassie beams at her. "My *good* friend."

I miss the kids the minute I leave; time spent in their company is utterly pleasant. It has given me a look at a form of human goodness, an innocence, both inspiring and tragic. I know there is anguish for the parents, even as they put on a brave face and tell me if they were forced to choose a disability for their kids, this would be the one. Besides the terrible medical problems (Laurel's had two heart surgeries) and the great likelihood they will never function independently as adults (and often die young), the emotional roller-coaster can be overwhelming. If the children find they can't soothe a playmate or if a baby gets upset in the market, they can become panicky and inconsolable.

"They have exaggerated emotional contagion," says Susan Hepburn, a researcher, petite and pixieish herself, who specializes in the disease. "They may instantly pick up on your emotion and say, 'You look frustrated today,' but they won't ask why or understand the context. Once they catch that someone's angry or sad, they're not sure how to proceed, how to figure out what they might say or do to help the other person." She stops and gropes for the right way to put it. "They don't know how to *think* about feelings."

Then there are those who are their polar opposites: people with Asperger's syndrome (AS), a less crippling form of autism characterized by a *lack of* empathic ability. People with AS often can do nothing *but* think about emotion. They tend to excel at logical, literal, systematic thought, yet are, in the coinage of Cambridge psychologist Simon Baron-Cohn, "mindblind," able only with extreme difficulty to discern other people's inner desires and intentions.

They must make their own reasoned analysis of the alien world of feeling to live in relationship with others, devising what an engineer might call "work-arounds" for their empathy impairment. Writes one mother with Asperger's: "Tone of voice, facial expression, body language—people give a dozen clues about their state of mind without uttering a word. Unfortunately, I do not always pick up on this . . . I therefore have great difficulty following a conversation, listening, being tactful, taking hints, making small talk, knowing when to use polite deception, and knowing what subjects are appropriate to talk about."

She describes not knowing how to emotionally bond with her children or intuit the meaning of one cry from another "unless it was an obviously alarmed cry." Instead, she worked out a system to manage this most primal of empathic relationships, a set of rules to use when the babies were upset: first offering her breast, then checking their diaper, then rocking them in a process of elimination until they quieted down.

But she was a good parent, breastfeeding her children even though she took no pleasure in it, because she reasoned, "I wanted to give them the best and nothing less." She questions whether her way is necessarily inferior. "Lack of empathy is not psychopathy, and it is possible to use reason instead. Sometimes it is better—how many things do parents do, not because it is wise or best, but simply because that is the way 'everyone' does it?"

Her sentiments are echoed on a Web site called Aspergia, which contends that adults with AS possess a unique set of traits that may have been shared by Mozart, Gregor Mendel, and Charles Darwin. (Bill Gates is often cited as a presumptive nominee for the AS Hall of Fame.)* Some of them wonder if what they call their "mutation"

---

* Simon Baron-Cohn argues that, although classic autism is an incapacitating pathology, Asperger's—a syndrome not officially recognized until 1994—extends right up to the borderline of normalcy. Indeed, it may cross over the line. One study he performed with Cambridge students indicated that the engineers, mathematicians, physicists, and computer scientists among them had a greater number of AS-like traits—strong abilities in rule-based systems, coupled with difficulty in empathizing—compared to their peers in the humanities, arts, and social sciences.

doesn't have a critical role to play in the evolution of humanity itself. "Wars are caused by strong emotions of affiliation," writes one. "They are sparked by bravado, nationalism, religion, hatred and xenophobia—all products of group allegiances. Could it be that the AS gene is telling us: Focus on individual development, and stop grouping so tightly that you might war yourselves out to extinction?"

Indeed, it's hard to argue that those they refer to as "neurotypicals," despite our "normal" emotional fluency, have done such a great job running the world. Why *not* let Aspergia—twenty million people worldwide, enough to populate their own Australia—take over for a spell?

I once met a citizen of the Aspergian diaspora. Sandra (not her real name) strode right up to a researcher I was talking to at an autism conference and plucked at the woman's sleeve. "Your blouse has a wonderful pattern," she said brightly as she stared at it closely— too closely, utterly intent.

A short, animated woman with a man's haircut and an androgynous look—she likes to refer to herself as "a monk"—she sat in the front row of a lecture about the dwindling resources available to people with Autistic Spectrum Disorder (ASD), freely expressing her outrage. "It's a human rights issue!" she exclaimed when a particularly egregious funding cut was detailed. "How can we change this?" she asked loudly. "Absolutely!" she shouted unself-consciously whenever the speaker made a point she found particularly on target.

She is earnest, agitated, possessed of a keen sense of justice, and not at all what I'd expected. "Autism doesn't exist in a vacuum," she explains. "I'm influenced by Roman Catholicism, the Midwest, postindustrial society, a degree in political science."

I mention that Asperger's is clinically classified as an empathy disorder.

"They say *we're* not empathetic?" she practically explodes. "Letting babies *starve* in this world—*that's* not empathetic! *Bombing other countries* is not empathetic!" She doesn't just converse; she expostulates. My first thought is, *Chill out*. But my second is, *Viva Aspergia*.

Sandra's the president of the sisterhood of her church. "They elected me," she says proudly. "We need to give help, not just get it. A lot of my friends come to me for support. I help them with the vicissitudes of life." She reels off the highlights of her social network, waving her hand as if diagramming its key nodes on an invisible blackboard. "I have three godkids. I have twenty-four nieces and nephews, and I'm proud of every single one of them. I work with the family of an autistic kid. I clean the church. I head a social skills group for autistics."

She knows she has certain deficiencies, but she reasons her way around them. "A professor taught me to read fiction by breaking it down into pieces of stories and characters. I need to chart the motivations. Things have to be explained in a logical manner. *Why* is that children's book hero called Captain Underpants?" (By contrast, I think of the Williams' syndrome adult who said she loved fiction "because I can put myself in that book and be right in there with the characters and feel them go through these experiences.")

"I know we all need each other in society," says Sandra, who has come to a Catholic faith in the rational tradition of Aquinas (was he another Aspergian agent?). "I'm always willing to help, because this is what the Master wants me to do." When she leaves, I hear her singing "Kyrie Eleison," precise and on-key, all the way down the hall.

It could be said that Sandra is *all* cognitive empathy: It is *logical* that we are not separate; it is a logical imperative to serve one another. The inborn drive for reciprocity and connection—for what the Vietnamese Zen priest Thich Nhat Hanh has called "interbeing"—is how we define our humanity. Watching someone struggle to attain it, against certain biological odds, is profoundly moving.

Speaking of her Williams' syndrome patients, Susan Hepburn says, "Their empathy makes them too vulnerable," and it's true. Even in normal people, one psychologist suggests, "the sense of self must be protected by an 'empathic wall' lest we be taken over by those around us." Williams' kids are without walls entirely. No stone wall against

70

neighbors, or against strangers, those unmet friends; no castle wall against the enemy; no interior wall to brick in the heart. They have broken down my own categorical walls: the ones that would define their condition as purely pathological rather than a poignant glimpse into our human capacities; that might deem them so wrong and the rest of the world so very right.

"I often have a feeling of wanting to just protect their naivete," admits Susan Hepburn, "to somehow miraculously change the world into a place where you *could* safely like everybody, and safely assume that everyone would also value you." She looks wistful, and I catch her mood—empathically, contagiously—feeling a bit wistful myself: What a wonderful world *that* would be.

Meeting these unusual people, I'm struck anew by how keen is our common desire to make contact. After all, we neurotypicals are not monochromatic. We each show up along a continuum from all heart to pure reason. We each have our own ways of reaching out to each other; we all burn with that ardent flame to, in E. M. Forster's words, "connect, only connect." But how much? How deep? How far?

*T*he great mystics see the continuum as a single circle, fusing the pure extremes of emotional and cognitive empathy into one blinding arc where the me-and-you distinction flares to transparency. This erasure of the border between I and thou is such a persistent perception that it can't be ignored.

Saints of all religions have presented it as an apogee of compassion,* one which they insist is attainable through inspiration, humility,

---

* The Latin root of *conscience* means "joint or mutual knowledge," the same root that underlies the word *consciousness*. Mirror neuron co-discoverer Vittorio Gallese goes so far as to suggest that the basis of consciousness might not be our vaunted "sense of self," but rather our "intersubjectivity," a sort of self-*and*-otherhood.

and spiritual elbow-grease. Said Meister Eckhart: "You need to love all persons as yourself, esteeming them and considering them alike. What happens to another, whether it be a joy or a sorrow, happens to you." Similarly, Shantideva recommends applying the thought "they are myself" habitually to every creature so that "one will come to care for them as much as one now cares for oneself." It does sound like empathy as an extreme sport, but we don't have to compete in some Compassion Decathlon for a heart of gold. We've all had, from time to time, an ineffable taste of nonseparateness, like the lovers in the Pablo Neruda poem:

> I love you in this way because
> I don't know any other way of loving but this,
> in which there is no I or you,
> so intimate that your hand upon my chest is my hand,
> so intimate that when I fall asleep it is your eyes that close.

Shantideva takes this lover's holiday from selfhood a step further: He maintains that there *is* no self (and therefore no other) in the first place. Buddhism claims that what we think to be the "I," the "me," is insubstantial—a puff of air blown into a balloon, the balloon locked in a box, the box secured in a vault, the vault in a bank, the bank guarded by police, the police employed by the government—a vast, impressive bureaucracy of ego to administer and defend a big empty *nothing*.

And if the self is unreal, so is all concept of "other," for the simple reason that the two terms have meaning only in juxtaposition to each other. Shantideva claims that to make a separation between "you" and "me" is just as impossible as "to cut the sky in two with a knife." He promises that those who "cast aside the ordinary, trivial view of 'self' " are sure to gain "an attitude of wanting to protect others as oneself, and to protect all that belongs to them with the same care as if it were one's own."

I struggle to understand this rather rarified notion of selflessness. What if it's not a matter of me being generous to you, but more that you and I really are two hands of the same being? If I refuse you when you're in need, it's like the right hand refusing to remove a thorn from the left on grounds that it's the *left* hand's problem.

You might try this exercise proposed by a Buddhist scholar to illustrate that the self-other dichotomy isn't all it's cracked up to be: *Put your right hand on the back of your left.* Try to feel the warmth and texture of the left hand's skin solely from the right hand's perspective, as if you've just placed your hand on your lover's. Feel how, from the right hand's point of view, the left hand becomes a fleshy object, an other.

Now try reversing it: Shift the focus of your attention to your left hand. Feel the right hand's weight and warmth upon it. Without changing anything but your mind, the left hand now feels like "I," while the right feels more like "other"—when, in point of fact, both are "me."

It's an imperfect experiment because you can easily (indeed, it's hard to avoid) experience both hands as very much your own. But even then, you may notice a peculiar flickering back and forth, like one of those Escher optical illusions that appears one minute to be a staircase going up and the next minute stairs going down (even though, because it's a single picture, both are true). Einstein himself once referred to our sense of separateness as "a kind of optical delusion of consciousness"—a delusion that limits our caring because it "restricts us to our personal desires and to affection for a few persons nearest to us." To live in the world we'd really like to see, he continued, we must undertake a deliberate change in perspective: "Our task must be to free ourselves by widening our circle of compassion to embrace all creatures and the whole of nature."

I've known a few people who make it seem possible. I met Brother David Steindl-Rast years ago when I was fresh out of the hospital for cancer surgery. I had gone to a conference but, in lingering postoperative trauma, found myself barely able to cope. People spotted my distress and for the most part gave me a wide berth. Maybe it was the raw surgical scar across my neck, as if I'd been decapitated and had my head sewn back on, or maybe the shell-shocked look in my eyes; but even in a crowd, I felt terribly alone.

Brother David was coming down a path from the opposite direction, gaunt yet radiant in his black-and-white habit. Perhaps touched by something he saw in my face, he paused, sat down on a low rock wall, and gestured me over by patting a space next to him. We talked; or actually, I talked. He encouraged me to unload the whole dump truck of my woes—his steady gaze told me he could take it. He was the first person who didn't flinch away. He seemed to be feeling not *for* me, but *with* me, harnessed to the same harrow I felt fated to pull across barren, rocky soil.

He conveyed a few words of advice and comfort—something about an "unknown guidance system," which kicks in when you're really lost—but mostly he shared my pain without trying to do anything about it. I felt taken into his heart in a way I can't fully explain. When he quietly told me, without a speck of dogma, that I shouldn't assume my suffering had no value, I never forgot it. I knew somehow that he had been there himself; that he had, in a sense, never left.

A tiny intervention, perhaps, but there doesn't seem to be much that's too small for him to notice or to care about. We've met again a number of times over the years, and I'm always reminded of his exquisite sensitivity to the living universe; feeling, feeling, always feeling. Once he described to me walking through a park and, seeing a scrap of two-by-four board lying on the grass, being overcome by "how hard it was for the grass to breathe; it felt like *I* couldn't breathe." When he lifted off the board, he told me, "I heard the grass rejoicing."

You might think, *Oh, brother, spare me.* But he's not of the quaking aspen school of spirituality. His mysticism is infused with a knowledge of the real world. I mentioned to him once how wrenching I'd found the beggars in India's Old Delhi, entire multigenerational families living on a single patch of sidewalk they'd claimed as their own. I couldn't imagine that the crumpled rupees I dropped in their hands could make a difference and had felt crushed by charity's impotence.

"Yes," he said softly. "I've seen those same people. It hurts the heart. Still we mustn't just regard them with pity, but see what they have to teach us. They take care of each other every day as an extended family. They practice values many of us have lost. We should help, yes, but our compassion should be connected with gratefulness for what they offer *us*."

The thought took me aback. I'd been looking at them as if through a one-way mirror. In fact, we were each other's reflections. *No self, no other.* I was reminded of the way one Christian writer differentiated two forms of compassionate love: "Charity extends the privileges of insiders to outsiders; while *agape* erases the line between insiders and outsiders entirely."

Brother David tells me his inspiration is the three Catholic rosaries known as "joyful," "sorrowful," and "glorious," which produce in him a "deep poetic stimulation of compassion." Contemplating Jesus' scourging, he feels a oneness with every beaten-down person in the world. It is not religious masochism, he says, pointing out that the earliest crosses were adorned not with Christ in agony but with jewels that symbolized, in place of unredeemable pain, "the triumph of suffering transmuted." When he meditates this way, he says he feels a fullness, a wholeness. There is no longer any part of life that can't be embraced.

Still, he says, "Sometimes, I have to protect myself. I can't take it all in." I ask him how he deals with it. "St. John's wor—," he says in a low tone that muffles the consonant.

"St. John's word?" I ask, thinking of *The Dark Night of the Soul*, that medieval masterwork of suffering transmuted.

"St. John's *Wort*," he corrects me, then laughs heartily, loud and long. "But his word, too."

*T*he last time I saw Brother David, he mentioned a dream he'd had the previous night. "I dreamed I was eating a pear," he told me. "A wasp landed on it. I brushed it off, and it fell into my glass of water. The whole dream was about trying to fish it out." A few nights before that, he said, he'd dreamed of an ant struggling in the middle of a pond. He was trying to rescue it with a branch, but every time he came close, someone threw a stone in the water and the ensuing ripple washed it back out. Finally it drowned, and he awoke feeling bereft. I thought of poet William Blake's comment on compassion: "He who would do Good for another must do it in Minute Particulars."

For in the end, empathy need not scale great spiritual pinnacles or be vetted with a psychological seal of approval. The Minute Particulars of relationship, in most cases, will do just fine. A friend once told me a story about his mother. On the first day she'd arrived in a new city, she had struck up a conversation at the train station with a woman making a stopover in the midst of a long journey and unthinkingly handed her a sandwich she'd been saving for later. It was the beginning of a twenty-year friendship. After his mother died, he'd happened upon a packet of the women's correspondence. One thing had particularly struck him, he said. "So many of the letters from this woman ended with the same words: 'I'll never forget that you fed me.'"

4

STREET RETREAT: THE DEBT OF LOVE

We're all in the gutter,
only some of us are looking at the stars.
—*Oscar Wilde*

A woman stands in line at the post office a few people ahead of me, and I am falling in love with her chestnut hair, which hangs long and glossy to the middle of her back. When she half-turns, I see her face is badly scarred. I flinch as a fantasy bubble pops. I know she catches that flinch; catches it constantly, from fools like me. My heart, wide open a moment ago, has shut with the faint click of a latch, like a music box closing in midtune. Why, I wonder, did it not sound a more sympathetic note?

A friend tells me that whenever *she* sees any human suffering, "My mind drops into my heart." She insists she's not just being poetic. It's an acute sensation, she says, physical and emotional, her judgments falling away, sympathies instantly engaged. I wish I could say the same, but I mostly tend to remain in my head, doing what comes most naturally: critiquing, doing due diligence, setting door policy.

I got an e-mail the other day whose title line read: "Affirm

77

Everything About Anyone." Yes, *exactly*, I thought: unconditional positive regard. It turned out to be an offer to spy on people via the Web, but no matter. Why *not* just affirm everything about *every*one, accept them in as-is condition, love them for who they are?

Last summer, I saw an immensely fat woman—350 pounds, at least—struggling to step onto a Manhattan bus. Wheezing with effort, perspiring through her floral print dress, she couldn't hoist her foot onto the platform. Her knee, encased in layers of flesh, wouldn't bend. The driver, with an exasperated sigh, bolted from his seat to try to shoehorn her through the door.

The passengers gaped and craned, and their gaze by and large was not benign; expressions ranged from embarrassment to scorn to a sort of horrified fascination. As schedules unraveled and tempers frayed, the irritation grew more audible. The blue, molded-plastic bus seats became an ad hoc jury room to reach a verdict on her human worth. The thought flashed through my mind as it did through nearly everyone's: *Why would—how could—anyone allow themselves to get so obese?* Then I saw the expression on the woman's face—mortification. And my heart broke—for all her hard days, and for all my hard thoughts.

Why was my first response not compassion, but instead a series of assessments that went off like a string of mental firecrackers before I even knew I'd lit the match? My judgment was so fused with my perception as to be inseparable: She became what I beheld. I was painfully aware of my mind—the mind itself—as a difference engine, cranking out the petty distinctions that keep people apart. And I wished I could dismantle the whole stupid contraption once and for all.

So I suppose I should have been glad when old Søren Kierkegaard showed up, clenching a monkey wrench in his ink-stained hand and hurling it unceremoniously into the churning gears. I knew him, of course; religious philosopher, bit of a crank, someone I'd lost touch with since college, when I'd written him off as some gloomy, angsty

Dane (*Fear and Trembling* and all). For years, he'd meant no more to me than any other Dead White Male of the Western Canon. But recently, on impulse, I'd rehefted one of his tomes and gained a new appreciation of this fiery eccentric who had shocked nineteenth-century society with his tirades against church hierarchy, sticking up for those "despised and rejected by men," proclaiming them nearest of all to God. As I discovered while reading his rhapsodic masterpiece, *Works of Love*, his pet peeve was smallness of heart. The chapter titles alone tell you what's on his mind (italics his): "You *Shall* Love;" "You Shall Love *the Neighbor*"; "*You* Shall Love the Neighbor."

Sir, yessir! I've taken to using *WOL* as a kind of oracle-book, opening it every few days to random pages. Today's selection is entitled: "Our Duty to Love the People We See," and enough said. I find myself nodding when Søren cites "comparison" as "the most dangerous acquaintance love can make." It is, he says indignantly, his Nordic blood heating to a rolling boil, "a noxious shoot"; a "cursed tree"; a "withered shadow"; a "swampy ground"; and, lest we forget, "a hidden worm." I take his point. I'm sick of watching myself weigh in on this and inveigh against that, going over all humanity with a fine-toothed comb. I do it with my eyes closed. Let someone's accent be Upper Adenoid, New Jersey, or Marblemouth, Georgia, and before I know it, I've placed a subliminal red checkmark next to their name and referred them to the credentials committee.

I have a friend who's marginally even more exacting. Though I know she has a kind heart, it's often covered by a brittle tortoiseshell of judgment. She grew up poor—"pedigreed trailer-trash," she likes to say—so of course poverty's her hot-button issue. Like many who've come up the hard way, she's put as much mileage as possible between herself and the dismal swamp of the past. She's even become a latter-day disciple of hypercapitalist Ayn Rand: By her reckoning, you're either roadmaster or roadkill. I've heard my friend espouse opinions about the downtrodden (and those who try to help them) so outrageously cynical it would make a member of the vast right-wing conspiracy blanch. (I know she partly does it to get my ultraliberal goat.)

She works in the PR trade, has a prestige address on her business card, is chic, svelte, and successful, and countenances no excuses for failure. But lately a downturn in the market has jumped up and bit her. She's been going through a prolonged bout of unemployment. She's by no means out on the street, but it's shaken her up.

"The other day," she tells me, "I turned into the alley behind my apartment, and there was this bum going through my trash bin. I had all the thoughts I usually do—disdain, disgust, and, on top of that, ir- ritation that I had to wait for him to get out of the way just so I could get into my parking space. I inched up behind him and was about to lean on my horn when he turned around. I saw his face, how ravaged this guy looked, suffering written all over him. And suddenly, I don't know, it was like breaking a spell. I felt this overwhelming sense of sympathy. I could just *feel* how ashamed he was, and then *I* felt ashamed, too. I rolled down the window and gave him a few dollars, and he almost cried, and I teared up, too. He was so grateful, it shocked me."

Fast-forward a few weeks, and she might have discovered *me* swan-diving in her dumpster. For here I am, with a week's growth of beard, in my rattiest clothes, a toothbrush in my pocket, living on the streets of Denver. I hadn't planned to be here. This week, I was scheduled to go to Cannes of all places, and thence to a farmhouse in glorious Provence, a dumb-luck invite only a dunce would turn down. But another invitation, this one from a group called the Zen Peacemaker Order to go on what they called a "street retreat," had suddenly come up in the same cal- endar slot. None of my friends thought there'd be much contest:

"If you don't get on a plane to France," one said, "then *I* will."

But Søren, old Søren, in one of my necromantic readings, had nailed my Achilles heel—snobbery—to the floor in one mercilessly deflating passage, mocking that person "who thinks he exists only for the distinguished, that he is to live only in the alliances of their circles, that he must not exist for other people, just as they must not exist for him." Of course, that's not *really* me. I live in a modest shack in the student badlands, drive a beater, have friends up and down the social ladder and across the zodiac; but still, when Søren skewers the elitist who tries to ensure he is "never among the more lowly"—who "will go about with closed eyes . . . when he moves around in the human throng"—I can't pretend I have no idea what he's talking about.

And since the point these days is to learn to *open* my eyes, along with that near-rusted lock on my heart, I knew what I had to do. The retreat rules were simple enough: Hit the streets unbathed and unshaven, without money or change of clothes, joining for the better part of a week the ranks of those whom life had kicked to the curb.

A stint of homelessness, a sojourn in the land of Ain't Got Nothin', Got Nothin' to Lose would be a way to get over my absurd sense of specialness. I'd be forced to relinquish my sovereign choices of food, lodging, and throng; be grateful to take what I could get. It's a spiritual exercise with a certain pedigree. After all, who were the Buddha and St. Francis but a couple of rich kids who'd opted to go out on the bum, seeking humility by dressing in rags, begging on the street, shucking whatever might separate them from anyone else's travail? St. John of the Cross told those who aspired to open their hearts to turn "not to what tastes best, but to what is most distasteful . . . not to desire the more, but the less . . . not to aspire to what is highest and most precious, but to what is lowest and most contemptible . . . to learn to know nothing, go whither you are ignorant."

The street retreats are the brainchild of Bernie Glassman, a man who has enshrined ignorance (which he calls "unknowing") as a central precept. A bearded, portly, former aerospace engineer or-dained as a Buddhist *roshi*, Bernie had been looking for ways to in-tegrate spiritual practice with compassionate social action. Sometime in the 1980s, he decided to spend a few months walking aimlessly around the inner-city neighborhood that abutted his meditation center, hanging out, talking with people in his cannily receptive way, listening to their problems. Out of this had grown, as naturally and prolifically as a zucchini patch, a sprawling multimillion-dollar social organization serving the rebuked and the scorned.

First there was the Greyston Bakery, which employed people just getting out of prison or off the street. The business grew, eventually snagging a contract to make brownies for Ben and Jerry's Ice Cream. But it soon came smack up against the endemic problems of the neighborhood. People missed work because of drug problems. Batches of dough were ruined because employees lacked basic math skills to measure ingredients or reading skills to decipher labels on cans. But each problem had suggested, after trial and error, its own solu-tion. The Greyston Mandala that emerged from Bernie's first street-scuffing walkabout now trains, employs, houses, and provides health services to hundreds of the formerly marginal, as well as offering care and housing to people with AIDS on the site of a former Catholic nunnery.

When Bernie's fifty-fifth birthday had rolled around, rather than resting on his laurels, he'd decided to spend a few days sitting home-less on the steps of the Capitol, figuring out what next to do with his life. During what turned out to be Washington, D.C.'s coldest, snowiest week in half a century, he had dreamed up the multifaith Peacemaker Order, a spiritual path based on just bearing witness and seeing what happened.

"When we bear witness," he wrote, "when we become the situa-tion—homelessness, poverty, illness, violence, death—then right ac-tion arises by itself. We don't have to worry about what to do. We don't have to figure out solutions ahead of time . . . It's as simple as giving a hand to someone who stumbles or picking up a child who has fallen on the floor."

You could say, Witness, *schmitness*. Fine for Bernie, with his track record of weaving straw into gold. But if he hadn't recommended it, I'd be hard put to justify my week of taking to the streets in a bum costume, as if I and my fellow retreatants didn't have somewhere better to go. All I could think was, at least for this interlude, there would be no better, and no worse.

*H*ere I was in Denver!" exulted Jack Kerouac in 1947 after hitch-hiking from New York. "I stumbled along with the most wicked grin of joy in the world, among the old bums and beat cowboys of Larimer Street." Kerouac managed to romanticize the down-and-out as the literarily up-and-coming, but those days are gone. His gritty cityscape—"smokestacks, smoke, rail yards, red-brick buildings, and the distant downtown gray stone buildings"—has given way to sports bars and brick *pied-à-terres*. The old Denargo market where he once worked hauling watermelons is now, almost predictably, the site of the million-dollar Jack Kerouac Lofts (which, says the sales brochure, "pay homage to a life of exuberant discovery, and offer a fitting home for those who are 'mad to live'"). Meanwhile the unfitting homeless, some of them the deinstitutionalized mad, are discovering a life less exuberant.

Denver has experienced a staggering 25 percent increase in homelessness. In a single year, hate crimes against the homeless population resulted in no fewer than nine beating deaths (with several *decapitations*). I feel glad I'll be traveling in a group of ten people, ranging from students to doctors, led by a fifty-two-year-old street-wise Buddhist social activist and Peacemaker priest named Fleet Maull. Fleet's a big guy, and despite his soft features and benign

83

expression, he looks a little threatening. With his old bulky coat and lumbering gait, the more belligerent street people tend to dodge him, as do the regular folks on their way to work.

We all gather to meditate each morning in a small park, an unkempt sliver of green down from the abandoned Sacred Heart School with its chipped Jesus statue and chiseled inscription from Mark 10: "Suffer the little children to come unto me and forbid them not." But it's forbidden to loiter, so we hit the ground walking, keeping on keeping on. After only a few days, the soles of my feet are already aching. *No wonder they shuffle*, I think, push-dragging the two anvils at the ends of their legs up and down the block. We're always on the ground, walking on it, sleeping on it. For them, it's a life; for us, with any luck, an exercise in humility.

Humility: from the Latin *humus*, meaning earth, ground, soil; the root of *human* and *humiliate* ("to lower the pride or dignity of"), as when we come down to earth with a crash, the ego one big purple bruise. I'd wanted to take this week to be a little less full of myself, see if innate kindness would arise if I moved out and made some room for it. But what is arising is my innate irritability. I can be impatient, and homelessness involves lots of waiting. Waiting for a soup kitchen to open, waiting for your number to be called for a meal, waiting for the rain or snow to let up or for a cop to stop looking your way. It's a different map of the world: Which Starbucks has a security guard who'll let you use the bathroom? How long can you linger in this place or that before you're rousted? It's a stray dog's life, sniffing around for a bone to gnaw, a tree to piss on, knowing nobody wants you, being wary of the company you keep.

My venerable friend Søren, in his tough-old-bird fashion, argued against harboring any delusions that "by loving some people, relatives and friends, you would be loving the neighbor . . ." No, he squawked, the real point is "to frighten you out of the beloved haunts of preferential love." Most of my new neighbors *are* haunted. Life has failed them, or they've failed it. A tall, stringy, young man with lank, black-dyed hair, tattooed like a Maori, tells me, "If you see Sherry, tell her Big John's back from Oklahoma." His eyes have the jittery glint of crank, each pupil a spinning disco ball, sending out fitful sparkles. An alcoholic Indian vet yanks open his shirt to show me his scars, the roundish puckers from shrapnel, the short, telegraphic dashes from ritual piercing at a Sun Dance, weeping over a life he no longer wants.

An angry-looking man approaches me to ask—to demand—that I give him a plastic fork, purpose unknown. When I demur, he stalks over to the dumpster and scrabbles through it unproductively.

"I'm sorry," I say.

"I'll just *bet* you are," he snarls, raising both middle fingers and staring with cold fury into my eyes.

I can't say I'm pleased to meet him, but WWKD: What Would Kierkegaard Do? "Root out all equivocation and fastidiousness in loving them!" *Sir, yessir.* The Buddhist sage Atisha recommended a prayer upon encountering those folks who mess with our minds: *When I see beings of a negative disposition, or those oppressed by negativity or pain, may I, as if finding a treasure, consider them precious.* It is good, Atisha said, when your comfy sweater of self-cherishing gets snagged on someone's rusty nail, unraveling as you try to pull away. Better, he said, not to pull away at all.

Every cerebral word of this homily is not running through my head as I step toward my new neighbor with a little nod of appreciation, hoping he hasn't stashed a ballpeen hammer in his coat. But he backs away, lip curled, then turns and runs, pursued by some host of invisibles. At least, I tell myself, I've managed to become more curious about him than repulsed, mindful that the more I amp up my judgment of others, the more I empower that ogre of criticism that grinds my bones to make its bread. I don't know how these guys drove their lives into a ditch or how to winch them out. I just try to stay present, to my heart's systole and diastole, my sympathies opening, closing, opening, closing.

The homeless. Street people. In truth, it's annoying they're out there, huddled in doorways, sleeping curled up against the wall of a building, declaiming their private jeremiads, deportees from ordinary life. What gives them the right to intrude into our space (sometimes their smell, supernaturally potent, intrudes first), to interrupt our train of thought or flow of conversation to make us feel that involuntary muscle-spasm of conscience? Why *don't* they get a job, pay rent for a roof over their heads?

But most are just downsized and luckless, in the talons of dire predicament, many so wounded and vulnerable they seem, if anything, too gentle for this world.

I fell in with a man named Fred who used to work in a livestock feedlot. "Rather feed 'em than kill 'em," he says mildly. He's a harmless-looking guy with a scraggle of graying beard, his soft face white as a daikon radish, wearing a cap embroidered with the Teamsters' logo of two horses and a wheel. It all started when his hours got cut, he tells me. Then the union bargained away his benefits. The plant closed down. He'd lost the house and then the wife. The kids grew estranged. The repo man grabbed the truck he'd counted on for sideline painting jobs. Fred seems abstracted, ruminative; he's understandably befuddled over his fate. How did he land here, anyway, snarfing down free church feeds and looking for day labor gigs as the months spiraled into nearly two years now?

He used to sleep in the alleys, he says, but it got too dangerous. "This winter was rough, man. There were guys out there who'd slit your throat for your sleeping bag." He finally found what he calls a "campsite" somewhere in the city. He won't tell me where; too many other pilgrims on *hejira*, too few oases. "It's got three walls and an overhang, almost like a room," he tells me, house-proud. He knows that the building super's wise to him, but he takes care to clean up, neatly stowing his stuff. The other day the super even left him a broom, standing it up against the wall, tacitly acknowledging his tenancy.

Our own sitting-room, when it's not a piece of pavement, is the Bus Terminal, aptly named for that percentage of its habitués who have arrived at their final destination and who are going nowhere fast. We can sit until closing time, keeping warm. When a lady comes by panhandling for the two dollars more she needs for a ticket, I let her pass, thinking I'll use the little money I've cadged today to buy myself a corndog. Then, feeling remorseful—*jeez, even at this level, I'm playing I've Got Mine*—I run after her and give her whatever's in my pocket, three big ones, and she hugs me like I'd handed her a fistful of pearls. I wish I'd had more. I want her to be warm, safe, and loved wherever she's going. And God, I hope when she gets there, she never has to come back.

*H*omelessness is a journey down the rabbit hole. The ordinary world vanishes. The roof over your head. The cash in your pocket. The food in your belly. Random acts of kindness become just that: sporadic, unaccountable, case studies for the Journal of Irreproducible Results. I'm amazed how fast my "real life" recedes. That night, as the terminal closes and the cold sets in, we trudge past a hotel where my girlfriend and I had stayed one New Year's, renting a suite with some friends, playing Scrabble and drinking champagne. I stop to peer in the window at the lobby's plush coziness, my breath making cloudy smudges.

We wander down the dark streets of the Five Points ghetto incongruously close to downtown's glittering towers, but the only glitter here is from shards of broken whisky bottles we sweep aside before laying down our cardboard next to some concrete walls. I notice they're pockmarked with bullet holes. Apparently our alcove is used for target practice by the local gangbangers, but it's the best squat we can find, with a generous overhang to keep out the weather.

"Do not judge your fellow until you have rested in his place," said Hillel, and I *am* trying, if you can call this resting, laying supine on a deconstructed lettuce carton, frost forming on my sleeping bag, still fantasizing about southern France and grilled squid, clinging to shreds of vanity. I realize this really *is* a meditation retreat, an active contemplation on the illusion of self-cherishing and worthier-than-others. Somehow, somewhere, the homeless fell down, and at this moment, I'm no different. We all fall. We are all fallen. It suddenly seems like the boundary I'd put up against them is the same membrane that separates me from everyone—even from those dejected parts of myself I refuse to grant a home.

Still, I tell one of my fellow retreatants as we settle in, "I'm laying here thinking I really deserve better. I'm telling myself, 'I'm never going to do this again.'"

He laughed. "I'll bet every other bum in Denver tonight is thinking exactly the same thing."

The next morning, we make our way down to the Holy Ghost Church, where you can get a breakfast of baloney and cheese sandwich with an *amuse-bouche* of mini-Snickers, plus all the hot bad coffee you can drink. I'm told that the line, snaking around the adjacent blue glass bank tower, is twice as long as last year. A church lady comes by offering wool hats hand-knit by members of the congregation.

These are the outposts of compassion, though too few and far between. We pass a Catholic Workers boardinghouse that puts up homeless families, and offer to help out. We slap a new coat of paint on the fence, and for once I'm Huck Finn, not Tom Sawyer. I hunt down prehistoric dust-bunnies behind the patched Naugahyde Barcalounger. In the parlor, a zinc tub sits near the woodstove, catching raindrops through the leaky roof. The manager, a careworn soul with fine spiderwebs around her eyes and an apron of wrung-out blue, gives us tea and a place to sit for a while, occasionally shooting us an enormous smile.

Then I set out walking with Fleet. My toes are now blistered, and so are his, but he's more stoic about it, padding them with Kleenex, laconic with his discomfort. We drift over to the Jesus to the World mission, where a stocky, tough-talking preacher is shouting aphorisms at the lunch crowd.

"Stop telling yourself what you *can't* do, and you *may* start knowing what you *can* do!" he bellows. "If I'm halfway *in* the storm, then realistically, I must be halfway *out* of it!" Most of it's pretty good stuff. When he says, "The first word out of your mouth that curses your life is 'I,'" the Buddhist in me approves, though I'm nonplussed when he walks up to a man at the end of my table and practically shouts in his ear: "If you don't repent, God may need to *kill* you to get your attention!" The man continues his meal unperturbed, the fire and brimstone so much hot sauce and pickle relish.

The preacher dials it down a little, lowering his voice confidingly. "When I was in prison, a man planted the seed of the Lord in me, and—"

"What was you in the joint *for*?" a man yells out.

"Traffic violations," he mumbles, momentarily offstride. "But that's not the point."

Fleet smiles faintly. Maybe it is, maybe it's not. Fleet's got his own story. He knows about the joint, more than a little.

F leet Maull was a thirty-five-year-old golden boy with a covey of beautiful girlfriends, a Tibetan guru, a yacht named *The Spice of Life,* and a penchant for thousand-dollar suits and lavish parties, all courtesy of a thriving cocaine-importing business, when he landed up in the federal pen. Convicted under the drug kingpin laws, he plummeted headfirst from cloud nine to the concrete floor of a steel cage, sentenced to twenty-five years without parole in the same Missouri prison where Robert Stroud, the Birdman of Alcatraz, had spent his last years.

Fleet was surrounded by hard-case, thin-skinned gangbangers, quickly noticing how a sideways look or casual remark could be seen as a diss, warranting a beat-down with a padlock wrapped in a sock, or worse. *I don't belong here,* he thought. He'd grown up in a close-knit Catholic family with all the upper-middle-class amenities: the big house with the sweeping lawn on a hushed, elegant street, the gleaming cars, the exclusive education. After dropping out of college, he'd worked awhile for his father's company, but he soon grew bored. Following the spinning compass needle of 1970s' hippie hearsay, he'd wound up in a Peruvian village in the shadow of Macchu Picchu, over-looking the vast, verdant valley of the Urubamba River, just east of Eden. Later, on a visit to Bolivia to renew his visa, he'd scored a kilo of coke through a source whose name a friend had scrawled on a slip of paper. It had been almost a whim, a lark, but soon the penny-ante drug deals to pay the rent on his Peruvian paradise burgeoned into the freewheeling smuggling operation that led to his big-time bust.

But landing in prison had catalyzed a remarkable transformation. "The minute the cell door shut," he says, "I had this profound experience of really, really deep regret and remorse. I began to come out of the drug and alcohol haze. I realized what I'd done to family and friends, to myself. It caused a kind of conversion experience, just this 180-degree turn. And I developed a profound desire to erase any kind of harmful things I'd done in my life and find a way to be of some benefit."

Thrown into a cramped unit, with 175 men sardined together on a floor built for fifty, he chose an upper bunk where there was enough headroom to sit crosslegged on a folded blanket and meditate. He re-members the moment he'd asked a prisoner to turn down the radio and got a venomous, in-your-face rejoinder: "Who the *fuck* do you think you are? This is *jail.* Your world don't revolve around *you* any-more." Fleet had been a dilettantish student of Buddhism before; now he became a locked-down monk, meditating in a broom closet amid the racket of blaring TVs, fights, and raucous games of slap-down dominoes. Years later, when good behavior earned him a private cell, he'd awaken every morning at 3 A.M. to meditate some more.

But he'd also begun to realize he was no one special. It hit him, he says, when he broke down crying one day talking on a pay phone to his former girlfriend. "I was wailing that I was no better than the rest of these people in here, waiting for her to contradict me. But she just said, 'Well, honey, *of course* you're not.' Being thrown into this hell-realm, not being able to separate myself from the environment, actually pulled me out of myself for the first time."

What affected him most was the Yard. Springfield is a high-security prison hospital with 300 mentally ill, 600 desperately sick, and 300 nominally healthy inmates to run the place. He'd watch the emaciated men dying of cancer and AIDS; the paraplegics and the quads, castaways from the rest of the prison system, marooned all together, and each alone, on this gray concrete archipelago. Fleet was still trying to distance himself. "I was better than *them*, at least; I still had my health." But after a while, he realized that was just the point: Their situation was so pitiably grim, and he was doing nothing to help.

The AIDS epidemic was accelerating, and its prisoner-patients had been isolated in the mental health wing in a secure unit for their own protection. Sometimes they were sent out to community hospitals to die shackled to their beds; most were fading away alone in the prison ward, facing the con's ultimate defeat, a death behind bars. Fleet, who had been delegated to run a film projector in the unit, smuggled in magazines, getting to know the men. Eventually he teamed up with a paraplegic prisoner to create a visitation program. It slowly grew into a full medical hospice, the first inmate-staffed program in an American high-security prison. Within a system built of, by, and for the crushing of the human spirit, they created for felons dying of cancer and AIDS an incongruous island of kindness.

It became a school for compassion, with once-violent cons caring for men who'd arrived at life's most helpless and vulnerable juncture.

In a place where the strong routinely preyed on the weak, it was astonishing, Fleet tells me, to see hardened killers washing their patients' emaciated bodies and changing their soiled bedclothes. Prisoner staff and prisoner patients talked and sat in silence, wept and prayed together, went through the long dying together up to the uncanny moment when the body's husk was quietly abandoned. If the dying patient was a Christian, then Fleet, a former altar boy, would recite the Lord's Prayer.

Four years later, in 1991, his National Prison Hospice Association became an officially recognized organization. By the time he'd completed fourteen years behind bars and mounted a successful appeal to get released, the model he'd helped create had spread through the federal prison system. "The hospice gives both guards and inmates permission to care," Fleet says. "It restores their humanity. They begin to feel, 'We're a community. We don't just let our guys die with nobody taking care of them.'" A prison chaplain at Springfield said the greatest transformations he had seen in his career were among the inmate volunteers.

Fleet himself remains a little impenetrable. Long years of circumspection and regimentation have left a mark. There are glimpses of the person he was before, the arrogant, macho dude who stepped on and over people in pursuit of selfish pleasure. But I get the feeling that person has been melted down, tempered, refined and recast; there's not a lot of the base metal left.

*T*he St. Francis Center is the best feed in town. Hot soup with chunks of real roast beef floating in it. Salad with tangy dressing and piles of fresh tomato slices. Hard-boiled eggs. Real fruit, even a few strawberries and, *pièce de résistance,* pumpkin pie. No sermons, all succor. It would have made St. Francis laugh to see the poor so honored in his name, remembering his days as a rake who loved to put out a big spread for all his friends.

Before St. Francis became, as it were, a holy bum, wearing the lowliest homespun of "beast color," sleeping where he could, he was a high-flying young bachelor in a city known then as the Babylon of Italy. A rich kid pursuing the troubadorial tradition of wine, women, and song, he was said to have lived "riotously," often playing the role of *rex convivi,* the host who underwrote the revels and banquets. His set led the medieval version of the urban singles life, Sex in Assissi.

But one day, out riding in a handsome new outfit, he saw a beggar and, his biographer says, "touched with compassion, changed clothes with him." Trading places with society's poorest and most beaten down seems to have liberated him from all judgment. He describes in his last testament how painful it had been to see lepers until he lived in their midst, but "when I left them, that which had seemed to me bitter had become sweet and easy."

The famous St. Francis Prayer is a paean to this confounding spiritual intention to turn exactly what we wish most to receive into that which we resolve to give: "O, Divine Master, grant that I may not so much seek to be consoled as to console; to be understood as to understand; to be loved as to love . . ."

Francis and his disciples, "careless of the day," wandering from place to place, sleeping where they fell, were essentially homeless beggars. So were the Buddha and his followers, who'd make the rounds with their wooden begging bowls. But the thought of doing what the Zen Peacemaker Order refers to as "begging practice" horrifies me. Sure, I'd done that high-class begging known as fundraising, my palm outstretched for checks written out to high-minded projects. But I'd always felt it was worth the other person's while; there were good deeds to show for it. Here on the street, I have nothing to offer. There is no mutual exchange, no way to ensure I won't feel indebted by some imbalance of boons. I'm a walking bundle of needs, and it galls me.

Besides, it isn't easy to get those needs met. Faces turn to stone at a plea for food money. Eyes flicker sideways, ahead to the middle distance, to the ground, anywhere but the empty space where I'm standing. The Confucians of the Sung Dynasty compared not feeling compassion for a stranger to not feeling your own foot has caught fire, and many of us have gone numb. (I think of an acquaintance of mine, an internationally known designer of leafy town squares in the New Urbanist style. "Of course," he once said to me ruefully, "the more open space, the bigger the quotient of 'bummage.'")

Bummage I am. I supplicate downtown pedestrians, dauntingly busy on their way from here to there, clutching purses and shopping bags and cell phones and lovers' waists. I recognize the filmy bubble of self-concept they carry, that protective aura of specialness. How often do most of us secretly say to ourselves that we're smarter, stronger, taller, more charming; have a cooler job, a more lovely spouse, more accomplished children; are (somehow) more spiritual, even more selfless? Anything is grist for the mill of selfhood versus otherness, of the gourmet flavor me versus plain vanilla everyone else. I, too, have achieved my differentiation at some cost and considerable effort; even here, I resist inhabiting the same universe as the full-time failures.

I've already arrived in one respect: My panhandling talents are nil. Each rejection thuds like a body blow. I can see the little comic-strip thought balloon spring from people's brows—*Get a job; I work!* It occurs to me to just forget it. Though we've agreed that during the week we'd each scrape up $3.50 for the bus fare home, throwing any extra into the kitty for the homeless shelter, I think, *Why put myself through it? I'll send a check when I get home.*

But I'm hungry now. I'm also starting to realize there's more to "begging practice" than meets the eye. Roshi Bernie Glassman has explained it with disarming simplicity: "When we don't ask, we don't let others give. When we fear rejection, we don't let generosity arise." I realize the street, much like a meditation cushion, has put my issues on parade, and the begging routine's got them goosestepping smartly past the reviewing stand. There's the Humiliation Battalion. The Fear of Rejection Brigade. The Undeserving Auxiliary. And of course, the Judgment Detachment, for I find I'm even judging my potential donors—are they good enough to give me a dollar?

My profound reluctance to ask passersby for help feels not unlike my aversion to calling friends when I'm needful in other ways, those times when I'm feeling sad, lost, lonely. I prize autonomy; I'm over-proud of it. I don't *want* to owe people for my well-being. Or just maybe I don't want to owe them my love. I wondered suddenly if I wasn't rejecting gratitude itself, that spiritual 3-in-1 Oil, said to open the creakiest gate around the heart? Aren't we all in debt to our parents, teachers, friends, and loved ones for our very existence?

But dear Søren Kierkegaard thought even *this* was a crock. Sure, he said, we *think* a person who is loved owes a debt of gratitude to the one who loves them. There is an expectation that it should be repaid in kind, on installment, "reminiscent," he says sarcastically, "of an actual bookkeeping arrangement." Instead, he turns the whole thing on its head: "No, the one who loves runs into debt; in feeling himself gripped by love, he feels this as being in an infinite debt. Amazing!"

Amazing. It is his most radical proposition: We owe those who elicit love from us for allowing us to be filled with the stuff. We owe a debt to those who suffer because they draw forth our tenderness. (Do I think that by avoiding others' suffering, I can hoard my stash of good feelings and not get bummed out? The helper's high phenomenon suggests the opposite: It's giving that turns on the juice, taps us into the infinite current.) Giving and taking start to seem less like zero-sum transactions than some universal love-circuitry, where what goes around not only comes around but comes back redoubled.

Still, "How would you like to enter into Kiekegaard's infinite debt of love?" is not going to win Year's Best Panhandling Line. I ask a stylish young guy—*No War: Not in Our Name* button on his fawn-colored, coat, canvas messenger bag in muted gray—if he can spare a little change for food. He calls out chidingly over his shoulder, "I don't give *on the street.*" Fair enough. But the bank building's LED thermometer reads 25 degrees, and the sun still hasn't gone down. I haven't had dinner. Sleeping on the street is a frigid proposition, and body heat requires calories. Then I realize I'm judging him and everyone else, defeating the whole purpose of the exercise. I make a point to mentally bless all comers and goers.

I approach a bearded guy in a fringed suede jacket. He declines, but hangs around as if waiting for someone. A few minutes later, hearing me unsuccessfully petition a half dozen more people, he comes over and hands me two dollars, cautioning *sotto voce,* "Don't tell anyone I gave it to you," as if worried I'd alert a Fagin's gang of accomplices.

I've now streamlined my pitch: "I'm sleeping on the street tonight, I'm hungry. I wonder if you could help me out at all?" Most people's eyes still slam down like steel shutters over a storefront at closing time, but then, " . . . Could you help me out?" and a man who's just passed me with a curt *No* pivots abruptly, yanked like a puppet by his heartstrings, and walks back with a green bill. "On second thought, I can." And I see in that moment how much more effort it takes to re-sist the raw tug of each other.

I strike out another twenty or thirty times before a crisp-looking gent crosses my palm with silver. "Thanks so much, it's chilly out tonight," I mumble, surprised after so many averted gazes. "It *is* cold," he says sympathetically, in three words restoring my faith.

Such little ups and downs are a roller coaster out here. There's scant insulation from the shock of existence—or from its bene-ficence. I'm able to feel, palpably, because it hovers constantly above my head, that the same sun shines on each of us, paupers or potentates, saints or souses. Beauty itself is available gratis, something I forget when I'm rushing along like the business guy in *The Little Prince,* "concerned with matters of consequence."

With nothing better to do and nowhere else to go, I can stand stock-still and gaze in wonder at a blue sky streaked with salmon clouds reflected in the windows of an office building, like some thirty-story Hockney painting. I awoke one morning to see we'd camped beneath a tree crowned with one leftover copper leaf burnished bright by dawn. I heard birds chirping mightily over the traffic and smelled, despite our steaming breath, the tang of portending spring.

"The gifts of the street," Fleet likes to call them. But of those gifts, Jesus was best of all. He came into our lives unbidden, heralded by an aroma of whisky and unwashed clothes. He'd approached us one day in the park like a shy deer, sidling up to the edge of our meditation circle, a youngish man in an oversized checked wool shirt worn *vato*-style. He'd dropped to a crouch, made an odd little genuflection, sat down, and introduced himself in short Spanish phrases: *Jesus. Jesus Martinez.*

He was from Chihuahua state, he said, having paid a *coyote* a few years ago to smuggle him across the border.

"Trabajo?" we asked. "Any work?"

"No tengo."

Jesus carries a black plastic garbage bag that serves as his all-purpose valise and storage locker. He'd worked as a gardener for a while, for a brother who was a contractor, but says he's been living on the streets a long time now, he claims by choice. "The sky is my roof," he says. "The grass is my floor."

He's got a misdemeanor rap for public drunkenness and a restraining order from his ex-wife ("I got mad and pushed her," he says, looking abashed) that keeps him from seeing his daughter. He's an illegal. He's worried about deportation. He's decided he'll just hang out with us for a while.

One of our group, Tim, a religious studies major from Maine, has forgotten to bring along a sleeping bag. The night has turned freezing, with the next day threatening snow. We hunker down, curled up together in a dog pile, but Tim goes to sleep shivering and anxious. The next morning, he wakes up warm. Someone, some anonymous Good Samaritan, has gently draped a sleeping bag over him while he slept. It's Jesus's bag, though he'd vanished in the night like an apparition. He'd opened his Hefty Sac and given away, with no assurance he'd ever see it again, the single most valuable thing he owned, becoming in that instant another of love's debtors.

Unpredictable as always, Jesus shows up again a few days later. Now he's talking to us more. Odd gems spill from his mouth. "Nobody has a heart with separate batteries—they all have the same source," he announces, adding that to convey the thoughts that fill his head using his poor English is "like trying to put an elephant through the eye of a needle."

He's a smart guy. "Why don't you work?" someone asks him.

"Work is always fighting, fighting. People fight for money. I'm a lover, not a fighter. I love life, not money." He claims he wants to attend seminary someday, maybe become a priest, and who's to say? Maybe Jesus is spending time as a self-styled Franciscan, careless of the day; or as one of those that Islam calls the *malamatiyya,* those who "draw blame," courting contempt by living like beggars to preserve their purity of heart. I don't want to romanticize him, but it's clear his story's not over yet.

As for us, we'll soon be going home, dispersing. And on our last day, in our last circle, suddenly Jesus is speaking English, simply, eloquently. "I've been watching you, not saying much, but I think you are true people. I feel you are with me, and I am with you. Because I was with all of you for these days, I didn't drink at all. Not once. So you have been good for me." He says it with no discernible flattery, but with a village courtliness almost quaint in its sincerity. "I wish you all a long life. I hope all of us will never die. I wish all of you to be happy."

Okay, I think. I've been waiting for the hustle to kick in. Here's the windup . . . and now the pitch. What does he really want? What will he try to scrounge? To my surprise, he asks for nothing from us; no money, no clothes, no place to stay. When one of our group, a doctor named Charlie, offers him his beautiful knit woolen gloves, a secret concession to luxury he'd smuggled along, Jesus refuses. He is persuaded only after Charlie unobtrusively dons his own filthy and torn ones, making it an exchange. Jesus wants no charity; compassion, he's clearly saying, is more than a gesture from the intact to the damaged.

And he's right: Sometimes, even in charity, the most open hand remains at arm's length. The story is told of the great Hasidic sage Reb Nachman, who was in the habit of using whatever money he had to pay off the creditors of people who had fallen on hard times. He'd saved many a man and woman from the fate of debtor's prison. But one day he ran out of money, was dunned for what he owed and, when he couldn't pay, was thrown into prison himself.

"Why, oh God?" he implored from the darkness of his cell.

And God answered, with a touch of irony: "So you could *really* know how much good you've done." It is a story about giver and receiver made one, in an exchange of places, in the bearing of witness, in God's own infinite debt.

God knew Reb Nachman; God knows I'm no Reb Nachman. Back home again, I'm delighted to be sleeping in my own bed. Bathed, shaved, fed, dressed, I take a walk on the mall with a friend. He looks at me askance as I press a dollar bill into a panhandler's palm, then, seeing how browbeaten the man looks, how downcast his eyes, peel off another two and chat with him for a while.

I'm trying to become insufferably virtuous, I tell my friend. How am I doing? Pretty good, he allowed; you're getting on my nerves.

Soon I'm giving money to the people with cardboard signs who stake out corners on trafficked streets, remembering when I was stranded once on the highway, having to scare up a ride with a magic-markered plea. One guy comes up to the window to recite his story as my car idles at a light. He's a former truck driver with a neck injury, he says, saving up for surgery. He seems so sincere, I believe him, though I'm not sure that really matters: I know he has his reasons. I hand him a bill and drive off. Then, feeling suddenly touched, I circle the block and cut recklessly through two lanes of traffic to give him another. "For your medical fund," I yell, practically hurling a tenner at him to beat the light. "God bless you, you and your family," he yells after me; and yes, I think, how Dickensian: oh, *kind* sir. But I also mentally thank him for helping me sink deeper into that debt that swallows all others and makes them small—small, and of no consequence.

I won't claim I've changed that much. Not in a week or two; not in a few months. But I do feel as if my inner pockets have been turned inside out, shaking loose some small change in my life. I've developed a soft spot. I can't help but notice the people at the margins, the invisible ones, the ones who used to be the extras in my movie. I know the feeling: *You in me, me in you.* It makes me an easy touch. The money I give out starts to mount up, twenty, thirty, forty bucks a month, unburdening my wallet, filling the heart's purse; but somehow, this is better than okay.

5

THE GOOD EYE

Whenever catching sight of others
Look on them with an open, loving heart.
—Patrul Rinpoche

The great Jewish mystic, the Rabbi of Berditchev, was known throughout nineteenth-century Europe as the Master of the Good Eye. It was said that he could see nothing of people's sins, only their virtues. He'd roust the local drunk from his stupor on high holy day, seat him at the head of the table, and respectfully ask for his wisdom. He'd *noodge* a man who'd publicly flouted the Sabbath by praising him as the only one in the village who wasn't a hypocrite. He extended his caring to all, whether powerful or impoverished, scholarly or simple, righteous or reprobate.

The Rabbi's inspiration was a Talmud passage that calls for everyone to be weighed "on the scales of merit" (*zechut,* from the Hebrew *zach* or purity). The meaning of *zechut,* explains one scholar, is "to intentionally focus on what is most pure in each person—to see their highest and holiest potential." It is a reminder that compassion is not just a gift, but a path. The Good Eye is a

ب_. it of perception, a transformative art that takes some practice.

My friend Rhonda, a nurse by trade and by calling, is something of a *zechut* artist. When she is warm to you (and she is to most everybody), you feel like a rare edition of yourself. I've followed her on rounds, watching the crankiest patients brighten at her approach; seeing even the most-needle-phobic relax and smile, as if her IV were an act of bestowal. She's another one of those people who coaxes your petals open. Rhonda says that she learned at the feet of a great teacher—her grandma Margaret, also a nurse and, from the sound of it, an unheralded Good Eye master.

One night Grandma Margaret was summoned to the obstetrics ward of her Arizona hospital. A Down's syndrome child had just been born, unpredicted in those pre-amniocentesis days, and the distraught mother was threatening to kill herself rather than keep the baby. When Rhonda's grandma saw the child, she felt a stirring and made an impossible leap of faith. "I'll take that baby home," she announced, "and I'll love her." True to her word, she raised a foster daughter who bloomed into a high-functioning young adult. "I didn't see any defects," she told Rhonda. "I saw a blueprint for perfection." Grandma Margaret once confided her greatest secret: "When I look at people, I see only the best part of them."

I used to think that people who regarded everyone benignly were a mite simple, or oblivious, or just plain lax—until I tried it myself. Then I realized they only made it *look* easy. Even the Berditchev *rebbe,* revered as a man who could strike a rock and bring forth a stream, was continually honing his intentions. "Until I remove the thread of hatred from my heart," he said of his daily meditations, "I am, in my own eyes, as if I did not exist."

He was, in a word, a man who didn't take the Good Eye for granted. Like many who give off that special ray of selflessness, he believed in tending to the heart, watering its roots, pulling ego's fibrous, prickly weeds by hand. The distinction between our ordinary eye and the Good Eye is, as is the one between ordinary sight and *in*sight, a quotient of conscious cultivation. It is the gist of the scriptural predicament, "You have eyes, but you see not." We have the necessary parts, but as the label on the shipping carton says: *Some assembly may be required.* Luckily, all spiritual traditions concur that it doesn't take a lightning bolt on the road to Damascus or a blast of enlightenment under the bodhi tree. The soul, luckily, is educable.

*L*ife offers up its own daily catechism, even if it's just seeing people in a little better light. Why not just resolve to give everyone the benefit of the doubt? "If we treat people as they ought to be," said Goethe, almost nailing it, "we help them become what they are capable of becoming." Or more to the point: Treat them as they already *are,* if we but had the Good Eye to see it.

Once, at a conference, I noticed a man striding toward me, his face alight. He seemed really happy to see me, but I didn't have a clue who he was. When he got closer, he pushed his glasses up to the bridge of his nose, peered at my face, looked down at my nametag, took a step back.

"I'm so sorry," he said, embarrassed. "You looked just like a friend I haven't seen for years. You even have the same first name . . . so when someone pointed you out . . ." He trailed off; the effusive warmth seeped away. I told him it was fine. His Good Eye had enveloped me in a gaze of anticipatory delight that made me feel golden. We wound up having lunch. He told me about his research (which coincidentally dovetailed with my own); he talked about the happiness and sorrows of raising a young daughter with multiple sclerosis *(for everyone is fighting a great battle)*. We still stay in touch.

Maybe we should all take off our glasses and hope for more cases of mistaken identity. For that matter, it might be *un*mistaken. Why *not* welcome everyone as some long-lost cousin, sprung from our African mother, bumping into each other again after a fifty-thousand-year separation. *Wonderful to see you after all this time—you look* great!

A friend of mine, a psychologist, works as a counselor to the obdurate, lethal men at Arkansas's infamous Tucker Max prison. She's well aware that most people look at her clients and see only dregs— "ugly toothless hulks," as she puts it—but she claims she can only see "radiant bulbs with these big lampshades blocking the light. I know they're supposed to be 'untreatable psychopaths,' but I feel like, *Oh, take that fright-mask off! It could come off in two seconds!*" It sounds absurd, but she's remarkably successful. In her presence, the toughest nuts crack wide-open; even their wary, death-row warders let down their guard and cry. She has an x-ray vision that goes straight to the human core.

"It's like there's this horribly thick suit of armor," she explains, trying to make me see it through her eyes, "and I know someone's trapped inside, so how do we get them out?" I ask her why she even bothers. "The joy!" she says, as if it's the most obvious thing in the world. "Just the joy of being with people when they show up as they really are."

If we can't see who people really are, say possessors of the Good Eye, it's just our ordinary eye playing tricks on us, focusing on differences and defects, blind to deeper connection. If we mistake each other for strangers, it's just blurry vision. The Good Eye is the corrective to Einstein's "optical delusion of consciousness." As with the rearview mirror that cautions Objects May Be Closer Than They Appear, we might be closer, much closer, than we think.

The sixteenth-century Tibetan meditation master Wangchuk Dorje recommended a practice he called "the Activity of Being in Crowds." Walking through a throng, he said, is a "good opportunity to check your progress and examine the delusions, attachments, and aversions that arise." I find the bustle of a mall an especially good place to check my Good Eye for jaundice. It's not just the plenitude of people, but of everything under that fluorescent sun that pushes our buttons. With everything winking merrily, beckoning with come-ons for instant gratification, and mirrors, mirrors everywhere (*it* is *all about me, after all!*), I go into a sort of mall trance. The mind itself gets into the spirit of things, hawking its tawdrier wares; my finicky responses to the goods on display merge with my reactions to the people I pass—little covetous twinges, subtle flickers of attitude, petty judgments on how people walk, talk, dress, and chew gum. And here a surge of superiority, there a deflating thought of inadequacy; here a lurch of desire for a sleek, well turned-out woman, there a picador's lance of envy at her undeserving boyfriend in the slobby polo shirt.

I return from these shopping expeditions with a discount grab-bag of those feelings the spiritual traditions agree most occlude compassion. I'm collecting a set of action figures based on Augustine's deadly sins (and can we just define sins as "biggest obstacles to selfless love"?). Yesterday I snagged Mammon, avarice (a Buddhist would call him *tanha,* craving), and today my favorite, Leviathan, jealousy, complete with light-up green eyes.

The Koran describes jealousy as a "veil" that beclouds the eye of the heart. Jealousy turns other people into sources of resentment: *If I had what you have,* Leviathan croaks mechanically when I push the little oval button in his back, *then I would be happy.* Jealousy tints everyone in bilious shades of envy. It presents a perfect paradigm of insufficiency: I am less because you are more. It's a zero-sum game. Jealousy's only hope is that the other person will be diminished, imagining that would free up proportionately more for itself. (It extends all the way to that uniquely German coinage, *schadenfreude,* gloating over another's misfortune, the Good Eye turned into the Evil Eye itself.)

But just as there are emotional toxins, there are also antidotes, remedies, what the apothecaries of yore called specifics. In Buddhism, the supreme medicine for envy is said to be *mudita,* or "sympathetic joy," which calls on us to feel happy about another's success. Easy enough when it comes to rejoicing for those we really care about: Every parent *kvells* over their kid's triumphs; a teacher exults when her favorite student aces the math exam. But to expand this feeling from a narrow circle to a wider arena is like pulling wisdom teeth.

I once witnessed an exchange between a Tibetan lama and a questioner on this subject. "Rinpoche," inquired a pleasant middle-aged man in a checked sport shirt, "I adore my son. He's a linebacker for his high school football team. I find myself rooting for him to just *cream* the opposing quarterback. Is there anything wrong with that?"

"Of course not," the lama replied. "You love your son, and you want his happiness, and he's happy when he beats the other team. This is only natural."

There was an audible sigh of relief in the room. The spiritual path may be challenging, but it's not *unreasonable.*

The man smiled. "Thank you, Rinpoche," he said, making a brisk little folding gesture with his hands.

The lama laughed sharply. "I was only *joking!* Actually, this is not at all the right attitude. In fact," he said, glancing at the man mischievously, "a good practice for you would be to *root for the other team.* See *them* winning, see *them* happy, see *their* parents overjoyed. That is more the *bodhisattva* way." The man thanked him again, this time with an ironic groan at a homework assignment that stretched past football season.

I have a wildly successful acquaintance next to whose perfectly

But by 2000, he found himself stretched to the breaking point. His company had, through a series of acquisitions, turned from a mid-sized shop into a lurching industrial titan. "I was trained as a researcher to discover things," he says, "not to manage thousands of people." He decided he needed guidance.

In the explosive-growth, quick flame-out world of the tech business, there is no shortage of advice for the entrepreneurially perplexed. Stacks of business bibles reveal how to turn companies into lean, mean, no-fixed-limit cash machines; armies of consultants feed CEOs' obsessive drive to play king of the mountain. But Ricardo was after something else. "I'd always been a seeker of depth, not height," he says in his lightly accented English. "I'd seen enough to be suspicious of the shadow side of power. I knew some of those Enron guys."

He turned to an old friend, Andre Delbecq, a legendary management consultant who had also come to his own crossroads. A sought-after executive trainer who also taught at a Jesuit college, Andre didn't like what was going on in the Valley. Its giddy, intoxicating ascendancy seemed to him foredoomed by its mounting arrogance. At the apex of the new Gilded Age, Andre took a year off to pore over the world's great spiritual teachings, seeking ways to inculcate that "paradox of perfect humility and perfect hope" that he believed was the hallmark of true leadership.

When Andre came down from his mountain (actually, a sailing trip off the Turkish coast), he invited Ricardo and a select group of CEOs to hear a presentation of his findings, promising them a management course that would change their lives as well as their business practices. It was certainly unorthodox. If most executive training is a regimen of psychological power-lifting and ego-steroids, Andre replaced yes-I-can with not-so-fast and no-you-don't: Don't be enslaved by your own ambitions; don't think only of the bottom line; don't, for a while, think at all—especially about yourself. Andre, who had always admired the Jesuits' openness to Eastern spiritual traditions, prescribed

109

on and other exercises—not, he stressed, as samurai _ slice off competitors' heads, but to get inside their own (and not incidentally, to learn some compassion).

It was the compassion part that Ricardo and the other CEOs found most challenging and most revelatory. Andre exhorted them "not to edit the place of suffering." He gave them assignments that plunged them into places they feared, having them spend time with Alzheimer's patients, prisoners, or the homeless in what he called "I-Thou encounters, just listening to and learning from, not judging anyone's value or worthiness."

He had the executives tell each other their personal stories, asking if anyone in their own family was struggling with disease, drugs, or mental illness or had found themselves on the wrong side of the law. The Titanium Men of Silicon Valley were astonished to discover that their most formidable colleagues and competitors were grappling with the same mortal complement of weal and woe. Andre became a sort of heart-coach, urging them to widen their sympathies by considering how each of their employees faced similar difficulties. He assured them that if they entered their workplace with what he called "compassionate presence," they'd discover the hidden life of their company.

A devout Christian who likes to wryly refer to himself as "an old sinner," Andre had scoured the world's religious practices, in the end deciding to teach his students the Buddhist meditation of *tonglen.* "There was no other discipline I'd found," he told me, "that enabled people to immediately grasp openness and humility for themselves." Ricardo found the practice—an imaginative exercise that calls for breathing in others' suffering and breathing out lovingkindness—edifying, even elating.

To put that vulnerability into practice in the business world, where dog really does eat dog and big fish swallow little fish and pick their teeth with the bones, had seemed like folly. But Ricardo had tackled it with his usual full-on commitment. At the time, the fate of his entire company balanced on a single excruciating choice-point. He had been negotiating to take over a large pharmaceutical company when discussions had turned hostile, finally reaching a bitter impasse. He put the talks on mental pause. "I decided I had to try to feel empathy for all parties, including the other side, the adversary. I needed an inner answer, not a spreadsheet answer." He had a realization that shocked him: "I saw it would be better for *them* to take *us* over."

"This would be traumatic for me, because I'd be disassembling the business I'd built over decades. But when I put myself aside and considered everyone else involved—our shareholders and employees, the *other* company's shareholders and their employees—I knew it was right." The decision was pure intuition, he says. People inside and outside the organization thought he'd gone crazy. In 2000, his company's financial bellwethers were surreally bright; every indicator pointed due north. But three months after the deal closed, the tech economy went south, and as Ricardo says drily, "It turned out in retrospect the direction I chose had been to everyone's benefit."

Big business is a combustible mix of giant egos and ultrahigh stakes, and it was not the only time Ricardo found his empathy skills called upon to turn the tide of a negotiation. When a deal was on the brink of failure because emotions between him and his counterpart had degenerated into "nasty, personal, real screaming anger," Ricardo sat down to meditate. On the morning of a critical kill-or-cure discussion, he recited, as he always did, the Jewish *Sh'ma,* a prayer of unity: *The Lord our God, the Lord is One.* He allowed the insoluble mess to recede from his mind. He put himself in his competitor's position, and something happened he says verged on mystical experience.

"I don't know what triggered it," he tells me, "but I felt an inner feeling of warmth flow from me to this other person. I seemed to snap into a mindset that was beyond thinking, beyond even, 'I'll put myself in his shoes.'" During that morning's conference, he felt a powerful physical sensation, "as if I was speaking from here and here—" he touches his heart and his gut, "and not from here," he says, pointing to his head. "I know the other guy felt it, too, because suddenly everything that was frigid had now, without explanation, turned warm. We easily settled every issue.

"When you open to another's pain," says Ricardo earnestly, "it opens the window to the soul, to God, to emotions that can dissolve the crust, remove the veil." He found that his practice led him to more generous policies for his employees. He backed benefits packages that cut into his profits because it seemed to him the right thing to do, only to find it also made the company stronger. Tonglen was, he realized, the spiritual equivalent of the catalysis at the very heart of his business. "You take in suffering, transform it to positive energy, and then offer that out into the world."

I happened to be present one of the first times the Tibetan meditation master Chogyam Trungpa sprang this bizarre-sounding practice on an unsuspecting Western audience. One student of yoga had raised his hand and asked, with some bewilderment, why it wouldn't be better to imagine breathing in love and light and breathing out all negative impurities. Ricardo, the creator of environmentally benign industrial processes, would have appreciated Trungpa's unhesitating reply: "Well, then you'd just be like a polluting factory, taking in all these good resources and spewing out your gray cloud on everyone else."

The practice *is* decidedly counterintuitive. Sometimes when I begin tonglen meditation, I feel a wild surge of resistance, a fear of (there is no other way to put this) contamination. The unhappiness of others feels contagious: I don't want to inhale their cooties. I'll think of someone I find creepy, one who hurt me, another whose burden *just isn't my problem,* and want to just forget the whole thing. But when it "works," the practice is so rewarding that I'm ready to throw myself in again. To stop dodging people's misery and discord, to discover I can give of myself with each breath and not feel depleted (in fact, oddly nourished) is a revelation. When I can stay with it, I notice I don't feel so guarded; my borders seem more porous. I'm less inclined to hold people at arms' length.

This is not a Buddhist infomercial. No salesmen will call. There's no pledge of religious allegiance. I admit to sometimes finding tonglen a moral challenge—gosh, do I *hafta?*—that I don't have the fortitude to meet. But at best, I find the technique radically simple and simply radical: an imaginative leap into otherness. There's a through-the-looking-glass moment, an almost audible pop as I seem to find myself looking at the world through different eyes. It enhances what some psychologists refer to as *intersubjectivity*, a shared space of experience. If our usual ego-identity is maintained by keeping the good and estimable stuff in here and the yucky stuff out there, then tonglen dissolves some of the rigidity of selfhood. It's not just about me or even *you in me, me in you;* it's more about *we in us*, or somehow, *us in It*.

When my mind has some downtime that I'd normally fill gossiping idly to myself, I instead try to take in others' suffering and broadcast my goodwill. It's my mental screen-saver: *tonglen in the morning, tonglen in the evening, tonglen at suppertime.* On the highway the other day, a college kid whizzed past at one and a half times the speed limit in a silver Hummer, honking wildly, blaring hip-hop from every window of his gas-hog, giving me the finger for good measure. I could feel my temper start to go off like a bottle rocket, my accelerator foot begin to twitch. Instead, I zeroed in on the back of his fast-receding head, breathing in his rage and frustration (which surely wasn't personal). I could almost feel his emotional claustrophobia, his agitated need for speed. I remembered being nineteen, riding the testosterone express.

What amazed me was that I didn't feel anger but some actual sympathy for the guy—along with a whoosh of inner freedom. Normally, when I feel hurt or affronted, my emotional choices seem to narrow.

I can either absorb the blow and feel wretched, or deflect it back to the other person (or later on some hapless bystander): It's like a choice between suicide or murder. With tonglen, I get to choose life.

Shambhala Mountain Center, an ink-brush painting of scrub pine hills, lazily foraging magpies, and skittish prairie dogs near the Wyoming border, has for decades been my place of retreat. It is dominated by the astonishing Great Stupa of Dharmakaya, a ten-story shrine whose gold-leafed spire shining in the sun suggests some unregulated spiritual broadcasting tower. Chogyam Trungpa, whose relics it houses, would have loved it and would have laughed. There is something both wondrous and absurd about exalted religious edifices that commemorate humble, profound insights: vast cathedrals to remind us the kingdom of heaven is within us; soaring monuments to the truth that's right under our noses; ornate memorials to those who reminded us the present alone is life's transforming moment.

On a recent visit, making my way down the hill after meditating before the stupa's gargantuan, faintly smiling Buddha statue, I fell in stride with an athletic-looking woman in khaki shorts hurrying down the path. When I mentioned my writing topic, she slowed down to talk. She had a story, she said, a simple one about meditation and compassion she'd been dying to tell somebody.

"I first started to meditate when my boyfriend dumped me," she said as I huffed along beside her in the thin mountain air. "I needed to sort through all the bad feelings. But I was afraid that I'd look inside and find out one thing: that I basically sucked. Gradually, though, I found it didn't matter if I thought I was horrible *or* if I thought I was great: I could drop my whole story and just breathe. It was a chance not only to explore myself, but get *over* myself. Meditation became this tool to not react in my usual way."

114

She was a ski bum, she told me, the "rabble-rouser and hell-raiser" in a family of perfectionists. Her older sister was the one with the high-powered, big-city job and the fantastic two-career marriage; the one who would come to her house and "just criticize everything about me right down to the stinky sponges in the sink. She'd drive me crazy until *wham!* I'd get combative and we'd have some huge, screaming fight."

During one of her sister's visits, they set out on a scenic drive. "Well, soon it was the usual: 'You're driving too fast! There's a beer can on the floor, the car is filthy!' And I noticed my habitual response coming up inside: *Who the hell are you to tell me how to live? Back off!* But this time the words didn't come out of my mouth. For once, I was able to just notice her, notice my own feelings, and breathe.

"When I didn't react, it made her even madder. She upped the ante. There was this onslaught of everything she could throw at me: '*I* make all the money in the family, it's me who'd have to scrape you up if anything bad ever happened to you,' *blah, blah, blah.* But even though I heard her anger and anxiety, I was able to slow down; and instead of getting defensive and lashing out, I just asked her, 'Are you okay, Carol?' And I meant it. I wanted to know.

"Well, she was so caught off guard, she didn't even have a retort. Instead, she started to blurt out everything about the screwed-up place her life had come to. How she was going to leave her husband—this decent guy who just wasn't quite right—how she'd be alone in the city, how she was afraid she'd never have children, and then she just broke down *sobbing!* And all the snotty comebacks I'd stored up just evaporated. I could feel the whole burden of my personality, her personality, our history, fall away, and like some beautiful plant springing up out of nowhere, there was just compassion."

Her story, like Ricardo's, confirmed for me a spiritual insight—call it, To Find Your Heart, Lose Your Head—that's as close to a universal principle as you can extract from the mystical traditions. The ego, despite its dazzling dance routines and ever-persuasive patter, is really a sort of trance state from which it is possible to awaken. And beneath its incessant inner commentary, behind the story lines and the beliefs that spawn them, beyond the passions that give those beliefs their emotional clout, there is a wellspring of pure compassion.

The great Hasidic rabbi known as the Maggid told his disciples that the best way to realize the love at the heart of the Torah is to "cease to be aware of yourselves. You must be nothing but an ear which hears what the universe of the word is constantly saying within you. The moment you start hearing what you yourself are saying, you must stop." The Buddha, in a radical act of reflection, suggested we disbelieve our thought process entirely.

Easier said than done, of course. If you want a little *aperçu* on that subject, try sitting stock-still for a while on a cushion or a chair; just sit there, observing the old inhale and exhale, trying not to get carried away by those broken-record thoughts yacketing in the background; just sit, dangling from a rope of breath above the morass of your charming personality, and you will soon be at one with a hundredfold generations of meditators who have discovered self-delusion's ripeness.

In seeking what Buddhism calls Big Mind, I confess I sometimes look inward and find new vistas of smallness. But my practice, such as it is, hasn't been all eddies and doldrums. Sometimes I can forsake the drone of internal gossip, opt for the unadorned Now. Then I find myself gazing into a void where, moments before, the bustling manufacturing hub of selfhood—that Rube Goldberg assembly-line cranking out endless iterations of Me, Me, Me—had been on track to fulfill its daily quota. I get acquainted with my mental habits—tics, really. I start finding my neuroses less dramatic than tedious; enough to tell them, when I'm really not in the mood for entertaining, to just buzz off.

Once, at a seminar, I heard a Westernized lama say that a meditator's state of mind should be like that of a hotel doorman. A doorman lets the guests in, but he doesn't follow them up to the room. He lets them out, but he doesn't walk into the street with them to their next appointment. He greets them all, then lets them go on about their business. Meditation is, in its initial stages, simply accustoming oneself to letting thoughts come in and out without grasping at their sleeves or putting up a velvet rope to keep them out.

Similarly, Sufi teachings specify that a certain impartiality is required to mount the "thrones of compassion." It is said one must remove the veil of *wahm* ("opinion," or "conjecture"). "The real heart," said the Islamic sage known as the Prince of the Illumined, "is that heart which is neither on the right nor on the left, neither above nor below, neither far nor near"—that is, beyond ordinary cognition and its incessant parsing of differences.*

No one would claim it's not tricky business. Such work, the alchemists used to say, is *opus contra naturum*: work against our natural tendencies, here the mind's impulse to classify this person as near, that one as far; this one a beloved, that one a rival. Various traditions call for cultivating detachment from the potent cues presented by the outer world (or for that matter, the inner one): Do you feel distaste when you see a particular person coming toward you on the street? Then regard that distaste as a thing apart, disconnected from its object, generated in your own heart and mind. By the same token, don't just swoon over that attraction that reflexively rises when you see her smile or hear his voice. Both are (in this practice, at least) obstacles, obscurations; they get in the way of a lovingkindness beyond mere personal preference.

It's not unlike the Christian practice of "discernment," which a theologian once described to me as "learning to see in a way that is consonant with God's way of seeing. As long as there's ego-attachment," she said, "we're seeing other people in a funhouse mirror. As long as our eyes are clouded by longing, needing other people to be this way or that for us, there's no such thing as compassion." I was fascinated. I'd always admired Christianity's emphasis on doing good; but here was

---

* A friend told me of visiting the Dalai Lama once in India and asking him for a succinct definition of compassion. She prefaced her question by describing how heartstricken she'd felt when, earlier that day, she'd seen a man in the street beating a mangy stray dog with a stick. "Compassion," the Dalai Lama told her, "is when you feel as sorry for the man as you do for the dog."

a practice of *seeing* good, one that resembled Eastern-style meditation. I had always wondered about the relationship between this inner Christianity and more churchly forms of worship. If I wanted to get a real insight, I was told, I should talk to Father Thomas Keating, the monk who had almost singlehandedly revived the contemplative method of realizing God's illimitable love.

*T*o get to Father Keating's monastery, you must pass, as must all good pilgrims, through a vale of temptation, in this case the Gulch of Glitz known as Aspen. I manage to ignore all its allurements (save a real New York–style Reuben with meltingly tender pastrami), heading out past the private airport where sleek personal jets take off and land with a purling roar.

All's quiet a few miles down a dirt road at St. Benedict's Monastery, its soaring, carved wood architecture at once a psalm to the earth and a paean to whatever lies beyond. Father Keating emerges to greet me, an eighty-one-year-old man in a simple plaid wool shirt, a watchcap plunked on his bald head. He could be an ancient mariner home from the sea or some ex-stevedore hired as keeper of the bell tower. There's a proletarian power to his posture, a tall man stooped at the shoulders as if from years of unloading cargo on far harbor wharves. For him, God's love calls for workmanly practice. "Jesus had a formula," he tells me as we sit practically knee to knee in his cramped office. "In the Sermon on the Mount, Jesus says, 'Pray to your Father, your Abba, your Daddy, in *secret.*' Go into your inner room at the center of your being. Close the door, not just to the external noise and distraction, but to the inner dialogue, too."

Keating speaks in lovely, loping, run-on sentences. Closing my eyes, his deep, creaky voice conjures some old cricket sachem, sawing a rhythmic evensong on long bowstring legs. "You have to silence the emotional programs that sustain who you think you are," he says, "allow the ego's self-reflective apparatus to fade out, put aside that false self based on childhood emotions—the reaching out for happiness, security, approval, affection, esteem, all those exaggerated needs we impose on others—and just do nothing.

"But not *just* nothing. Rather nothing of our *own*, but everything of what God proposes we do. God prefers this kind of love—not what you're willing to do, but what you're willing to *receive*. Our lack of confidence in his great love is the only problem." Although this isn't a particularly funny remark, he smiles with such gentle irony that I can't help but burst out laughing, feeling some perfusion of high seriousness and puckish joy.

"We say that when you enter prayer, *nothing* is worth thinking about," he says, peering out through his enormous round glasses, "whether it's a sense-perception, memory, plan, concept or image. It doesn't mean no thoughts, but to disregard them. They're placed in the 'cloud of forgetting,' which contains the ultimate knowledge of what is, but which is unknown to the intellect."

I suggest to him it must be hard for someone who is so clearly an intellectual to relinquish all thought and center himself in the heart. He smiles. "All you need is a willingness to suffer, and a willingness to love." All the rest of it, he stresses, is the "false self" and its gnat-cloud of petty thinking that obscures love's ultimate Source. And as far as he's concerned, organized religion has too often swarmed with the gnats instead of soaring with the angels.

"Such a shame what we've done to the Mystery," he murmurs with a sigh, "with all our naive loyalties!"

T he history of religion is not an uninterrupted purview of the Good Eye. Alongside its numberless good deeds are uncounted (and unaccountably) bad ones. It's tragicomic to hear, at the dawn of the twenty-first century, *imams* promising Paradise to infidel-slayers, pastors invoking a Prince of Peace who sounds more like Rambo, rabbis sanctifying biblical land-grabs, Buddhist priests blessing military juntas. (I recently heard a cleric who surely spoke for sectarians everywhere decree from the pulpit, "Everyone is created by God, but not everyone is a *child* of God.") A good organizational consultant would counsel the world's major faiths to reexamine their original mission statements: The core business of Jesus, Inc. or Allah Ltd. or Moses Corp. or Buddha LLC is surely not to sell tickets to heaven or peddle get-out-of-hell-free cards, but to distribute every kernel of wisdom from their ancient storehouses that might help us to love each other.

We *are* slowly emerging from millenia of holy know-it-alls beaning each other with their Infallible Books, passing judgment with their Divine Laws, and trying to enforce competing copyrights on Ultimate Truth. The question of whether a deity once responsible for global flooding and serial smiting incidents is keeping tabs on our celestial credit reporting agency is moot. The God of our times is no longer some Big Eye in the Sky, but the Good Eye itself. He is turning into what Nietzsche, who preferred deities of blood and thunder, once sneeringly called a "changed god . . . Now he counsels 'peace of soul,' hate-no-more, forbearance, even 'love' of friend and enemy . . . [N]ow he is merely the good god."

I'll take him. So will, it seems, a lot of other people. In churches, synagogues, temples, and mosques around the world, there lately has been a quiet revival of the inner traditions for transforming the heart. Just as the formula for baking a loaf of bread is similar across cultures, the same techniques for compassion seem to crop up everywhere: Loosen the bonds of discursive thought. Extend the circle of caring. Cease armoring against suffering. Wish for others the same happiness you wish for yourself. Be a tender-minded steward of Creation.

"Religious stories are training," a rabbi once told me, "not just rulebooks." At their best, the practices we call spiritual are tried-and-true ways to unplug from the ego's Matrix and awaken from delusory life; to shut the biased and nearsighted Squinty Eye, and open the Good Eye wide. The Little Prince said it as well as anybody: "It is only with the heart that one sees rightly."

Such seeing, however, may require deliberately redirecting the gaze. Awhile back I decided to unplug my TV. I didn't have it in mind to return to reading by kerosene lamp and entertaining company with silhouettes and lively games of whist. I just wanted to clear my head of mass culture with its endless parade of imaginary characters who not only clutter the mind but, I began to think, subtly sidetrack the heart. In my TV's old corner, I've created a small shrine, an experimental compassion lab. In place of test tubes, Bunsen burners, and chemical reagents, I've arrayed candles, incense, and homemade icons. I could have gone Zenny and no frills, I suppose, but I decided to bait the hook a little, grab my own attention with a few shiny lures. I enjoy the musky smells, the warm votive flicker like some inner pilot light. Like the Jewish tradition of putting honey on a book so a child associates learning with sweetness, I need to fool myself a little. At this point, I'd at least rather watch my shrine than *The Sopranos*.

I've propped up photos of friends and loved ones, little endorphin triggers, jump-starts for the heart. I've included some pictures of people I really don't like. I try to breathe in their suffering, breathe out my goodness. I remind myself I don't need to reserve a stash of happiness for my exclusive use. Like digital data, infinitely replicable because it has no substance or extrinsic cost, I can afford to give it away, even to those I deem undeserving. There's more where that came from.

To all of which you might well say, "So what?" Don't just sit there, *do* something. The world is on fire, or it's drowning. Too many people are tragically dying; too many lucklessly born. And it's true: The Good Eye should guide the Good Hand, set the Good Feet in motion. But I believe that old existentialist Camus had it right: "We all carry within us our places of exile, our crimes, our ravages. Our task is not to unleash them on the world; it is to transform them in ourselves and others." Inner transformation doesn't supplant outward action, but nourishes it. I project less on others of my own need for redemption. Do-gooding becomes more alloyed with be-gooding. The Good Eye is not merely a gaze but a creative force, like the penetrating sunlight that quickens a buried seed.

Next to pictures of my family, I've placed a photo of Juan, a seven-year-old Salvadoran I've started sponsoring through one of those international aid agencies. He stands there in his faded Spiderman T-shirt, his mouth determined, his stance a straddle, as if braced for something. His blue pants are covered in dirt. His fly's unzipped. Behind him is a wall with charcoal drawings of volcanoes and trees; next to him stands his mother, Ana Rosa, a Mayan-looking peasant, formally dressed, stolid and unsmiling. Juan writes a few words on lined paper about his small village by a lake. He says he wants to be a doctor when he grows up. He's become part of my orbit of caring, a link to the larger human family. I send my checks, yes, and little notes of encouragement, but I try to send something else on wings of breath.

Am I getting anywhere? Is there anywhere *to* get? These days I can feel unexpectedly pierced by something I'll hear, something I'll see, some stray thread of feeling I might have overlooked. I've placed a few eyedrops in the Good Eye. I'll sometimes feel a soft explosion of warmth or ache in my chest and think that it's my heart shaking off its torpor. I hear it murmuring; maybe someday it will shout.

6

HEART SCIENCE, HEART'S MYSTERY

I will take the stony heart out . . .
and give them a heart of flesh.
—*Ezekiel*

Man will become better when
you show him what he is like.
—*Anton Chekhov*

hat is the Heart, but a Spring?" asked the seventeenth-century materialist Thomas Hobbes. He wasn't waxing poetic about an upwelling of liquid gladness or praising tender buds of feeling burst forth anew, but making a case for the heart as a gearworks—a mechanism that, however marvelously constructed by that intelligence he called the "Artificer," was as devoid of sensibility as a clock.

This view has held sway for centuries, though it's deeply at odds with our felt experience. When the psychologist Carl Jung, on one of his perennial quests, visited Chief Mountain Lake of the Taos Pueblo, the tribal elder told him he judged the whites to be quite mad. "Why is that?" Jung asked.

"They say they think with their heads," the chief replied.

"Of course," said Jung. "What do *you* think with?"

Mountain Lake pointed to his heart: "We think *here.*"

I've always taken this idea—the wisdom of the heart and all—to be a metaphor, albeit a charming one. But in cultures the world over, it takes on a peculiarly literal cast. Among the Sufis, for example, the physical heart is a container for *al-aql,* the intellect, and *al-fouad,* a second, "sensitive" heart that can see into the hearts of others. Aristotle claimed the heart was responsible for "the power of perception and the soul's ability to nourish itself." In the Eastern Orthodox tradition, the heart is not only the core of a human being but is identified with the mind itself. Similarly, the Japanese have two heart-words: *shinzu,* the physical organ, and *kokoro,* "the mind of the heart."

Does the heart have a mind of its own? Neuroscience has long known that the two hemispheres of the *brain* think somewhat independently—the right side being, in a sense, more heartful, specializing in emotional-intuitive functions; the left leaning more toward rationality and logic. The idea of heartfulness as an independent form of cognition was illustrated, albeit inadvertently, in a widely reported 1986 experiment. A test group of college students was first shown a documentary about Mother Teresa. Immediately afterward, their saliva revealed increased levels of S-IgA, an immune system–boosting hormone. The conclusion reached in the popular press was, "Compassion makes you feel good *and* it's good for you."

But the media reports overlooked a strange fact: Most of the students said they'd found the film *depressing.* After seeing it, they reported a *decrease* in feelings of love and friendliness and an *increase* in "overall negative mood." They found the plight of the poorest of the poor, the sick and the dying of Calcutta's slums, deeply dispiriting. Mother Teresa's rigid religiosity made some uncomfortable. The surprise was this: Both the students who had negative reactions *and* those who had positive ones showed the *same* immune system boost.

What's going on here? The experimenters surmised that while conscious judgments were taking place in the left brain, the right brain was responding to the emotional thrust of the film—images of altruism and compassion—and translating them into physiological responses. The left brain was put off by the film, but the right brain was turned on. While the former was supplying its usual up-to-the-minute bulletins of judgment, the latter was beaming get-happy messages to the immune system. It was as if the students were literally of two minds, and when push came to shove, the *heartful* mind had the final say.

The heart itself may be smarter than we think. It not only receives impulses from the brain but *sends* information to it via the vagus nerve. The heart generates its own hormones and releases them into the body. It even broadcasts its own electromagnetic field thousands of times more powerful than the brain's. And while scientists once thought the heartbeat was as monotonous as a metronome, its rhythm under resting conditions shows odd irregularities that, when carefully analyzed, seem to correlate with specific emotions.

This latter claim remains controversial, but according to scientists working at an organization called the Institute of HeartMath, that organ pulsating in your chest cavity really does know a thing or two. And the institute, whose scientific board includes Joe Kamiya, the father of modern biofeedback research, along with an impressive array of cognitive biologists, cardiologists, brain physiologists, and biomedical engineers, claims to have the data to prove it. They have set out not just to study the heart, but as one of their researchers told me, "to maximize the heart's influence on the brain" (or as another put it, admitting it sounded like "squishy" science: "to illumine the mind with the heart's knowing").

*T*his all sounded good to me, so when I was invited to visit their campus nestled in the northern California hills, I (or was it my heart?) leaped at the chance. I was scheduled to interview a few of the scientists at HeartMath's sprawling, 160-acre spread (the grounds of a former corporate retreat named, appropriately enough, Satori), but first I'd been pencilled in for some hang-time with the organization's enigmatic founder, "Doc" Childre.

I'd been prepped for this meeting by a mutual friend, who described Doc as an eccentric genius who once claimed to have lived a year without food, like some supernatural Taoist hermit. Those days were over, she informed me. He now liked a good smoke, a cold beer, and as a man of the South, favored his barbequed shortribs slow-roasted.

I'm told Doc likes to meet people at night, and am led by flashlight to a barn where I'm directed to climb a ladder to a loft, its beams decked with strings of white Christmas tree bulbs. I find Doc is sitting in an old club chair. With his gray beard, faded plaid shirt, and a bandana wrapped around his head, he looks like Willie Nelson. He turns down the dimmer on his party lights—"they'll look brighter in a minute," he says, his accent a mouthful of Carolina river pebbles—then pours me a cup of warm whisky and one for himself, fires up a nonfilter, and pops the top off a tall frosty one.

"If you can't have your cake and eat it, too," he pronounces with a croaking laugh, "why'd they bake the damn cake?" And we're off to the races.

Truth to tell, I don't remember much of our conversation. As the evening took its course, my notes are in a progressively shakier hand. I remember sitting there companionably with the reclusive guru of HeartMath in his Batcave, finding him immensely likable, as he talked elliptically about "domains of higher frequency emotions," the "heart's nervous system," the "access codes to holographic dimensions," and "bringing the heart to the street."

I do remember one koan delivered by the flare of a Bic held to the tip of a Pall Mall: "Love's not enough," he said, the flame underlighting his bewhiskered face. *"It's the care that puts it in the real!"* It wasn't exactly technical, but Doc's ideas, backed by some hard research, have been showing up in such august publications as the *American Journal of Cardiology.* Cardiologists had for years been studying subtle, beat-to-beat irregularities in heart rhythm called *heart-rate variability* (or HRV), mostly as a diagnostic tool to measure nervous system aging and emotional stress. But Doc had added a key insight. Different HRV patterns seemed to correlate with specific emotional states, in particular those that psychologists call the *qualia,* such as compassion, love, and forgiveness.

Measuring inner states with instrumentation is nothing new. EEGs have shown that alpha and theta rhythms in the brain are associated with the calming effects of meditation and yoga (known generally as the "relaxation response"). But HeartMath's research added a new wrinkle. Measures of heart rate variability show that the patterns generated by altruism and compassion are distinctly *different* than relaxed meditative states. Researchers claim that states of mind (or better, states of heart) that have more to do with caring about others than with seeking inner peace actually have greater health-promoting effects on the immune system and autonomic nervous system. "Love and caring," says HeartMath researcher Rollin McCraty, "drive the entire bodily system to oscillate at its resonant frequency," a purported state of harmony between brain and body he says he can scientifically measure.

McCraty, a wiry biophysiologist with a thatch of reddish hair, square gold-rimmed glasses, and a gold tooth that seems to flash in synch with his level of enthusiasm, takes me on a whirlwind tour of his biophysics lab, pointing out his spectrometers and cell-culturing rooms; his supersensitive, shielded confocal microscope for directly observing DNA; his towers of tall, silvery, sixty-channel processing units and assorted boxes whose blinking amber diodes and ebony and brass knobs give them a retro, Jules Verne–ish look. All told, he can measure damn near anything having to do with the heart. Using a technology called *spectral analysis,* for example, McCraty has shown that positive feelings create orderly "coherent" frequency patterns in the heart's electromagnetic (EM) signal that correspond to coherent rhythms of heart-rate variability. Not only that, he says, but the heart's EM field signal affects the *brain's* own electrical rhythms; and not only *that,* but one person's coherent heart frequency can affect *another* person's EEG and—well, you get the drift.

McCraty, a confirmed cardiophile, can riff with authority all day long and deep into the gloaming on the heart's incredible powers, filling in the big picture piece by puzzle piece until he gets your own heart racing and your brain puffing along behind on stubby little legs. Which, by his reckoning, about sums up the case. More often than not, the heart leaps first, leaving the brain to play catch-up. He cites evidence that some sensory information is routed to the heart *before* it arrives in the brain. The heart, he says, sends far more messages to the brain via its ascending (afferent) nerve pathways than the brain sends down the heart's mail chute through its descending (efferent) ones.

"Emotion," he says succinctly, "is faster than thought."

This model—let's call it The Heart is Quicker than the Mind— seems to be showing up everywhere. Primate researcher Frans de Waal's "perception-action model" suggests that in both apes and humans, emotions—including the empathic instinct—trigger a physical response *before any conscious decision has been reached.* Psychologist Jonathan Haidt has put forward a similar heart-over-head hypothesis (which he calls the "social intuitionalist model"). Haidt believes we first have an "emotionally tinged intuition," followed by intellectual justifications for what, in effect, the heart's already decided. When Thomas Carlyle noted a few centuries ago, "It is the heart that always sees, before the head can see," he may not have been far off.

The heart is now known to influence the brain via everything from neurotransmitters to pressure waves. It sends signals to the brain that activate or inhibit the cortex itself, giving the heart a neural vote (and maybe a veto) on cognitive functions, as well as its own back-channel influence on emotional centers like the amygdala. Nor does it always have to go through the brain's bureaucracy, because—did I mention?—the heart turns out to have its *own* brain of sorts, some forty thousand neurons and support cells arranged in an intricate architecture resembling that of the cortex. Research indicates that this heart-brain can learn, remember, and sense. The heart-brain even secretes its own dopamine, a component in the pleasure circuits that strongly influence our behaviors, suggesting our heart may play us like a violin. It is also known that the heart generates its own supply of oxytocin, the so-called "cuddle chemical," which, though it has a half-life in the bloodstream of only seconds, can create a lifelong imprint. Could it be that the heart strikes up love's music and the brain, that happy fool, dances to its tune? More often than you think, your heart really is the boss of you.

Using only the inner science of contemplation, mystics and meditators throughout the ages have made the same discovery. When the fourteenth-century monk St. Gregory Palamas wrote, "Our heart is the place of the rational faculty," he wasn't just speaking of the heart-as-metaphor but, according to one contemporary Greek Orthodox archbishop, "this spiritual heart located in the bodily heart as in an organ." The Hindu *Upanishads* describe a "self-luminous Being who dwells within the lotus of the heart, surrounded by the senses and the sense-organs, who is the Light of Intelligence"—an image strikingly like that of a cognizing brain ringed by its perceptual organs.

The relatively new field of neurocardiology has discovered that the heart *does* have its own sensory organs: Some of the heart's nerve ganglia receive information directly from the skin (giving new meaning to the phrase "you touched my heart"). There are forty nerves from the heart to the muscles governing subtle facial expression. What is inscribed on the heart may indeed be written all over face. (It may also explain why changing your facial expression can also change your mood; when you smile, are you giving your heart cause to rejoice?)

To get an idea how far all this diverges from the original (and still influential) insights of the early psychophysiologists, consider that Walter Canon, the father of psychosomatic medicine, once claimed that a severed head, if kept alive, would have a full range of emotion and cognition. *Hey, who needs a heart?* Would-be cryogenic immortalists flash-freeze severed heads, figuring that would be all you'd need to reconstitute yourself as an upstanding citizen of Alphaville. Cyberneticists talk about downloading the software of the human personality into indestructible robot brains and bodies in some postmodern version of the Tin Man. The ancient Egyptians, decidedly more low-tech in the eternal preservation department, knew better. Though they removed the other major organs (including the brain) during the process of mummification, they left the heart, which they considered the seat of the soul, intelligence, *and* emotion, where it belonged, to ensure that resurrection would be worth all the trouble.

*D*oc Childre realized that the heart doesn't exert its uplifting influence on body, mind, and spirit entirely on autopilot: It's helped by conscious intention. He and his researchers discovered that, just as imagining holding your hands in front of a campfire causes your palms to measurably heat up, so creating a mental image of the heart glowing with warmth produces a distinct physiological effect—in this case, one that seems to correlate with feelings of calm and lovingkindness. Simply giving the heart your full attention, that is, seems to produce physiological patterns that correlate with compassion itself. HeartMath researchers have noted that these "coherent" patterns of heart-rate variability are associated with positive effects on autonomic nervous system balance, cardiovascular efficiency, and reduced secretion of the stress hormone cortisol. Other tests have revealed that coherent HRV patterns produce greater increases in cognitive functioning than even the relaxation response, giving the expression "putting your heart into it" new scientific heft. (The implications for human performance have not been lost on the corporate world: Hewlett Packard, Shell, Sony, Boeing, and Glaxo-SmithKline are using HeartMath training for stress management and enhanced productivity. A federal pilot grant is funding HeartMath in nine school districts, based on preliminary evidence that it increases standarized test scores.)

One of HeartMath's PR people explains a training technique called Heart Lock-In: "Shift into the heart, activate a positive emotional state, lock on through the breath," she commands, "then bring your brainwaves into alignment with the heart rhythm." It sounds like a Vulcan courtship ritual, but I sort of get it. In the Hindu yoga traditions, it is said that whatever part of the body we concentrate on draws *prana,* or life-force, to that spot (think of the last time you made love). But HeartMath's instruction to stay with "core heart-feelings" rather than "head-thoughts" doesn't play to my strongest suit. How can someone like me learn to see with the eyes of the heart?

"Easy," researcher Rollin McCraty offers, "I'll show you."

He sits me down in front of a biofeedback-equipped computer that displays changes in heart-rate variability as dynamic graphics in a videogame. "It's the opposite of games that encourage aggression," he explains as he fits my finger into a pulse sensor that will pick up my HRV readout. Rather, he says, the point of this game is to train players to generate the physiological states associated with love, care, and compassion. When my heartbeat hits the magic love-frequency, the barren black-and-white landscape on the screen will bloom into a colorful flower garden.

As I sit before the screen, doing my best to germinate some love-seeds (*uh-oh:* compassion performance anxiety), I manage to entice a few sprigs to poke up from the digital dirt, though it ain't exactly the Tuilleries. McCraty taps the keyboard and another screen appears, this one of three bar graphs representing low, medium, and high HRV coherence. I try simply meditating; but, to my surprise, this mostly produces readings in the low end, with a little blip of activity in the center column.

"Now try focusing in your heart," McCraty suggests. "Think of someone you love."

I do as he says, imagining my daughter's face, and am amazed to see the medium graph rise like a soufflé and spill over into the high range. "That's great," he says encouragingly. I decide to try my hand, or at least my finger, at another game in which coherent HRV readings are synched to the movement of a colorful hot air balloon. Putting a little love in my heart, I quickly attain liftoff and am soon wafting over a bucolic landscape on a self-generated breeze of affection (is this energy-efficient transport or what?). But then my focus drifts. My balloon nearly shears the roof off a farmhouse before clunking to the ground.

I take off the sensor and hand it to McCraty. He takes a deep breath, inserts his trigger-finger and, the local top loveslinger, does everything but crack his knuckles. Soon enough, his balloon is up, up and away, sailing blithely over every obstacle—stone walls, houses, treetops, mountain ranges—and into nothing but blue skies.

Being stuck on the ground having to eat his pixie dust has my competitive juices going. Here I am, a reasonably adept meditator, but I'm getting pasted by this . . . this *heart-jockey.* I try again, slipping my finger in the little harness, but it's no go. My alpha-male mood creates a severe deflation event, and my balloon crash-lands in a haystack, refusing to budge. We could try another game, McCraty says, suggesting something about "make the bunny kiss the deer," but I decline, resisting an urge to sulk.

When he sends me back with a home-version kit for practice, I hook it up right away to my computer. I'm amazed that after playing around with it only a few times a week, I actually start getting better; at least, my readings increase. So does a feeling in my chest I can only call the warm fuzzies. Yes, there's something a little absurd about sitting in the glowing cathode twilight, entrusting my heart to the gondola of a digital blimp—I mean, *get a life.* But I find to my surprise that as I walk through the day, even this little bit of practice really *does* make me feel different. What I might call head-centered consciousness seems to look out at the world from a narrow turret, surveying the terrain, evaluating, while this heart-awareness has a more tender, inclusive gaze, like some mental *I ♥ You* button. Now and again, I find myself slipping into states of mindless (yet not at all stupid) beneficence.

Of course, this hardly requires a machine, and as the novelty fades, I'm disinclined to cuddle up with my computer on a daily basis. Besides, does the heart really *need* formal training? We know we've mastered the basics. When we see our child's face and experience that heart-bursting feeling that would make us gladly lay down our lives. We're *supposed* to love our kin; we're *designed* for it. Why make an extra effort to feel it for neighbors and strangers? Why tamper with human nature?

*B*ut the activation of the heart through deliberate practice is a venerable tradition. Until awakened through concentration and prayer, said the early Christian patriarch St. Markarios of Egypt, the heart's greatest potentials lie dormant. For the uncultivated, he wrote in *The Philokalia,* "The heart is a tomb, and there our thoughts and intellect are buried." But with attention and intention, mystics claim, it can be transformed: We can learn to see with the heart, think with the heart, judge from the heart, live through the heart. *The Way of the Pilgrim,* a nineteenth-century work revered in the Eastern Orthodox Church for reviving the meditative tradition of the Desert Fathers, describes a practice called the Prayer of the Heart. Its anonymous author has been identified by some scholars as a wandering, crippled Ukranian mystic whose order included characters like Blessed John the Fingerless and a 125-year-old forest-dwelling hermit named Righteous Melchizedek. The book's author promises that by reciting the words "Lord Jesus Christ, have mercy on me, a sinner," many thousands of times, the prayer will become "self-active," eventually synchronizing with the heartbeat itself, producing a flow of constant compassion.

The Pilgrim claims he was taught by an old cleric in an isolated monastery, a *starets* (literally, an "old one"—a guru) who instructed him in practices that contemplatives of any Eastern tradition would recognize: visualization ("forming a mental picture of His constant presence"), mantra ("a constant interior Prayer of Jesus"), clearing the mind of thoughts, and focusing on the heart. "Sit down alone and in silence," the starets told him. "Lower your head, shut your eyes, breathe out gently, and imagine yourself looking into your own heart. Carry your mind, your thoughts, from your head to your heart." The Pilgrim was urged to repeat the prayer frequently, matching each recitation with his outbreath. Taking a job as a gardener, he practiced the "self-acting spiritual prayer" thousands of times a day until finally he attained the purpose his starets intended: "to reach the realm of the heart."

Fans of author J. D. Salinger will remember *The Way of the Pilgrim* as the dog-eared tract clutched by Franny Glass when, home in pieces from a disastrous college love affair, she sprawls on the family couch, lips moving in breathless, unceasing prayer, determined to install in her soul some final principle of mercy. Franny is the author's lampoon of a religious fanatic (her brother, alarmed that she will "either be in a nut ward or wandering off into some goddam desert with a burning cross," finally manages to talk her out of it). Salinger was right in one sense: It *is* cruel to force the psyche into unbearable strictures (the quality of mercy is not strain'd). But it was the whole notion of repetitive religious practice that struck him, as it does many of us, as so much medieval mumbo-jumbo. In a recent article on contemporary religion, I noted an interview with a thirty-nine-year-old former altar boy, out jogging on a Sunday morning that once would have found him at Mass. "I don't see how something like a few repetitions of the 'Hail Mary' are going to solve any problems," he said.

The consensus among the world's spiritual traditions has always been the opposite. Some Tibetan Buddhist practices call for a hundred thousand or a million repetitions of prayers and visualizations. To remove the "locks" upon the heart, some mystical schools of Islam call for chanting over and over again one of the ninety-nine Beautiful Divine Names of God. Such customs make us free spirits uneasy: Isn't this just so much high holy brainwashing? But the contemplative traditions claim that we are already brainwashed by habitual thinking, and each day is a new trip to the laundromat. After all, aren't many of our whirling thoughts just repetitive mantras to our own minor gods and personal demons, variants on "I'm not good enough" or "I'm too sexy for my shirt?" Aren't we *already* reciting our daily matins of hope or regret, our incessant prayers for success and true romance, the same load of socks swooshing past the mind's little round window on automatic wash, rinse, and spin?

To change this inner drone calls for training in new cognitive habits, though we're more likely to exercise ("do reps," in gym parlance) for well-cut abs than a well-tempered heart. It takes effort to detach from the cavalcade of small thoughts and vain imaginings, the rehashing of slights and plotting of triumphs, the cataloguing of merits and demerits that constitute our self-centeredness workout tape. I know for myself that I've already done enough spadework via countless such thoughts to dig myself into a ditch of churlish habitude.

Why not, then, visualize myself as a loving bodhisattva dispensing boons with a thousand arms rather than as a grab-it-all-with-both-hands mogul? Why not deliberately call to mind examples of human kindness rather than filling my head with the daily news and its forlorn proofs of human folly? (In either case, I am forming a picture of the world that influences how I feel and what I do.) I learned my ABCs and do-re-mi's by rote; I can at least recite May All Beings Be Happy a few times a day.

A change of heart is rarely a one-shot deal. As the seventeenth-century French philosopher Blaise Pascal observed, "The strength of a man's virtue should not be measured by his special exertions, but by his habitual acts." Science is now validating this observation, and more. Substitute for the word *virtue* the term *neuroplasticity*—the newly discovered ability of the brain to alter its very structure through mental training—and Pascal was right on the mark.

*L*ondon's boxy black cabs, with their room-sized interiors and foldout jump seats, are, compared to American Yellow Cabs, marvels of comfort and convenience. But that's not the only difference. A New York taxi driver can learn enough about his city's rectilinear grid to get his hack license in a few days (though that plastic-encased mug shot may mean you know where you're going better than he does). A London cabbie, by contrast, must spend years acquiring what is reverently called "the Knowledge" before he or she is certified. On a trip to London, my driver explained how he had biked through the city's twisting, medieval biways month after month, memorizing every corner and cobblestone, in order to pass the stringent licensing test. "I've got this town's whole bloody street map, down to the last lamppost, etched right here on my brain," he said with a finger-tap to his forehead.

His claim may not be exaggerated, according to a study by the University College of London. Researchers there discovered that the longer the cabbies had been at their jobs, the larger was an area of the brain—the right rear hippocampus—crucial to storing mental maps of the environment. There had been, they concluded, a "redistribution of gray matter" based on intensive learning and prolonged mental habit. The study added to a growing body of evidence that what we habitually think and feel actually resculpts neural tissue. "If you do something, anything, even play Ping-Pong, for twenty years, eight hours a day, there's going to be something in your brain that's different from someone who didn't do that," notes Harvard neuroscientist Stephen Kosslyn. "It's just got to be."

What about compassion? There's a saving grace when compared to Ping-Pong: We're prewired for it. Empathy is integral to the human operating system, and building upon its substrates can result in surprising demonstrations of our human potential.

In recent experiments at the University of Wisconsin, a European-born Buddhist monk named Matthieu Ricard was placed inside a functional magnetic resonance imager (fMRI), a device that shows, in real-time and in crystalline detail, the brain's dynamic processes as they occur. Inserted into a beige tube with racketing, whirling monster-magnets, Ricard turned to a meditation he described as follows: "Let there be only compassion and love in the mind for all beings—friends and loved ones, strangers and enemies alike. It's compassion with no agenda, that excludes no one. You generate this quality of loving, and let it soak the mind."

As he did this practice, his brain showed a dramatic increase of activity in the left middle frontal gyrus, an area associated with joy and enthusiasm. In another series of tests, Ricard proved to be adept (two standard deviations above the norm, a scientifically unprecedented variance) at perceiving split-second changes in the facial muscles' expression of emotion, an ability strongly correlated with empathy. Most telling, when he was shown a film clip of severe burn victims having dead skin painfully stripped from their bodies—a sequence used in psychology labs to reliably trigger the instinct of disgust—he reported instead a sense of "caring and concern, mixed with a not unpleasant strong, poignant sadness." Ricard (called by the pseudonym "Lama Öser" in the study) modestly insists he is a monk of no great ability compared to others in his monastic tradition.

What if you had spiritually trained yourself so that whenever two roads diverged in a yellow wood, you'd reflexively choose the one most kind? Tibetan Buddhists believe that for anyone who practices diligently enough, compassion can become second nature, an unhesitating reaction to virtually every situation. At the Wisconsin lab, a tape of a woman's bloodcurdling scream was unexpectedly sprung on another monk in the midst of his compassion meditation. Rather than eliciting the predicted negative emotional reaction, his scan showed an unexpected activation in the left prefrontal area of the brain, a region associated with *positive* emotion. A warm response to others' suffering had become so ingrained as to be automatic.

At a 2003 conference at the Massachusetts Institute of Technology, neuroscientist Richard Davidson, who oversaw the groundbreaking Wisconsin experiments, presented the results of a series of follow-up studies. Davidson, who spent time in Asia studying meditation when he was younger and retains the air of an enthusiastic grad student, flashed a PowerPoint slide of a bell curve rising like a red mountain out of a flat landscape. It was a graph, he explained, charting 150 people's normal brain state. For the great majority, the brain tended to purr along in some Goldilocks zone between left prefrontal (positive emotion) and right prefrontal (negative emotion) activity.

But there was one tiny data point at the far edge of the chart, a solitary pilgrim wending his way from the looming red peak of statistical normalcy toward parts unknown. That point was Matthieu Ricard, who had been scanned while practicing deep compassion meditation. His reading was literally beyond the curve in the area of positive emotion—the most extreme such result ever documented.

At the MIT meeting, as Davidson shared the stage with the Dalai Lama himself, he quoted the Tibetan leader's contention that "the wiring in our brain is not static, not irrevocably fixed. Our brains are adaptable." Davidson seemed nonplussed when his statement was met with a spontaneous outburst of applause mixed with actual cheers from an audience of usually sedate neuroscientists. It was as if he had not just announced intriguing lab results, but promulgated a declaration of human independence—which in a sense he had.

The meeting was epochal in one respect: It was the first formal exchange between cutting edge Western brain science and traditional Eastern mind science, two hemispheres of knowledge sending forth early neural tendrils of some new corpus callosum. Davidson points out that psychology has spent nearly its entire history studying negative emotions, positing that fear, sex, and aggression were baselines for human functioning. Meditators, on the other hand, have been learning how to deliberately elicit positive emotions for millenia. It was as if Tibetan society had invested twelve hundred years in a top-priority Inner Space Program. For eras, while the world blustered through the age of steam, spit electricity's cold fire in the face of the night, unleashed the railing demons of the atom and circumnavigated the moon, Buddhists had sat calmly by the flickering light of millions of yak-butter lamps, doing essential R&D on the energies of consciousness itself. The results, now documented in the lab, prove in the words of psychologist Jerome Kagan, "Joy and serenity are not slavishly tied to our physiology. We are not programmed neurons over which we have no control. We are collaborators in the generation of our thoughts and emotions."

The person who sets out to develop what the Dalai Lama calls the Good Heart is trying to encourage certain propensities and override others. No one would suggest it's easy. I sometimes wonder if contemplation is, for human beings, as fundamentally new a way of cognizing as the bonobo Kanzi's leap into symbolic understanding. He's on the very brink of thought, while our project may be to see *through* thought itself, thus earning our full name: *Homo sapiens sapiens*, the creature that is aware of being aware.

But the monks insist their state of mind (and heart) isn't dependent on any superhuman evolutionary leaps. It's been accomplished through a Himalayan version of the old joke, "How do I get to Carnegie Hall?" (or in this case, the Potala Palace): "Practice, practice." They have, comments one scientist, "mastered a metacognitive skill of noticing a reaction and being able to channel it." It's not just a matter of adopting a new idea, as if we could pop a new program into our mental hard drive, click Install, and add instant functionality. It's been estimated that to acquire the mastery that actually alters the brain—to become a chess expert or a good violinist or, presumably, a journeyman bodhisattva—takes some ten thousand hours of practice. But there's still plenty of room for us amateurs. Every little bit of metacognition helps.

I've met Matthieu Ricard on a number of occasions. He does not emanate palpable sun-rays; rainbows don't sparkle in his eyes. He is a man of wizardly intellect who as a graduate student at Paris's Pasteur Institute made original discoveries in genetics. At age twenty, Ricard had seen a film about Tibet and was transfixed by the faces of some of its great meditation masters. He traveled to India, met a famous teacher in Tibet's "wandering yogi" tradition, and spent summers studying in India while he completed his biology doctorate. Powerfully drawn to the spiritual life, he finally left France, took monastic vows, and continued an intensive discipleship, doing long retreats and becoming a translator for the Dalai Lama.

Ricard is affable and direct, though I wouldn't call him inordinately warm. He's too down-to-earth to come off as a mystic. An impression of roly-polyness reveals on closer look a man who, at nearly sixty, has the barrel-chested stolidity of a wrestler, though his only grappling has been with the subtle doctrines of his adopted religion and the workings of his own mind.

When I tell him ten thousand hours sounds like a bit much, he mentions several new studies in which groups of people will be taught compassion techniques while their progress is monitored. "My rough prediction," he says, "is that you'll see a sharp upward curve, maybe the most dramatic change, in the first six months." He chuckles drily. "On the other hand, meditation's not the seven-day cure for self-centeredness—more like seven years!"

When I ask him if he thinks some people are predisposed, perhaps even genetically so, to be kinder, Ricard, who keeps up with the news from biology's frontiers, enthusiastically cites a recent animal experiment. Baby rats from a genetic line that had been bred for fifteen generations to be "superanxious" were placed with mothers bred to be over-caring. "If these babies spend just ten days with the over-caring mothers," he says, "their superanxious genes don't get expressed. They grow up normal. That's amazing, fabulous—just think what potential we humans must have! Even if 50 percent of our character is genetic, the other 50 percent is plastic. You're not just stuck with what you are. Nothing's graven in stone. Learning can radically change you."

I press him on this: Isn't it just harder for some people to learn to be kind, while others seem to have a positive talent? "Yeah, yeah, *oui*, of course," he says, sounding a little impatient. "Look, *I'm* not instinctually compassionate in my nature. Unfortunately for me." He tells me an illustrative story: Once he was being driven on a high, icy pass in eastern Tibet to attend an important gathering. Darkness and bad weather were closing in. His party was already hours late. "At one point, we passed by this guy sleeping by the road, which was okay with me, because we were in a terrible hurry. But I was traveling with a friend who is one of those extraordinary, spontaneously empathetic people. She made us find a place to turn around—not so easy on those narrow roads—and go back. It turned out he was just drunk.

She's one of those whose empathy *makes* her take care of everyone who needs help. She could care less about some big important project. I could react by passing the guy; her, never."*

I'm reassured, I tell him, that a man who has proven he can play his brain as dexterously as an accordianist in a polka band still has to make a special effort to be a Good Samaritan. "Listen," he says, "none of us is born with full knowledge. Take love: Most everybody can love in the normal sense. Your family loves you; you love your family. A friend treats you well; you feel affection. If he's mean to you, maybe you don't. Well, what about a total stranger or even an enemy who treats me badly? Can I have genuine love and compassion for them? I think the world really needs that kind of learning. We spend all these years getting regular schooling or job training. If just a little of this mind-training came into mainstream education, it would be a big, big, *big* contribution."

He elaborated on this theme on a panel at the MIT conference. "In the West, we think freedom means that every thought that arises in my mind, I'm going to do it. So we are the slave of every thought." Citing anger, compassion's fiery nemesis, he remarked: "The point is to learn not to jump into that chain reaction, but instead just let the feeling be, look at it—what *is* that? Why should it multiply that way?

---

* I spoke with Dr. Lobsang Rapgay, a former Tibetan Buddhist monk who got his psychiatric training and joined the UCLA faculty, as he was completing a study on moral reasoning and compassionate activity among Tibetan monks, using his psych grad students as a control group. "It's hard to figure out if some of these lamas are actually making the leap from studying and meditating on compassion to actually *doing* it," he told me. "They will do their practices, be kind to a stranger on a pilgrimage, throw a fish back into a lake, and so forth. But when I posed survey questions like, 'If you were asked to take five days away from whatever you're doing to help a sick friend, would you?' the grad students mostly said sure, while some of the lamas said they would instead opt to keep on with their practices. The grad students often scored higher on the empathy, sympathy, and love scales." When I told this to Matthieu Ricard, he made clear he was a strong partisan of the traditional meditation disciplines. "Maybe at first, it's like you're just laying down the plumbing and the electrical wiring in a building, so it may not directly help anyone. But when the building is finished, it's more powerful than just helping people one by one on the street— it's like a hospital. It makes sense to train to be a better person and to get rid of self-importance—then you're able to be genuinely helpful to everyone, no strings attached."

It is like stopping a forest fire at the first spark, because later it is harder to control and the fire just spreads."

I once observed a group of violent offenders in an anger management class. One woman, who had been convicted of second-degree battery, talked about her struggle against her automatic responses. She described the "pictures I get in my head when my boyfriend is late getting home—that he must be cheating, so by the time he comes back, even if he's innocent, I'm really mad at him." She was touchingly insightful about "where my anger takes me," noting that when these images appeared in her mind, "my breathing speeds up, I hold my breath, clench my fists, start talking to myself, getting angrier, imagining how I'm gonna mess him up." Now, after therapy and training, she finds there are times she can interrupt the cycle by picturing she is saying to her anger, "You're *not* going to take me there," enduring "the uncomfortable feeling I get when I *don't* do something, 'cause it's in my comfort zone to violently act out." Hers was a poignant variant of what each of us struggles with in our own way: applying the gift of free will toward becoming a better person.

"Freedom is the freedom to not be carried away by an emotion," one of the MIT neuroscientists remarked. But then he added, "It's also cultivating the ability to love."

In the Buddhist system, this cultivation of beneficial patterns of heart and mind is known as the "accumulation of merit." Though sometimes viewed as simply doing good deeds or performing prayers to accrue "good karma," merit is more than just a stockpile—it is a living principle. The flow of thoughts, images, and feelings that form our consciousness is said to be a "mind-stream." Whatever we drop into it tends to keep circulating, whether a rusting beer can or a lotus petal. The idea is to place more positive intentions and loving thoughts into the stream while refraining from tossing in any more junk, thus purifying the waters and restoring what Buddhists consider the mind's natural ecology of benevolence.

Whatever our religious persuasion, practice, or lack thereof, the nonnegotiable terms of life seem to be much as Gandhi described:

Your beliefs become your thoughts

Your thoughts become your words

Your words become your actions

Your actions become your habits

Your habits become your character

Your character becomes your destiny

One Buddhist analogy compares each of us to a person living in a hovel beneath which is buried a magnificent treasure. Someone shows up at our door with an ancient treasure-map and tries to convince us to dig it up, but we refuse to take the trouble, not able to imagine such a thing, let alone believe it would be worth tearing up still serviceable floorboards to find out. Because we don't recognize the wealth we already possess, we live in unwitting, needless penury. If we would just dig deep and keep digging right on the spot we're standing, insist the great teachers, we'd discover we're all compassion billionaires.

*A*fter the XVIth Gyalwa Karmapa, leader of the Kargyu Order of Tibetan Buddhism, died of stomach cancer in a white room full of beeping machinery in a hospital in Zion, Illinois, his monks propped him up in meditation posture and refused to let the body be moved. He was clinically dead, but there was apparently some unfinished business. As doctor after baffled doctor confirmed by palpating the holy man's chest cavity, the Karmapa's heart remained persistently, inexplicably warm.

"The monks called me in about twelve hours after he died," an attending physician, Dr. Ranulfo Sanchez, told me when I investigated this wild-sounding story. "The body was cold, but the area over his heart was still normal body temperature. It was really very strange. I can't explain it. None of us could." Though medical personnel were dumbfounded, the monks showed no surprise. It was a sign, they said, of the great lama's indestructible compassion. After three days, the Karmapa's heart grew cold, and the body, now a shell, was removed for his funeral in Sikkim.

Whatever one makes of this tale, the Karmapa was certainly a big-hearted man. A friend of mine named Alan remembers being with him when a songbird suddenly crashed headfirst into a picture window and fell to the ground. The Karmapa, an animal lover who kept an aviary in his monastery, asked him to bring it inside. "As far as I could tell," Alan told me later, "it was kaput. Its chest wasn't moving. I couldn't feel a heartbeat." The Karmapa took it gently in his palm, stroked its feathers, blew on it. "Suddenly, it stirred, looked around with its beady eyes, and hopped off his hand." Alan was astonished. "Maybe it had just been comatose; I'm no veterinarian. But I'll never forget the tenderness the Karmapa directed at that creature." Another friend told me of going to a pet store with the Karmapa who, saying he felt sorry for the mice and crickets about to be fed to the snakes, instructed him to buy them and release them in a nearby national park.

The Karmapa was above all a people-lover, and the feeling seemed to be mutual. When he stayed in hotels, the staff invariably fell in love with the big, moonfaced man in the sleeveless maroon robe, the maids and bellhops spontaneously lining up by the elevator each day to receive his genial benediction. I once watched him bless a crowd of several thousand people, one by one, touching their foreheads with his heavy ritual *dorje* and, when his arm tired, lightly tapping them with his empty Coke can, gazing at each who passed with equal delight. I was reminded of a line from Shakespeare: "My crown is in my heart, not on my head."

I'd met the Karmapa a few times. We'd talked for a bit, but all I remember is his warmth, like the radiant heat of a woodstove, his laugh (jolly really is the only word), and his wide Cheshire smile. And something else, some unmistakable emanation that made you feel just great—encouraged about your possibilities, affirmed in the rightness of your existence (and for that matter, everyone else's). I once spent a night sleeping on a couch in the living room of a ski chalet his students had rented for him during a visit to Wyoming. I'd awakened at 5 A.M. to the sound of his chanting. I peeked in on him as he leafed patiently through folio sheets of prayers, reminding me of times I'd watched my Orthodox Jewish grandfather reciting his morning *Sh'ma*. Here was the Karmapa, believed by his followers to be a supreme bodhisattva of compassion—a man who, according to tradition, had already been on the job for sixteen lifetimes—still practicing, practicing, always practicing.

His posthumous heart trick is beyond explaining. But I can't help but feel it was a gift, one final summoning of attention—*look, love's mystery, the sweet spot, the stillpoint!*—that last bloom of warmth a homing beacon, some small proof of a power as deathless as the poets have always claimed. A final communique in the vernacular of the flesh, a mute prayer, a silent sutra, unforgettable: *At the end of our upward striving, all things come to rest in the heart.*

7

THE GIVEAWAY

> Whatever joy there is in this world
> All comes from desiring others to be happy
> And whatever suffering there is in this world
> All comes from desiring myself to be happy.
> —*Shantideva (8th cent. B.C.E.)*

*H*arold Mintz is a big, sweet galoot. He insists on picking me up at the train station so I don't get entangled in the color-coded sailor's knot of the Washington, D.C., subway grid. When I slide into the front seat of his car, he gives me a broad smile and punches my arm, like I'm the buddy he was out shooting hoops with last weekend. He's a large-boned man, six foot five, dressed in a boomer-casual outfit of khakis and plaid; with his walrus moustache and thin gold earring, he could be a hip off-duty fireman, the kind who'd tell you a knock-knock joke while he resuscitated you from smoke inhalation. When his wife calls on the cell phone ("Yep, got him, honey!"), his ringer trills a few upbeat bars of "Zippety-Doo-Dah" (*my oh my, what a wonderful day!*).

The forty-six-year-old sales VP is as gregarious as a golden retriever and just as convinced the world means him well. He knows why I'm here: a field trip to observe, in its native habitat, the rare *Altruistus americanus*. Except, Harold tells me as we walk through the front door of his tidy brick Georgian, I've come to the wrong place.

"Well," I point out, "that *was* you who gave away your kidney to a total stranger." He shrugs, smiles a little.

Harold's is one of those stories that sounds to skeptical ears like tabloid fare; vaguely freakish, possibly pathological, completely unlikely. Here, *ecce homo*, is a man who donated his kidney—one of two spongy organs shaped like, well, giant kidney beans, that nestle cozily on opposite sides of your lower back—to someone he didn't know from Adam or Eve.

Evolution, master of redundancy, has seen to it you only really need one kidney, but if both of them go, you're toast. Fifty thousand Americans in renal failure are now awaiting kidney transplants. Only twelve thousand per year will receive them, some from relatives, but mostly from cadavers. (Nephrologists derogatorily refer to the poor-quality kidneys they're forced to use in the shortage as "crumbs.") Several thousand patients die each year, waiting. A healthy, transplantable kidney could scarcely be more precious. A few years ago, a man tried to auction his on Ebay: Before they shut it down (human innard–peddling being illegal), the bidding had reached $5.7 million.

The idea of making a bodily sacrifice on another's behalf, with its undertones of myth and martyrdom, is unsettling and not a little awe-inspiring. The first live organ donor of record, the god Prometheus, gave up his liver to bring humanity the gift of fire. There's Christ's oblation on the Cross and the offering of his flesh as love's ransom. And there is the *Jatakamala,* a treasury of the Buddha's deeds of compassionate sacrifice, beloved Asian children's fables that make even the Grimm Brothers' more disturbing tales look as tame as the Teletubbies. In one story, the Buddha plucks out his own eyes and gives them to a blind man. ("To the virtuous," says the text, "no suffering exists but that of others.") The fifth-century

148

itinerant monk Faxian describes a great gilded *stupa* in the ancient kingdom of Taxila (Chinese for "the severed head"), commemorating the Buddha's gift of, yes, his *head* to a man who, presumably, had lost his own.

But Harold Mintz insists he's got his head securely screwed on his shoulders, right, tight, and certifiable. He shows me his psychiatric evaluation, a donor prerequisite, as proof. "The docs said I'm as sane as anyone. And I'm definitely no saint. The best part of this story is that I'm completely normal."

"Okay, then, why'd you do it?" I ask again.

"You tell me," he says, stretching out comfortably on the living room floor and popping one of his wife's homemade lemon squares in his mouth. He offers me one. It's dizzyingly rich, so lubricious with butter that it's less a pastry than a myocardial infarction grenade. *It's not because you're a health nut,* I think.

"Dominoes," he says, propping himself on one elbow. Above him is a wall-sized painting, a piece of outsider art depicting large, enigmatically floating baby heads. He reaches for another lemon square. "Dominoes," he repeats, his mouth full. Seems his dad was an architect, and as a child, Harold loved to imitate him by creating elaborate setups of dominoes. When he could no longer stand the suspense, he'd give one of his just-this-side-of-Vegas creations the barest nudge and watch enthralled as gravity set off a clacking chain reaction.

"It was beautiful," he says. "When that happens in real life, we call it fate." And it does happen, Harold insists, sure as you're born. His donation was, as he sees it, scarcely of his own doing, but a case of one thing leading to another by the push of some greater index finger.

One domino, he says, was his father's death from cancer at age fifty-six. Harold had felt a sheer helplessness that "ripped my heart to pieces, seeing this linebacker-sized man just shrink away. I remember looking at his glasses on the nightstand after he died, sobbing my eyes out, wishing I could have done something, anything." A few years later, at the mall on Valentine's Day, Harold passed an elderly couple sitting at a fold-up table with a hand-lettered sign that read, Help Us Save Our Child. "I was there to buy some pants, not hear some bring-me-down story," he says. "But when I saw people whipping past them without even looking, I had to double back." The couple was searching for a matching bone marrow donor for their leukemic daughter, and Harold eagerly agreed to be tested. To his intense disappointment, a near-match turned out to be a hairsbreadth miss.

Not long after that, he says, another domino fell. Flying cross-country, he saw an in-flight movie about a high school football player who had donated a kidney to save his sick grandmother. Harold had felt so moved, he'd jotted down the 800 number at the end of the rolling credits. (As he tells me this, it rings a bell: I'd seen this film— one of those based-on-a-true-story heartstring-tuggers—somewhere before.) Soon after, Harold happened on an article about a white schoolteacher in North Carolina who had given a kidney to a black student using a relatively painless new laparoscopic procedure.

It was a revelation. "You can give away your spare and save a life? And your race doesn't even matter? How great is *that*?" Impulsively, he resolved to become a donor. Then click-clack, another domino fell: He found out that one of the few anonymous donor programs in the country was in a nearby town. He signed up, went through a battery of psych tests ("laying on the couch blithering about myself like some *New Yorker* cartoon"), and after passing the medical screening, was elated to get a go-ahead. His wife, he says, was "not so enthused about anyone taking things out of my body. But by the time I finished explaining to her that it's *ER* for real—that I could be part of this medical miracle that saves someone's wife or mom—she was bawling her eyes out."

Ethiopian refugee Gennet Belay, wife to Tsegaye, mom to Meseret and Abiy, had been on dialysis three times a week for over a decade, enduring over forty operations to keep her alive, her name going nowhere on the endless list of would-be kidney recipients. To Gennet, an accountant, her life felt like a wall clock set at five minutes to midnight, the seconds ticking past. But two weeks before Christmas that year, she found herself being wheeled into an operating room in Falls Church, Virginia, while Harold was trundled into an OR near his home in Georgetown. With the reggae music he'd chosen thumping softly in the background, surgeons made a few small slits below his navel, threaded in a small video camera, inserted their retrieval instruments, and gingerly jockeyed out his kidney. It was then rushed across state lines and, essentially, repotted like a prize azalea. When Harold awoke from anaesthesia, he was awestruck to hear a nurse say, "Your kidney's inside someone else, peeing up a storm!" Two months later, at a banquet arranged in their honor by the transplant consortium, the two oddly intimate strangers were introduced for the first time. Their families have since become friendly, having dinners together, talking often on the phone, exchanging holiday cards and birthday presents.

"It's a fairy tale," Harold says, "a tearjerker with a happy ending, just like that movie." I suddenly remember where I'd seen the film, and it gives me a slightly eerie sensation. My friend Anna wrote it, I tell Harold. I'd watched it in her living room. "Great," he says, "tell her what she did!" A half hour later, in one of those rare strokes of cosmic bureaucratic efficiency, my cell phone rings and Anna's name shows in the little window. Just calling to say hi, she says. "Here, someone wants to talk to you," I tell her, handing the phone to Harold.

"Did you ever think your movie'd actually save a life?" he yells happily. I can't hear her end of the conversation, but by his *There you go!*'s and *Is that cool or what?*s, I know she must be gratified. "So, how do you feel about that?" he finally asks her, putting the phone to my ear so we both can listen. "You were behaving the way human beings *should* behave," she says, "and usually don't." Anna's Hungarian family had to flee first the Nazis, then the Communists; humanity hasn't always shown her its most felicitous expression. Now we all feel unexpectedly swept up in a vortex of shared elation.

151

"Dominoes!" Harold exclaims triumphantly after we hang up, as if pronouncing one of the seventy-two names of God; and indeed, under his umbrella of goodwill, I can't help feeling that Anna's call has revealed a piece of that pattern Hindus call Indra's Net: the universe as an infinite web of jewels, each one reflecting all the others. Still, I tell him, I don't entirely understand why he did it.

"Anyone, if they'd experienced the same things I had, would've done the same," he says flatly. If only *I'd* known his father; run into the leukemia lady at the mall; seen Anna's film . . . Well, it would likely have been me on that gurney.

But that's just the point, I tell him. It *wasn't.* I've seen what he's seen. My sister had leukemia, my marrow was tested, wasn't a match; they tried my brother, it didn't work; she died. We all wept for years. I've seen the same tearjerker movie, watched the disease-of-the-month telethons. But Domino F, in my setup, is still inches too far from Domino G; when it falls, it just falls flat.

He shakes his head. He's not buying it. This is a guy who called up his four best friends before his operation and suggested that they *all* go in and donate their kidneys. "It'll be fun," he told them. "We'll wake up in the hospital together and eat strawberry ice cream." He still seems perplexed that each found a plausible-sounding reason to beg off.

I will give my kidney away eventually; both of them, in fact, having signed that driver's license consent form committing them and other choice parts to needy others—someday. Just not now. I've got mild paranoia as it is: What if I'm prised out of a mangled wreck and carted off to an ICU so eager to harvest my vitals that, like a modern version of Poe's premature burial, they're tempted to just toe-tag me DOA?

"Look, I admit not everyone's going to be a living donor," Harold says. "Not everyone's going to run into a burning building, either. But if you came across someone in real serious trouble, wouldn't you want to help?" He starts ticking off hypotheticals in a practiced rhythm. "What if you could give up an organ to save your child? No question, right?"

"Sure," I say.

"Okay, imagine I fall down right here on the floor in front of you. I'm writhing in pain—" he flops down on the carpet for effect, "—sudden renal failure, your kidney's a good match, you can save me. Wouldn't you do it?"

I look at him lying there, miming a poor helpless creature with its legs in the air. He's making a piteous expression—*"wouldn't you?"*— with his scrunched eyebrows. I laugh, think about it a minute, then realize, "Okay, I would." I feel like I'm taking a pledge. It's exhilarating and vertiginous.

"Good," he says, sitting up. "So, what if it was your assistant—the girl who called me, what's her name, Dana?"

Dana's a lovely person, smart, funny, dedicated. But what if my daughter needs my kidney someday? He reminds me that in this exercise, Dana needs it *now.*

"Maybe," I allow cautiously, "if there was no one else closer to her."

"What if it was your neighbor?"

I don't say anything, mentally temporizing.

"The next-door lady who once clipped your hedges for you?" he prompts. "Took care of your mail when you went on vacation?" Harold's in sales mode, and in his line of work, he's what's known as a closer. My kidney wakes up and squirms.

"Maybe, maybe not," I say, sounding, to my ears, a little petulant.

"Okay, then what about someone four blocks away, some deserving person who—?" I hold up my hand, telling him I'll take a raincheck. I really *don't* know. He gives me one of his genial armsocks. "Good answer, I like that, it's honest."

W hat Harold has described is the basic instruction manual for all compassion do-it-yourselfers, aspiring bodhisattvas, and saints *manqué*. Step One: Recruit the heart by thinking of those you love the most, tapping a reservoir of deep concern. Step Two: Let it flow, extending until it reaches neighbors, strangers, even enemies. Step Three: Repeat. Never stop. But after years of spotty meditation practice, I still struggle. Why does it come so naturally to Harold?

Seriously, I ask him, where did you *get* this stuff?

From nowhere, he says—I should take it at face value that he's no one special. To him, giving is not all that complicated. There's no reason anyone can't wake up one fine morning and jump in the deep end. Besides, he says, look at the things he's gotten from his generosity: like that time at the Transplant Olympics, where he and Gennet and other living donors and their recipients trotted into the stadium like tag teams, each of them wearing half of the same heart pin, and a crowd of five thousand jumped roaring to its feet. "The cheering, the confetti, the balloons dropping . . . it felt great!" he says. For Harold, such public events are a further extension of his giving, a way to shine a spotlight on living donation: "I'm just saying, if I can do it, they can do it." Ever the salesman, he wants more bang for his buck, to save first one life, and then, as the news ripples out, more and more.

Some might accuse him—and have—of grandstanding, of getting more bang for his own ego. As he well knows. He sent me an e-mail, teasing and maybe just a little anxious about what I might write: "Hi! Just checking on how that 'people who do good things but aren't *really* as good as other people might think they are' thing is going?" And it's true: I'm still trying to wrap my mind around what he did and why.

A few years ago, the French film *Amelie*, about a young woman who traipses through Paris secretly improving people's lives, was a surprise hit. I have friends who were deeply annoyed by the character, a kind of Holly Golightly whose martini seemed to have been spiked with Ecstasy. Maybe it was her unseemly glee as she spied out the results of her do-gooding, a hint of what we mistrust about such people: It's not just out of the goodness of their hearts—they're also getting their jollies off.

The motives of people who seem exceptionally unselfish or downright self-sacrificing have been debated for centuries. "The humblest man alive," wrote Bernard Mandeville, a satirical eighteenth-century Dutch philosopher, "must confess that the reward of a virtuous action . . . consists in a certain pleasure he procures to himself by contemplating his own worth." Or is it really a case of low self-worth? Exhibit A might be someone like Joseph Cornell, the avant-garde artist whose cunning shadow-boxes are in museum collections the world over. Cornell had lived his entire adulthood with his mother and his disabled younger brother, Robert, who was a victim of cerebral palsy. A recent biographer writes:

> "The sacrifices that Joseph made on Robert's behalf were certainly valiant, yet the self he inhabited was so diminished he could not afford to think of his deeds in such generous terms. The truth is that his mother made him feel that his own needs were unimportant beside Robert's—that he should be ashamed of having needs in the first place . . ."

But Harold seems to have no problem taking care of his own needs. He just likes to take care of other people's, too. The good news, it occurs to me, is that though there's *some* x-factor I can't put my finger on, maybe Harold differs from most of us only by degree. He's uncomfortable with the word compassion, he says. "It makes it sound like I'm not just like everyone. But I am." He reminds me of my friend Tasha, a hairdresser at the local salon, who has spent the past two years braving international red-tape hell to adopt an abandoned baby girl from China. When I tell her it's an act of kindness, she pooh-poohs it: "It's not like we're selfless. We want to make a family." I've noticed how many people who do good are embarrassed to be tagged as do-gooders. They're more in the mold of what Hispanic tradition calls the *santas sombras,* the hidden saints, who quietly go about their good works and may turn out to be that neighbor who, come to think of it, has always been a little on the super-friendly side.

S teve Aman let himself get written up in the paper once, but he's not sure he liked the sensation of seeing his name in print. He, too, donated a kidney to a stranger but tells me, "I turned down *Good Morning, America* and all the rest of them. That isn't what this was about."

Steve lives a long way from Harold's manicured D.C. exurbs in a flyspeck town by the Erie Canal, a place where the granite quarry sits next to a graveyard that's slowly filling with its products and the main drag is Judy's Coiffure and Krafts, the Chill 'n' Grill, and a long defunct dry cleaner called Dry Cleaner's. It's no poverty pocket—there's a gentleman farm here and there, and Steve's got a good patch of acreage—but it's the boonies. The weathered blue house across the street, shuttered and abandoned, looks like the Bates Motel.

When I show up, Steve's talking to one of his neighbors, a grizzled man in a sweatshirt with raggedly severed sleeves, the tattoo of a dragon on his left bicep.

"I'm gonna need to cut up some trees that fell during that weird spring ice storm," the man is saying.

"My friend Becky's got access to a splitter; I could ask her if she'd make you some logs."

"Good, that oughta get us through next winter."

Steve's place has a funky, laid-back ambience. There's a stuffed buffalo head above the Cardiomax exercycle, and below it a prostrate dog so mangy and inert I first take him for a cast-off throw rug. A faux-crocheted "East, West, Home Is Best" hangs on the wall. As we settle down to talk, I note the telltale kindly guy gestures. He sees me washing my eyeglasses and unthinkingly hands me a paper towel; when he makes me some tea, he puts a small ice cube in my cup so it won't be too hot. Compared to Harold's brash bonhomie, Steve is more self-contained, interior. He wears a hearing aid with a little antenna sprouting from it, and glasses as big as shop goggles—your high school chem teacher (which isn't far off: he's a former chemical technician for Kodak). If Harold's a garden-club tulip, Steve's a modest jack-in-the-pulpit whose late-blooming path of generosity was more roundabout, if no less certain.

Steve wasn't a particularly generous soul when he was younger, he says. He was a severe introvert. "I would've been happy taking my wife and kid to the woods and being a recluse," he says. He remembers always feeling inwardly like an idealist—"a dreamer," as he puts it—but never felt it possible to be one in the world. Though he'd been "ecologically minded" ever since he'd read Rachel Carson's *Silent Spring*, there he was toiling for over a decade in the Kodak lab with "all those nasty carcinogens." He'd kept his head down, an employee-of-the-month type, toeing the company line, reliably punching the clock.

Except that he had become an alcoholic. It was his AA sponsor who had introduced him to a self-help group called Lifespring, where, he says simply, "you learn to love yourself and accept others." The courses gave him what he calls an "aha experience." The core of it, he said, was "dealing with the fear of not having enough." It led him to realize that "whatever I had *was* enough. I was sufficient just as I am. And that made me see that I don't need to hang on so tight—that I have things I can give."

Sometimes all that is needed is a channel, some pipeline for pent-up goodness, a wire for love's current to flow. Steve, at age forty, began giving blood for the first time in his life. "I had never thought that people could get gratification from donation with nothing in return," he says. At some point, he says, "I decided I didn't have to be afraid what would happen to me if I didn't follow the regular path." He left his job and began working full time at a tree nursery, finding that he had "green in my veins." He did some volunteer work for environmental groups. He bought a parcel of land "to preserve it for the next generations."

"It wasn't that I was so selfish before," he says, "but I hadn't explored too many ways to share." Now Steve would do something to help out and discover he got back more than he gave. That felt so good that he'd try giving some more. The feedback loop grew into a virtuous circle. Tortoise step by step, he experienced a gradual "unfolding of gifts," and, in an echo of Harold, he says, "the dominoes began to fall." His wife, Mary, a medical technician, had become interested in her part-Mohawk heritage, and together they began to explore Native American philosophy, attending the ceremonial Sun Dance. Steve was floored by the dancers' sacrifice as they pierced their skin with slivers of bone attached by leather thongs to a Maypole-like post. "It takes real generosity of spirit to undergo that pain and discomfort, dancing for four days with no food or water, offering your flesh for the sake of the people." His biggest inspiration, though, came from a central tenet of the Native American life called the Giveaway. "If you have something you don't use," he explains, "then you put it someplace where others can take it if they need it." Steve says his lifesaving deed was just that—a giveaway. As he sees it, he had an extra kidney and figured he'd drop it off in the community free box.

The story wasn't much more complicated, at least to hear him tell it. One day, he'd seen an item in a Rochester paper about a man who had put out a desperate public plea for a kidney. Steve had been longing to take another step, "to do something important for someone really in need." This looked like an answered prayer. He zapped an e-mail to the man, who turned out to be a former TV broadcaster whose wait for a donor transplant had lasted nineteen touch-and-go years. A few months later, they met for lunch. "I think he had to make sure

I didn't want anything from him," Steve says. "But it really wouldn't have mattered *who* he was." They turned out to be a perfect match, and the operation went smoothly. The whole thing, Steve says, was "really no big deal."

I ask to see his scars from the new, less invasive extraction method, and he accommodatingly pulls down his shorts to show me a thin scalpel line above his groin. It gives me a twinge to look, but he swears it was mostly painless. He knows people see him as heroic but says, "I didn't do anything above and beyond." He has a motto that in anyone else's mouth would sound like stilted white-guy Indian-speak: "To be a hollow bone, grateful to be used for Spirit." He says it without sanctimony, but is Steve just too self-effacing—too grateful to be *used*, period? In an indigenous culture, he would be prized for his humility; a shrink might diagnose him as a case of fuzzy boundaries.

*I*n the early 1960s, when "harvesting" a kidney meant slicing a foot-long incision across a patient's back, occasionally snapping a rib, a New York hospital sent out a public appeal for donors. They netted nine people willing to undergo the procedure on a stranger's behalf. According to one monograph, all reported "positive emotional benefits, with no regrets or psychological complications after donation." But the project was abruptly terminated because, the report said, doctors "remained suspicious of these donors' psychological status and motivation." The decision reflected more than medical ethics. It was a snap referendum among medical professionals on whether extraordinary acts of compassion were compatible with mental health. How many people could there really be out there, uncertified by haloes, who were capable of such high-end selflessness? There *had* to be something wrong with them. The pilot project was shut down, and no further reports were heard for forty years.

Then, in 1999, an organ procurement nurse named Joyce Roush happened to be in the audience when a Johns Hopkins surgeon described a new, less traumatic kidney extraction method. She felt so inspired, she volunteered on the spot. "It was an instantaneous decision," says Roush, "and one I never had second thoughts about." She was matched to a thirteen-year-old boy from Maryland. When the media trumpeted the successful laparoscopic surgery, the hospital was astonished to be deluged with dozens of people clamoring to offer their kidneys, too.

It ignited a tiny (just over two hundred, so far) but growing trend, one so new it's still searching for the right sobriquet. Some use the studiously neutral term *Non-Directed Live Donation*; others, the arms-spread-wide *Benevolent Donation*; or the religiously tinged *Good Samaritan Live Donation*; or the mysterioso-sounding *Altruistic Stranger Donation*. The labels describe with varying nuance the Scarlet Pimpernels of the transplant world, those who perform a feat so spiritually swashbuckling, one newspaper dubbed it "the ultimate gift of human kindness." If they remain strangers, it is because compassion itself remains something of a mystery.

In surveys conducted around the world, between one and five out of every ten people say they would willingly donate a kidney while they were still alive. Who *are* these people? What motivates them? How many would really step up to the plate and knock one out of the park, and how many are just taking practice swings out of some wishful moral virtuosity? (One study drily notes a cardinal truth: "Reported intentions are not necessarily highly correlated with actual behaviors.")

I once saw a sign, a little professional homily, at a nurse's station: "Sympathy sees and says, I'm sorry. Compassion feels and whispers, I'll help." What are the x-factors that distinguish the altruistic from the merely sympathetic? The answer might contain a golden key to human nature itself.

*H*e's a Giver," a friend once remarked about a mutual acquaintance. I'd never heard anyone parse people that way. In my intellectual New York Jewish family, it was the march of human folly, not the roll-call of charity's armies, that was fodder for dinner table repartee. The crowd I ran with was self-anointed urban smarties: People got points for being bright, talented, funny, attractive, socially deft, and nice, in approximately that order. I've wondered if the super good-deed-doers aren't different from most people in some crucial respect. Are their dominoes preset to fall in a kindlier pattern? Did some combination of genes and upbringing give their generosity a hairtrigger threshold?

As I was skimming a foot-high stack of papers I'd collected on kidney donors, one snagged my eye with its tart, no-nonsense subtitle: "Lunatics or Saints?" it read, cutting to the chase. The principal author was Canadian researcher Antonia (Toni) Henderson, a vivacious, animal-loving psychologist who, when I called her, had just returned from taking her Rhodesian ridgeback, a dog bred to hunt lions, to a "tracking class" for search-and-rescue training. Over a period of years, Toni has been doing her own tracking, interviewing would-be donors by the dozens. When I tell her what a blast I'm having with the people she calls Living Anonymous Donors (LADs for short), she effuses, "Me, too! I started interviewing them with all these cautions and caveats, but they just boggled me: Wow, this world's a cool place to be!" I know what she means. Spending time with the Givers is part of my strategy to jump-start the heart, hooking my cables to their twelve-volt Diehards, sharing current with motors already humming at maximum torque, inducing my own to turn over.

Toni has spearheaded a series of studies as part of an ambitious effort to create the world's first large-scale kidney donation program with standardized practices and protocols. "It's been a hard sell," she says in a tone of diplomatic understatement. The first funders she'd approached were big pharmaceutical companies. "They thought anonymous donations were ridiculous: What kind of person would want to do such a thing? To be fair, this isn't your usual Hippocratic Do No Harm. You're proposing to take an optimally healthy person and physically compromise them. There has to be at least a clear psychological benefit. A father-to-child transplant, sure, that's a no-brainer. But when someone says, 'I want to give my kidney to a *stranger*,' the surgeon has no idea why. I'm not sure I do, either; I mean, *explain* these people to me!"

Maybe it's a tautology, I suggest: If there's really such a thing as a true-blue altruist, they do selfless deeds because, well, that's just what altruists *do*, like finches trill and sockeyes thrash upstream. The fact is, no one really knows. Though there are now some sixty hospitals in the United States willing to accept volunteer donors, there is still no precise agreement on who these people are or what really motivates them.

The hairsplitting is not just an academic exercise. A medical system in an organ shortage crisis that goes slack in its definitions—which mistakes, say, a person with pathologically low self-esteem for a Good Samaritan—risks exploiting a weak spot in someone's psyche just to fill a quota. And a few transplants that began as happy stories have wound up as cautionary tales: In one reported case, a donor made harassing demands on his kidney's new host, who finally had to get a restraining order.

In her initial study, Toni made a first culling by simply waiting to see who among the ninety people who had first called to offer their organs were committed enough to slog through the paperwork. Confronted with endless questionnaires and lengthy interviews, half dropped out, sorting in a stroke the genuinely motivated from the merely well-intentioned. The half that remained were eventually divided into two groups: one assessed as having the right stuff (LADs) and the other, the equivalent of astronaut training wash-outs, designated as "non-LADs." Interestingly, there were some similarities in both groups: 24 percent of the LADs said they "cannot bear another's suffering," as did 14 percent of the non-LADs. But the question of whether they had a consistent history of altruism (community work, giving blood, bone marrow donor, etc.) turned out to be the clincher. Nearly half the LADs answered in the affirmative compared to, well . . . exactly 0 percent of the non-LADs.

LADs, in other words, walk their talk—they do philanthropy, deliver Meals on Wheels, volunteer in homeless shelters, perform that steady stream of good works that invisibly keeps society running. (Perhaps this is the real message of the mythic sacrifices of the demigods and saints: Altruism is something you offer in the flesh, committing the kinetic potential in your leg and arm muscles, not just your voicebox.) Quotidian stuff, some of it, but that was the point: Whether by temperament or force of habit, they had developed an everyday practice of actively caring.

But are they just self-sacrificing neurotics? (How many Jewish mothers does it take to change a lightbulb? None: "Don't bother, I'll just sit here in the dark.") Victims of a martyrdom complex, atoning for some nameless guilt? In Toni's study, the LADs scored no differently on the "neuroticism" scale than the average population. "I'm trained to detect pathology," she says, "but these folks are psychologically healthy. In fact, I was surprised by how many of them clumped on what I'd call the 'saintly side' of the spectrum. They really *are* motivated to make the world a nicer place." I become aware that Toni and I are now giggling conspiratorially, like two people in on a delightful, mildly illicit caper: Just thinking about the LADs has given us a compassion contact high.

Toni then decided to embark on a larger-scale study, asking a thousand randomly selected adults living in Vancouver whether they'd be willing to donate a kidney to family members, friends, or strangers. Once again, most never bothered to complete the screening process. Of the group of 250 who did, only 50 stuck it through to the follow-up. Of those, 16 were adjudged to be committed LADs.

It might be thought of as a down-and-dirty census of the seriously kind. If we were to idly wonder what portion of humanity (in western Canada, at least) are dyed-in-the-wool Givers, the answer would seem to be: 1½ percent. One person out of seventy—one person, say, on your typical suburban square block—who would go beyond neighborly greetings and friendly favors and even laudable charity to put their bodies on the line for you. Skeptic that I am (and daily try not to be), I find these decent gambler's odds; I would have hazarded only one in a thousand. If you're sunnier (or a better handicapper), you might have guessed one in ten. Either way, it's a nontrivial question: How common we believe kindness-without-a-catch to be in this world shapes our outlook (jaundiced or rosy), our ethical premises, our religious sentiments, our parenting styles, our social policy preferences—everything having to do with living with our fellow human beings (to say nothing of how we regard *ourselves*). In trying to create a gold standard for kidney donors, Toni has inadvertently created something even more interesting: a frequency analysis and quick-sketch portrait of the contemporary altruist.

Some of the features that jumped out were what you'd expect. Respondents scored high on the category she dubbed "tender-minded." ("If I can do something for someone else to alleviate their suffering," one said, "why *wouldn't* I?") But they were tough-minded, too: prone to "question authority and to entertain new ethical, social, and political ideas." They had an "insatiable intellectual curiosity and . . . a willingness to think outside the box." They were, in other words, iconoclasts, not looking over their shoulders for consensus before plowing ahead; independent enough to step out of the crowd and do what many people—including friends and family—deemed outrageously stupid.

In my own less scientific observations of the LADs I met, I've noticed a certain willingness to work without a net. Steve Aman talks about the times he's "stepped into the unknown," plunging into radical life-changes on pure faith. Harold Mintz is an avid skydiver and a bungee-jumper. Comparing notes with other donors, Mintz concluded, "We're risk-takers" (a skeptic might say risk-seekers). His bungee-jumping credo could be a metaphor for how Givers tend to function in the world: "You have to get your body to leave the safety of the platform and launch into thin air." But his risks are also calculated—he prefers bungee-jumping because "you know you'll get yanked back before you go *splat* on the pavement."

I got an impression of people who live in the here-and-now. "I don't do what-ifs," says Harold. "I make decisions based on today. If someone needs my kidney now, they should have it. If I need a kidney down the line, then someone will step forward later for me." Nurse Joyce Roush, when asked if she's worried a family member might someday need the organ she's given away, echoes Harold with uncanny precision: "I've never lived my life by 'what-if.' If that 'what-if' happens, there will be an answer then."

Toni's study also noted "a highly integrated spiritual belief system, though not necessarily based in an organized religion." If Harold, for example, could be said to have a religious philosophy, it's probably the Great Domino Theory, some belief in a Force that works with sure-handed certainty in human affairs yet welcomes all the help it can get. Steve told me, "The heart is the Creator part that lives in each of us. I believe in it, even when my head tells me a different story." Even those with more traditional religious beliefs held to a Just Do It brand of faith. "If I had ten kidneys," said a Methodist pastor in Alabama, "I'd give away nine of them. I never felt like it was courageous. I just knew it was right. I don't know how a Christian could *not* do this."

Despite what might sound like transcendental leanings, they were not like Voltaire's Candide, bumbling through life with utopian naïveté, lambs among the wolves. Rather, I observed a strong streak of pragmatism and tenacity. As he pursued each step leading to his donation, Harold says he "pushed hard, as if there was a marathon runner in front of me. I was going to do whatever it took, no matter what." Steve wasn't shy about playing hardball when one hospital balked at the unusual procedure, letting them know he'd take his case and his kidney elsewhere. Nurse Roush, the pioneering donor, shouldered her way through obstacles (including her husband's initial opposition) to become a figurehead and tireless proselytizer for the lifesaving procedure. They reminded me of an Emerson quote I keep on my bulletin board: "Truth is handsomer than the affectation of love. Your goodness must have some edge to it, else it is none." They had an instinctive knowledge that a helping hand requires a certain strength of grip, one that can't be exercised wearing bunny-shaped mittens.

In spite of their generally clear-eyed assessment of reality, "trust" was also a remarkably high-scoring measure among the LADs. According to Toni's study, "They believe that others are not maliciously intentioned and will treat them with honesty and benevolence." It struck me that it was not that they wanted to make the world a nicer place; they think it already *is*. They live in the sort of parallel universe where Harold might genuinely believe all his friends would jump at the chance to go into surgery with him and have a post-op ice cream party. Nurse Roush, too, assumes people are, well . . . more like her. "I had this mental image that once they knew it was available, lots and lots of people would line up to do this," she laughs. "That it would be like when Elton John tickets go on sale in Fort Wayne."

I get the impression that trust is the strong center pole: trust in others; trust in the future; trust in a higher power, in fate, in the heart; trust in a universe so provident they can afford to give things away rather than clinging to what they have, because such providence is inexhaustible.

I'd started with an image of them as natural-born saints; or else as moral alpiners, strivers huffing and puffing toward the shining white summit of Mount Virtue. But they seem to find the summit in their own backyards. As they would have it, their neighbors (and that includes you) are good; the *world* is good, its ugly spots no more than blemishes on a fresh-picked apple, little affecting its savor. They exemplify how to live in the world as if it *is* the benevolent place we wish it were. Some of us are just dragging our feet owning up to it.

*P*ete Dubrowitz, the man now playing host to Steve Aman's kidney, answers the door in the frayed jeans and stained work shirt of a serious weekend gardener. He guides me back to a postage-stamp yard engulfed by a riotous raised-bed cornucopia. A dozen varieties of peppers dangle from their stalks, gleaming like red, green, and yellow Chinese lanterns. (He informs me they thrive on a vile-sounding brew he calls "my special potion—Coca Cola, beer, dish soap, ammonia, and mouthwash. Plants love it—pesticide and fertilizer all in one!")

Pete's face looks older than fifty-three; with thin, sandy hair and hawk's eyes, it's the mug of a second-card pugilist, a stand-up guy who refused to take a dive and has been put through the wringer. Pete recites in his still-mellifluous newscaster's baritone a litany of the failed operations, the endless dialysis, all the miserable death-cheating crises: "I flatlined twice. I had to throw the priest out of the room in the middle of last rites."

His quest for a living donor had been a last-ditch gambit. Even his terse newspaper ad was a stripped-to-the-basics last hurrah: "Wanted: Your Spare Kidney," followed by his e-mail address. The less-is-more ploy generated a flurry of local publicity, and responses ran the gamut. "One guy said I could have his kidney for twenty-five grand. Another wanted visitation rights! Another one said, "Hey, it'll be fantastic. We can go to church together *every single day*." Pete winnowed the roster down to six. Steve was number two.

"Steve was just so unassuming," he says. "He had no agenda. It was basically, 'I have a spare part; if you can use it, you can have it.' After the immune-factor screenings, my doc asked, 'Where did you *find* this guy?' The chances of a match like this are one in ten million." As fate would have it, Steve and Pete had even gone to the same high school. (Donors all seem to have these crazy-odds stories. Harold told me he discovered that he and Gennet had unknowingly once lived in the same condo complex at the same time, and for all he knows might have bumped into each other on the elevator.)

"The enormity of what Steve did—I mean, who *does* this?" Pete marvels. Certainly not him. He freely admits he had been what's known in the business as a media whore. "The stuff I used to do was lowest common denominator, just grab viewers fast, cheap, and easy. I could've gone to any city and slapped together a half-hour local news show: eight minutes of commercials, six minutes of national, then a minute and a half for a local murder-suicide or some building burning down. It's like rubbernecking at an accident; people can't look away."

"Okay," Pete says, changing the subject, "so I went after my third kidney transplant." He glances at me a little defensively. "The neighbors were saying, 'Why does he deserve three? Just because he's the TV guy?'" His eyes narrow. "To which I say, 'Screw you, I'm not counting!'" He catches himself and softens. His life, he says, took a radical turn after the operation; Steve's act of compassion knocked him for a loop. He tried hard to stand pat but found he couldn't keep grubbing along as a Class-A cynic with Steve's giveaway pulsing inside him.

His new life lease is more like a new incarnation. He's gone from a jaded media hard-ass to the director of the city's Big Brothers, Big Sisters program. When he talks about it, the downmarket news palooka vanishes. His face looks transformed, lit up: "I've had the five most rewarding years of my life. I've taken the health I've been given and helped kids—we've just doubled our numbers! Before, I couldn't look at myself in the mirror. My TV station had this spinning blue earth logo, but what damn good was it doing for anyone? Now, in my little piece of the world, I change lives every day. I tell Steve all the time, his part's playing its part in all this."

"Steve and I," Pete says, talking about him like the brothers they are under the skin, "we're pushing to create a blind-pool national registry of living donors." He pats his lower back, giving Steve's kidney a proprietary attaboy. "I gotta tell you: *This* is the gift that keeps on giving."

8

THE ALTRUIST

If there is any kindness I can show,
or any good thing I can do to any fellow being,
let me do it now, and not defer or neglect it,
as I shall not pass this way again.
—*William Penn*

f there's a facet of human nature that, when you hold it up to the light, shines bright enough to blind you, it's altruism. A selfless deed, witnessed up close, is like a lamp blazing up from darkness before your pupils can adjust. We're a little bedazzled by people who don't seem to be out for themselves, who do good unto others without stopping to consider if others will do good unto them. The altruist lives in this world, with its grubbiness and inconstancy, but doesn't always seem entirely of it.

We each know ourselves to be capable of selflessness. We'll lay aside our needs—even lay down our lives—for our nearest and dearest. But beyond the charmed circle, we tend to parcel love out, weighing who deserves what (while placing a subtle thumb on the scale of *what's in it for me?*). Altruists seem to have inscribed in their very bones the great writ of all faiths: Love the stranger. They don't just give themselves to family and very best friends, but to pretty much anyone who asks, sometimes till it hurts. It's not just the amplitude of their caring that amazes us, but its consistency. We can see, steadfast in their hearts, what is more sporadic in our own. Are they for real? we wonder. The whole proposition seems a tad unnatural.

To give without gain, the altruist's creed, goes against the basic instinct of self-interest—an instinct with a several-billion-year pedigree. Biologists get into high dudgeon just thinking about it. Evolution, asserts biologist George Williams, "can honestly be described as a process for maximizing short-sighted selfishness." Looking out for Number One is the motive force rippling up the phyla from paramecium to paraprofessional. Most evolutionary biologists concur there can *be* no such thing as selfless altruism. What seems like a generous deed is just a strategy to get others to help *you* (a principle, called "return-benefit," that has been observed even in vampire bats). The theory holds that most self-sacrificing behavior in nature, including human nature, can be attributed to "kin-directed altruism." When a parent gives up comfort, food, or life itself for their child, that feeling of selfless love is based on a compelling instinct to preserve the carriers of their genes.

Biologists support this stance with observations that the amount of caregiving given by one animal to another often correlates with eerie precision to the percentage of the giver's genes that the beneficiary carries. Though evidence is spottier in humans, one oft-cited study of twin children revealed that identical siblings, who share all their genes, cooperated and helped each other more than fraternal twins, who share only half.* Any seemingly altruistic action, it is claimed, must be driven by this desire to enhance one's own survival

---

* There is a wealth of anecdotal evidence of mutual sacrifice in the annals of twin lore, some of it mind-boggling. I recently heard the director of a national twins organization tell the story of a member who planned to pay a prison visit to an identical twin brother doing life without parole, then secretly substitute himself, taking on the final portion of his twin's sentence as his own.

or that of one's genetic "conspecifics." Darwin went so far as to write that any trait not based on genetic fitness but solely "for the good of another would annihilate my theory, for such could not have been produced through natural selection."

The altruistic stranger kidney donors seem to exist as if to confound theory. They do not set out to benefit themselves (in fact, there is some detriment); their recipients are not kin, or even friends who could give "return-benefit," but unknown persons often not even in their community. Altruism has become a hot-button issue because it poses a central mystery. Writes Frans de Waal: "We are facing the profound paradox, that genetic self-advancement at the expense of others (which is the basic thrust of evolution) has given rise to remarkable capacities for caring and sympathy." That paradox has lodged like a chicken bone in the throats of some theorists: They can't completely swallow it, but they can't quite cough it up. As science tries to get to the bottom of human nature, altruism presents a parallel challenge to scale the heights.*

When I was researching the kidney donors, I did an informal poll among my friends: Do you know someone who, no matter how rough the going got, would act for your welfare even at the expense of their own? A woman I know described a sort of two-step early pregnancy test for compassion she uses to gauge people: "First, would they risk hiding me from the Nazis in their attic? Second, if we all had to hide out together and there was only one candy bar to live on, would they share it with me?" When I asked who among her friends made the cut, she could only name one, then added, "I know he'd want to share the

---

* Richard Dawkins, who has been called by critics a "fundamentalist" and an "ultra-Darwinist," is these days doing a little public chin-scratching: "The easy altruism is kinship altruism, reciprocal altruism," he told the host of a London radio show. "But I think there's a harder problem still—what you might call real altruism, altruism which couldn't conceivably *ever* have been thought of as hoping for reciprocation, giving money to charity in secret and insisting that your name is not publicized. Even giving blood for which you get precious little reward—that kind of giving." He hastened to add: "But we've got to [explain] it in a Darwinian way because we are Darwinian products. We've got to make the best of our Darwinian explanation, and that's sort of the best shot I can do at the moment."

candy, but his *wife* would talk him out of it!" It would take a compassion Olympian to surmount her high hurdles.

She's not alone in applying tough standards. Social psychologists, too, use a tight mesh to separate "pure" altruism from helping behaviors that, examined more closely, are as subtly contingent on getting as giving. The filter is exceedingly fine. Psychologists suggest we may help others in order to alleviate the shame or guilt we'd feel if we *didn't* help; or we may do a good deed not for outward recognition but *inward* self-esteem; or an altruistic-seeming deed may help us avoid public censure for appearing to be mean-spirited (this one comes with the charmingly convoluted theoretical moniker "self-interested refusal to be spiteful").

Some researchers, though, claim to have sieved out one gold-standard group that helped others even when they themselves had everything to lose and nothing to gain: Gentile citizens of Nazi-occupied Europe who rescued persecuted Jews. Here were people who really *did* hide people in their attics, risking their own lives and those of their loved ones to save total strangers from annihilation. There was not even, as with some kidney donors, a possible payback of community acclaim for their deeds. The only recognition they could expect was betrayal to the SS by a craven neighbor.

This line of research was begun by Samuel Oliner, an investigator with unique qualifications. As a Jewish boy in Poland during World War II, he was sheltered by a Catholic peasant woman after his parents and every inhabitant of Poland's Bobowa ghetto were machine-gunned into a mass grave. Emigrating to America after the war, he became a college professor specializing in the study of the Holocaust. He began his pioneering focus on what he called the sociology of compassion after a German student came to him in tears, asking to drop his class because she couldn't bear her feelings of guilt. Assuring her that she was not to blame for the "cancer of the Third Reich," he resolved to search out those who had shown compassion even in the face of Nazism's insidious, metastatic growth.

Take Stanislaus, a man from a poor Polish Catholic family who had saved dozens of Jews, teaching himself bricklaying so he could build false walls and hidden entryways to conceal them around Warsaw, secreting them even in his own house, feeding them from his and his mother's own meager ration. Asked why, he answered: "When someone comes and says, 'I escaped from the camp,' what is the alternative? One alternative is to push him out and close the door. The other is to pull him into the house and say, 'Sit down, relax, wash up. You will be as hungry as we are because we have only this bread.'"

Oliner and his wife, Pearl, studied both rescuers and a control group of bystanders who had failed to act, interviewing some eight hundred people in seven countries. They found that rescuers had a particular characteristic: They were unusually empathetic. "What distinguished rescuers from nonrescuers," the Oliners write, "was their tendency to be moved by pain. Sadness and helplessness aroused their empathy. More frequently than others, rescuers were likely to say, 'I can't feel good if others around me feel sad,' 'Seeing people cry upsets me,' 'I get very upset when I see an animal in pain.'"

I thought of Toni Henderson's kidney donor study: Her LADs were found to have ". . . an extraordinary empathy, such that they could understand a stranger's suffering, and felt compelled to do what they could to ameliorate it." I began to wonder if both rescuers and kidney donors pointed toward a *type* of person who is more likely than most to act compassionately. It could be argued that the LADs' gesture was one-shot heroism, plugging Joe Death with a silver bullet and riding off into the sunset. But like Oliner's rescuers, whose often spontaneous decision called for years of elaborate logistics and perseverance, kidney donors, too, said their first reaction to help required dogged follow-through. Sometimes several hospitals turned them down before one would accept them. A transplant required planning and testing, personal expense, overcoming objections from friends and family, and losing work time for convalescence. They risked medical complications from an irrevocable decision with lifelong consequences. Some later became public advocates, donating additional energy, time, and funds to the cause. And like the rescuers the Oliners studied (many of them non-Jewish Germans or Poles who could have safely remained bystanders), they didn't *have* to do it.

The rescuers' stakes were infinitely higher, of course, and not surprisingly, few chose the risk: It is estimated that out of Europe's seven hundred million people, only about half a million were active rescuers, saving some one million Jews. But I began to wonder if the LADs were not the same *sort* of people. LADs and rescuers alike claimed they performed their altruistic deeds almost choicelessly, because it seemed to them, beyond any risk-benefit calculus or even moral deliberation, the only thing they *could* do.

S o, okay: You're jogging around the park and out of the corner of your eye, you see a child fall into the city duck pond. You feel an instant booster shot of adrenaline and without thinking leap in, grasp her by the collar, and paddle safely back to shore. You're a hero. Are you an altruist? Those who are adept at teasing out the nuances of why we do such things might say: Well . . . sort of. You might not ordinarily be particularly selfless, but in the immediacy of the moment, you react to save the day. And as they say, that ain't just chopped liver.

But social scientists set the bar for "true" altruism (if such a chimera exists) yet higher. One criterion is an *ongoing* pattern of good deeds. Kidney donor Harold Mintz, for example, had given blood in high school and then gone on to organize entire blood drives. He had sought for years to find a way to act on his deep sympathy for people with incurable illnesses.

But even here, a purist could quibble about whether he was strictly selfless. Harold certainly makes no bones about the personal satisfaction his do-gooding has given him. About his high-school heroics, he told me: "Hey, when you gave blood, they let you out of fifth period, and the *cheerleaders* made brownies for you!" He enjoys the attention from being what he calls "a poster boy" for kidney donation. The psych report Harold showed me reads, "He has insight into the narcissistic rewards of his altruism." A psychologist might pounce on him as living proof of the principle that "psychological egoism" (sociologists call it "rational selfishness") underlies even the most generous gesture. And there is that matter of the selfish gene's dear love of kin: Biologists would claim that when Harold speaks in schools and churches, garners glowing PR write-ups and a certain *eclat,* he enhances his and his family's biological fitness by gaining allies and status. Though this doesn't sully the magnanimity of his act, it creates some theoretical ambiguities.

Sociologist Kristen Renwick Monroe was well aware of these arguments when she set out in the Oliners' footsteps to study Holocaust rescuers. If Samuel Oliner is the grand old man of altruism studies, Renwick is the field's spitfire. Once, after listening to a group of skeptical biologists and economists insist that all altruism was disguised selfishness, she burst out that they were "trying to stuff a fat lady in a corset—you get her all laced up and she looks great, but it distorts the underlying reality. Saying altruism is just kin selection or group selection or reciprocal altruism is just an attempt to smuggle in self-interest and say theirs isn't really altruism at all."

Auguste Comte, the eccentric nineteenth-century French visionary who coined the word *altruism* (literally, "other-ism"), didn't deny there were self-serving motives for generous behavior. But he believed these existed side by side with an instinct to live unselfishly for others. The emotional part of the brain, he proposed, harbored the altruistic drives* that coexisted with egoistic ones. Comte, a

---

* The debate over whether it is thought or feeling that generates our moral sensibility may never be resolved. But it is sure to take on new life as brain scans are used with increasing sophistication to map cognitive functions. A recent PET scan study may have vindicated Compte: It showed that while subjects confronted with a technical problem used the brain's higher cognitive centers to solve it, a *moral* dilemma lit up the *emotional* areas of the brain.

utopian who wrote tracts on the moral evolution of humanity—an old etching shows a man with high, noble brow, his yearning, vitreous gaze fixed on the future, in one eye the glimmer of a tear—went on to establish the field of sociology and to found the philosophy of positivism. But his views on altruism were soon eclipsed by the Darwinian revolution. Ever since, the concept of altruism has been a sort of scientific pariah: odd man out in modern sociology (which assumes people are self-interested "rational actors"); sob sister of psychology (which tends to focus on ego-integrity); invisible man in economic theory (to assure the best work from our fellows, wrote Adam Smith, "we address ourselves not to their humanity, but to their self-love").

With the work of the Oliners, Monroe, and others, the subject is being rehabilitated, part of a debate about whether humankind is at least as cooperative as it is competitive. The question is a vital one. Among the underpinnings of any society are its assumptions about human nature. If we consider it a scientific fact we are fundamentally egoistic, our educational system will teach children to be self-assertive individualists, relegating kindness to a secondary value.* Our business culture will enshrine maximal self-interest, with any small gestures toward the common good pegged to larger trade-offs. A theory can become a society's self-fulfilling prophecy.

Monroe wanted to find a way to challenge accepted theory, teasing out a thread of "pure" altruism from more normative social behaviors. She decided to compare a group of Holocaust rescuers with two other groups, entrepreneurs and philanthropists. The entrepreneurs, the "rational actors" of the social sciences, turned out to have a charitable

---

* I recently witnessed an illustration in microcosm: Deirdre, my friends' six-year-old daughter, wanted to give an adored playmate the greatest birthday present she could imagine. As she scoured her room, her eye fell on her own "bestest" Barbie doll.

"Here," she told her mother. "Will you help me wrap her?"

Her mother was appalled. She called in her husband. "We can't let her just give away her favorite toy. She has to learn to value her own possessions, respect what makes *her* happy. Besides, she'll just cry for it back tomorrow."

Husband and wife argued a little, but in the end, the Barbie went back in the closet.

streak, but it did not generally extend beyond their immediate kin. The other group, philanthropists, was generous in conventional terms, but cautious not to give away so much that they couldn't pass on the great bulk of their wealth to succeeding generations. Both entrepreneurs and philanthropists imposed subtle and not-so-subtle obligations on their recipients, their behavior generally conforming to predicted kinship and returns benefit considerations.

But Holocaust rescuers were another story. They offered what Monroe calls "dramatic refutation of the kin selection hypothesis." As Monroe explains: "Every single rescuer knew they were endangering their family members through their attempts to help Jews. Under the Nazi policy of kith and kin, the rescuers' relatives, including even their youngest children, could be killed because of their actions. This meant . . . those who shared the rescuers' genes could be killed because of the rescuers' actions. The Nazis thus attempted to use biology to deter rescuers, but did not succeed."

Altruistic stranger kidney donors, too, seemed to flout natural law by privileging a desperate stranger above their own kin. And as in Dickens's savage caricature of the charitable Mrs. Jellyby in *Bleak House* (who gave money to starving children while her own went hungry), they sometimes incurred social mockery and even hostility.

In 2003 a Jenkintown, Pennsylvania, professor of Renaissance literature named Zell Kravinsky, who'd made his real estate fortune in student rental properties, decided to give one of his kidneys away, specifying only that the recipient be an African-American woman. He was turned down by two hospitals before Philadelphia's Albert Einstein Medical Center agreed to perform the procedure. ("I had to convince them I was doing it," he says, "because it is logically and morally compelling to save someone's life if you can.") He emerged from a successful operation to discover that the path of altruism does not always run smooth.

Kravinsky's wife, a psychiatrist, threatened to divorce him, especially when it emerged that he was also giving away most of the family fortune to endow hospitals. People he'd known for years turned a cold shoulder. The *New York Times* was moved to editorialize, "His brand of altruism borders on obsession, perhaps even a sort of benign madness." When Zell remarked on a talk show that he could, in theory, conceive of donating even his *other* kidney if it were the only way to heal, say, someone who was creating a cancer cure that would save millions of lives, the conservative host seemed on the verge of bashing him with a chair: What about his wife and kids, to say nothing of his *own* life?

Zell recognizes his views are a little extreme. In our conversations, he struck me as a stringently (and not exactly joyously) idealistic man in difficult straits. In a poignant and self-reflective letter, Kravinsky told me his deeds have caused considerable family turmoil: "I've just now come from a tearful session with my oldest son, who feels passionately that those very acts reflect my lack of compassion for him. The issue is complex, more so in his mind than in mine; my zealotry simplifies everything but leaves a complicated trail of tears that runs all the way from the hospital to my doorstep and up the stairs where I, my wife, and our four children sleep, none so fitfully as I."

In a response to one online critic (Kravinsky stirred up a hornet's nest in the chat-room world, which seems to self-select for staunch individualists), he wrote: "I would go through fire for my kids, literally, and I would do the same for yours. If we can only agree that *all* our kids are, equally, of a preciousness beyond speech's capacity to declare it, then maybe no kids will get hurt, or feel diminished . . . Perhaps I'll feel a bit underdeveloped until the eyes of other men's children provoke the same stir in my heart as my own children's faces . . ."

Here may be the crux of why some people are put off by kidney donors: What kind of person would put a stranger on a par with his own family? Harold Mintz told me, "One friend from Ireland was really upset with me. He said, 'Your wife or daughter might need that kidney someday!' My boss got angry and yelled at me, 'How could you do this to them?' People can be *so* opinionated," he said, rolling his eyes. Nurse Roush admitted her own family did not immediately climb onboard her decision. "Honestly," she said, "my husband just about threw up." Zell Kravinsky's seventy-seven-year-old mother complained to a newspaper reporter: "You can give money; you can give service. Body parts are quite another thing. You give them to family members, and even that's a great sacrifice . . ."

It's a perennial question about the amplitude of compassion and the carrying capacity of the heart: Do we only have a fixed quota of loving to allocate between family and the world at large, so that if one receives more, the other gets less? Does the cup that runneth over contain just so much milk of human kindness? Writes one researcher: "Brother love in the literal sense comes at the expense of brotherly love in the bibical sense. The more . . . we bestow unconditional kindness on relatives, the less of it is left over for others."

Conversely, does altruism leave less room for ordinary affection? I have a friend, a real estate agent, who is a giver *in excelsior.* She has dozens of people in her life whom she seems to love unconditionally (bailing them out of serious crises, taking their late-night phone calls, loaning them money, incurring their eternal gratitude (which she brushes off as unnecessary and even unwanted).

"Do you love me? Really love me?" her husband asked her the other day.

"Of course, I *really* love you," she replied, puzzled. "Why do you keep asking?"

"Because you *really* love *everybody,*" he said, his feelings spilling out in a burst of hurt and annoyance. "It doesn't make me feel special!"

According to at least one study, such feelings might sometimes be valid. In a study of UCLA students, researcher Belinda Campos found that a factor she called "love of humanity" had relatively little overlap with romantic love (.23 correlation, to be exact), with family love, or even with friendship. This data could be read in different ways. It *could* mean that the tightly bonded "we" of romance, family, or friendship simply crowds out concern for the "they" outside of the charmed circle. It could mean that humanitarians do indeed have less left over for their intimates.

Sociologist Kristen Monroe calls the "pure" altruists she studied "John Donne's People," after the poet's declamation that "no man is an island, entire of itself; every man is a piece of the continent, a part of the main." Perhaps Donne's perception of an interconnected humanity provides some more final insight into what makes altruists tick. Monroe believes the key to the Holocaust rescuers' activities is their unshakable sentiment that "all human beings belong to one . . . family . . . forming such a central core of their identity that it left them no choice in their behavior toward others."

I heard it again and again in conversations with kidney donors. "Humanity's a family thing," Harold said. "My brother, my boss, someone a town or a country away, it's the same." Steve Aman confided he was preparing for a Mohawk ceremony called "making relatives" in which he would tie a ritual family knot with a man, a hard-luck case, he'd met at a Sun Dance. "Guy's in his mid-thirties, had a tough life, is about to get a heart-valve replacement. I want him to know I'm really there for him." A West Virginia postman donated a kidney to a man on his rural route he saw only once a month, explaining to his somewhat astonished wife that the people to whom he delivered the mail "are like family to me."

Could it be that the "other" for whom the kidney donors made their sacrifice was the same "other" as for the Holocaust rescuers: humanity itself? If so, when others accuse them of neglecting their families, they might well reply in all sincerity, "But everyone is my family." Maybe altruists don't so radically refute the kinship hypothesis, after all. Everybody shares the same genome. We *are* all kin. They may just be the ones who know it bone-deep.

Still, many people find altruists suspect, even irritating. "I think it makes people feel guilty," said one of Kravinsky's still-loyal friends about all the flak. "I don't think I'm a bad person. I give money to charity, and I think I'm fairly generous, but on the other hand, when I look at what he's done, I can't help but notice a little voice in the back of my head saying, *What have* you *done lately. Why haven't* you *saved someone's life?*"

His comment may cut to the quick of why altruists stir up uncomfortable feelings. If *they're* normal, then maybe I'm deficient, so there must be something wrong with *them*. Their lights are on so bright, we find ourselves looking down for their feet of clay. What are they up to, anyway? Which category of too-good-to-be-true should we check off: people-pleaser, queen of denial, religious nut, other? After their noble come-ons, their freebies of grace, what will they try to finagle in return? When we look behind their boons, will we discover a little sell-by-date stamp?

Yet we hope there really are folks with immaculate motives, because our own (I'll speak for myself) are so often sullied. That such people really exist inspires a sense of relief—that we might lay down our defenses, purge the heart's archives of the clutter of old betrayals, let trust bloom anew. I want to believe we live in a benevolent human universe, not the wised-up world of the Eurythmics' corrosive oldie: "*Every*body's looking for something." I want to declare an open-door policy of the heart; it gets wearisome scrutinizing everyone through the peephole before sliding the deadbolt free.

But when I bring up altruism in conversation, I encounter some distress at the notion there could be people who are somehow congenitally kinder. It's one thing to acknowledge, say, musical prodigies, but quite another to speak of kindness virtuosos. We tend to view compassion as neither a talent nor a skill but a quality of the moral sphere, where we are all, in principle, equally endowed.

I respond by saying that I admire these epitomes, and yes, I try to be more like them, but I'm realistic; I doubt I'm going to *be* them (not in this lifetime, anyway). We may all be handed the same instrument, but we're not all destined for the concert stage. I can enjoy the fact that I play decent twelve-bar blues at the same time as I'm acutely aware (inspired, even) by what the more gifted can manage with the same ten fingers and eighty-eight keys.

But there is a point where the analogy between inborn talent and compassion breaks down. There are too many cases like Ebenezer Scrooge, an apparently unendowed wretch who lived his life "self-contained and solitary as an oyster" and only to wind up a joyous, self-less dispenser of boons to all. In the moral sphere, we are all remarkably capacious, for the very reason given by the philosopher Mengzi: "All men have a mind which cannot bear to see the suffering of others." A Buddhist might say, with a slightly different spin, that all beings have *bodhicitta,* the 'heart-mind' of compassion. It doesn't matter where we start; compassion is indwelling and available. Buddhism often uses the analogy of water. There is water that bubbles clear and sweet straight from a mountain spring; other water that must be scooped turbid from a muddy ditch. But even a cup of ditch water, once cleansed of its impurities, is in nowise different from a carafe of Evian.

Studies of Holocaust rescuers and LADs reveal, in fact, people who seem to genuinely believe they are no better or worse than anyone else, but had simply responded with ordinary kindness. And though Toni Henderson's volunteer donors scored high on the scale of "humanitarian values," most were not grand crusaders, seeming to dwell more in the realm of private deeds and personal conviction. Still, there is no use pretending their viewpoint wasn't unusual (if it weren't, there would be tens of thousands more kidney transplants and millions more Jewish survivors). Monroe makes the odd observation that rescuers' fellow-feeling was not constrained by "personalistic or empathic ties to family, gender, and religious, national, or ethnic groups," nor even by ordinary emotional affinities: "Women were not more likely to help other women," she writes. "Children and babies were not particularly cherished because they were more innocent."

If anything, the decision to risk themselves for others was curiously impersonal.

Monroe had this dialogue with one of the rescuers:

"Q: Would you help somebody you don't like?

"A: Absolutely.

"Q: Would you help a person that you thought was terrible?

"A: If something happened to that person, certainly. If I can help somebody, I will be happy to do it."*

"Q: Was empathy part of your rescue activities?

This attitude is remarkably similar to the Buddhist concept of "boundless impartiality," described in one text as "giving up hatred for enemies *and* infatuation with friends." It resembled, too, St. Thomas Aquinas's *caritas,* which extended even to enemies because, in his reasoning, if one loves God and God loves all, then one must love everyone whom God loves. Harold Mintz pretty much summed up the *Summa Theologica* when he remarked, "Even if my kidney had wound up inside a total jerk, it'd still be cool."

It sounds almost *too* cool: Where is love's passionate, exclusive attachment to specific persons? But love of humanity, abstract to most of us, seems for the altruist to be as palpable as that "real love" that we (and our genes) so wildly applaud. "There are such helpers in the world," said the poet Rumi, "who rush to save / anyone who cries out /

---

* Monroe claims that not even empathy was necessary for those she calls "pure" altruists. She quotes from another interview:
  "A: Meaning what?
  "Q: Feeling that 'this could be me.'
  "A: No, never even thought of it.
  "Q: You didn't think of that at the time?
  "A: [Shakes her head no]
  "Q: Did you feel sorry for the people? Pity?
  "A: I don't know. I didn't feel anything to be honest."

Like Mercy itself / they run toward the screaming." Perhaps the plight of a patient scarred by fruitless operations, captive to dialysis, clinging to life under a medical death sentence, evoked the same powerful response in such helpers as seeing a Jew in a ghetto consigned to liquidation. Do some people have an internal, trip-wired alarm system that simply says, *Attention . . . life imperiled . . . must . . . save?*

Is it possible, in other words, that what most of us feel as a stirring (which we heed with such fidelity as we can muster), is experienced by some as seizure by an irresistible force—one with the same inevitability as the whoosh of air that declares nature's abhorrence for a vacuum? Something in their makeup, something more like an instinct than an idea, seems to draw some people choicelessly toward those in need.

In 1902, the biologist Peter Kropotkin, a former Russian anarchist who'd escaped the clutches of the czar's prison when his friends organized a daring daylight prison break, wrote about the symbiotic animal behavior he had observed in the frozen wastes of Siberia. Citing Darwin's little-noted ruminations on the enhanced survival conferred by cooperation, he argued that more crucial than the "law of mutual struggle" was what he called "mutual aid." Kropotkin puzzled over the helping impulse in humans, concluding that love and sympathy were too narrow a reading of the "moral feeling" (which he described as an "unconscious recognition . . . of the close dependency of everyone's happiness upon the happiness of all"). Kropotkin explained: "It is not love of my neighbor—whom I often do not know at all—which induces me to seize a pail of water and to rush towards his house when I see it on fire; it is a far wider, even though more vague feeling or instinct of human solidarity and sociability which moves me."

Is this the same instinct that sent the firemen rushing up the stairs of the burning World Trade Center towers? It may have also been duty, a binding *esprit de corps,* a refusal to believe they were walking into a deathtrap, and sheer valor. But storming up the stairwells, story after story, they revealed that it is in our nature to love each other heedlessly, come what may. I can't help but feel that it is they, and not the egoists, who point most directly to who we really are and what we each might become.

*W*here does this tenderness come from?" asked the Russian poet Marina Tsvetayeva. How do we account for altruism? Is it a special gift, like a green thumb or perfect pitch? A perspective picked up from one parent or a gene cadged from another? The product of religious epiphany or of life's on-the-job training? Is it taught (through pedagogy) or caught (through emotional contagion)? Bought through reciprocal benefit, wrought through practice, or brought into the world as a genetic endowment?

Biologists speculate that evolution selects for some, but not too many, highly selfless individuals in a given species grouping. (Too many, the thinking goes, and they'd *all* become prey.) The least disruptive scenario as to how altruism may have evolved is that although, as one scientist puts it, "self-sacrifice is counterbiological" for any given individual, generosity among members of an animal colony (or a kinship-based clan) who share genes would lead to more *overall* genetic success. (As Darwin himself put it: "Those communities which included the greatest number of the most sympathetic members would flourish best.")

I can't help but wonder if just as there are genes predisposing people to temperamental traits like shyness or risk-taking, there are also "altruism genes." Maybe *these* are the people who spend their lives succoring the sick, feeding the hungry, clothing the naked, comforting the abandoned, making peace between enemies, scarcely thinking of their own gain, even placing themselves in harm's way. As one Holocaust rescuer told Monroe poignantly: "Life is possible because a certain number of people are not selfish and believe in sharing with others." She added, "If there is not love and sacrifice, no concept of others, then maybe life would be possible in some ways, but it would be a terrible tragedy."

Most social theories hold that altruists are the product of moral example, the power of which has even been demonstrated in the lab. In one experiment, children watched an adult play a miniature bowling game and win tokens that could be exchanged for toys, then give half of her winnings to poor children. A second group saw the adult win the tokens but use them all for herself. Observed later at play through a one-way mirror, the children who had witnessed generosity behaved more generously than the other group. The impact of this single "exposure" to kind behavior was noted in their play even four months later. Experiments have also revealed that children who are shown TV programs with positive messages about helping others exhibit more "prosocial" behavior.

Early cultural influences are formative. Hopi children are taught at an early age that nothing is more important than having a "Hopi good heart." This ethos includes having trust and respect for others; being concerned for everyone's rights, feelings, and general welfare; seeking inner peacefulness; and practicing conflict avoidance. Even social factors such as whether a person lives in a small town or a big city have differential effects on altruism. In one study, a child was placed by experimenters on a busy sidewalk and instructed to tell pedestrians she was lost, then ask them to call her house. In a small town, three-quarters of passersby stopped to help; in a city, only half. This may relate to Oliner's concept of "normocentric" behavior, the way that beliefs, models, and values absorbed from parents and communities become an internal compass of what "normal" people just *do*.*

---

*The African term for humanness itself, *ubuntu*, means "a person is a person through other persons." The social ethic is so pervasive that in 1997 a South African government white paper officially recognized *ubuntu* as central to "the rights and the responsibilities of every citizen in promoting individual and societal well-being."

In Monroe's study, both the "rational actors" (entrepreneurs) *and* the Holocaust rescuers reported growing up with role models who had transmitted virtually identical moral messages: "honesty, fairness, justice, equality, respect for other people." Were the rescuers somehow predisposed to take it to heart? But their attitudes, and ultimately their behaviors, were quite different: Why? Monroe notes in passing one peculiar observation: Altruists' deep humanitarian perspective was "evidenced at an early age." It again raises the question of whether there is some factor in the altruistic personality that can't be solely attributed to family upbringing, cultural influences, or moral training.

Psychologist Lawrence Kohlberg, who established a widely accepted schema of stages of moral development, noticed that children classified as highly gifted also used a higher level of moral reasoning than their peers, reaching a peak by their teens that only 10 to 15 percent of adults *ever* attain. Their helping behavior was exhibited so early in life that he reluctantly conceded it could not be entirely explained by his model of age-specific stages. Are some of those we deem altruists not just people who have done diligent moral labor, but some special revelation of latent human potential?

Indeed, such people, as they make their unusual presence felt in a family or community, are often uniquely regarded. Tibetans refer to exceptionally bright and compassionate young children as *tulkus,* believing them to be reincarnated *bodhisattvas* who have practiced great kindness through a garland of lifetimes. They are given special instruction and placed in positions of spiritual leadership. Every society has taken note of children who are exceptionally giving at a very young age, even in families and cultures that do not particularly encourage it. Sometimes, almost inexplicably, a lotus appears in a daffodil patch. The tenth-century St. Luke the Younger (known as the Wonderworker for his legendary healing powers) was born the third of seven children to simple farm folk. He was said to be so naturally tenderhearted as a boy that he would give his supper to the hungry and strip off his own clothes to hand them to beggars. (Whether he made his parents tear their hair out or they recognized him as a budding holy man, they must have loved him, entrusting him with sowing his father's fields even though he "was wont to scatter half the seed over the land of the poor.")

In our culture, special children often fall under the heading of the "gifted." Indeed, descriptions of young saints, *tulkus,* altruists, and the highly gifted sound strikingly similar. For while the popular image of the gifted child has more to do with intellectual talent than tenderness—the "little professor" type, the mathematical prodigy—social psychologists have also remarked upon an extraordinary quality some call "moral sensitivity." Linda Silverman, a specialist in gifted education, writes: "We have dozens of cases on record of gifted children befriending and protecting handicapped children, becoming terribly upset if a classmate is humiliated, becoming vegetarian in meat-eating families, crying at the violence in cartoons, being perplexed why their classmates push in line, refusing to fight back when attacked because they considered all forms of violence (including self-defense) morally wrong, writing poems of anguish at the cruelty in the world, and fighting injustice."

She describes Sara Jane, who, at two and a half, brought her piggybank to her mother after seeing a TV report of a Russian earthquake that had left hundreds homeless, saying, "Mama, send them my money." The following Christmas, she asked her parents to donate all her gifts to poor children: "I have everything I need. I wish you would give my presents to some little girl or boy who won't get any." At age six, she organized donations for a soup kitchen. This sort of active moral response coupled with caring is not unusual, even in play. I was told of a gifted nine-year-old who was so upset to discover that, in a computer game called Neo-Pets, unwanted digital creatures were euthanized by "Dr. Death," she created original software to save them. Her "adoption agency" program allowed her and other children to rescue, "groom," and then give away the pets. She seemed little interested in the stated objective of the game, which was to acquire as many creatures as possible for her own private menagerie.

One theorist claims that such children see the world in a way that constitutes a "qualitatively different new intelligence" he dubs "caring thinking." This includes not only "advanced cognitive abilities" but "heightened intensity of perception, of feeling and of experience, motivated by an intense social and moral conscience."

Pitirim Sorokin, the founding chairman of Harvard's sociology department, who, like the biologist Kropotkin, had escaped the czar's prison, devoted his career to studying human goodness. He took note of certain people he categorized as Fortunate Altruists: "Such individuals are loving and friendly from childhood. In the course of time they grow graciously in their love behavior . . . similar to the growth of beautiful plants." Sorokin, whose singular passion was the progressive "altruisation" of individuals over a lifetime (and of humankind over millenia), cites the eighteenth-century Quaker John Woolman, who, recalling killing a robin as a child, later wrote how he had been "seized with horror, at having killed an innocent creature." Woolman grew up to be a forceful antislavery abolitionist, belying the notion that people who seem "hypersensitive" are by nature also too fainthearted to be effective. Such early bloomers appear in all times and places. They grow up to be people with an acute empathy for the downtrodden; a reflexive belief in one humanity; an intense thirst for justice; a tendency to cast off status and privilege; an osmotic pull toward others' suffering; and a gardener's faith that the watered seed always flowers.

From what source, then, does altruism spring—not just in the "fortunate" and the "gifted," but in all of us? Is it possible that we owe as much of our moral activity to inborn instincts and emotional circuitry as to early pedagogy or the starry realm of conscience? The newest (and oldest) theories seem to agree on this much: The heart leaps first, slipping past the cognitive gatekeeper. Writing on the self-less impulse in the third century B.C.E., Mengzi noted: "Even nowadays, if men suddenly see a child about to fall into a well, they will without exception experience a feeling of alarm and distress. They will feel so, not as a ground on which they may gain the favor of the child's parents, nor as a ground on which they may seek the praise of their neighbors and friends, nor from a dislike to the reputation of having been unmoved by such a thing."*

As one Holocaust rescuer put it, "The hand of compassion was faster than the calculus of reason." If we see someone about to stumble off a curb into traffic, our arm will shoot out and yank him to safety without a second's hesitation. There is no need—and no time—for "perspective-taking," thinking how crummy we'd feel if we didn't save him or imagining the bystanders' applause if we did. It is as if we each possess a moral reflex similar to those instant physiological reflexes mediated by the spinal cord (for example, jerking back from pain—only in this case, toward it!).

Psychologist C. Daniel Batson, who was a skeptical grad student during what he wryly calls "the dawning of the age of Aquarius," was convinced that altruism was a rational, ego-driven strategy, a chip off the old ice block of calculating self-interest. After ten years' worth of rigorous lab studies, he did an about-face, concluding that the "egoistic" hypothesis was not borne out by scientific evidence and that what he calls "empathy-altruism" is a prime force behind good deeds.

---

* Darwin used an almost identical example (and drew an almost identical conclusion) in *The Descent of Man*. Noting that people who had never risked their lives for another will spontaneously jump into a torrent to save a stranger, he took such deeds as evidence of "the greater strength of the social or maternal instincts rather than any other instinct or motive, for they are performed too instantaneously for reflection, or for pleasure or pain to be felt at the time. Moreover, if we are prevented by any cause from so acting, distress or even misery may be felt."

He defines empathy in the Greek sense of *empatheia,* "feeling into," and empathy-altruism as a "motivational state" that bypasses conscious moral reasoning. That is, it is not a case of putting oneself in another's shoes ("perspective-taking"), but a direct, swift intuition he compares to a mother's unthinking response to her child's need. Pascal's famous quote, "the heart has its reasons of which reason knows nothing," often relegated to Valentine cards, may yet be pinned to the neuroscientists' corkboard.

Batson believes that the egoistic theory has held sway so long because it provided what he mockingly calls an "Eden of simplicity," a single explanation for a complex range of phenomena. Expelled from this narrowly bounded paradise, science can at last embrace a "pluralistic model [where] both egoism and altruism have legitimate claims." This model is appealingly fluid, closer to our actual experience of a sliding scale from me-me-me to you-you-you. "Contrary to the beliefs of virtually all [research] psychologists," Batson sums up, "concern for the welfare of others is within the human repertoire." Hosanna: It's official.

*B*atson's notion that the self can do a disappearing act—that between the perception, the feeling, and the helping hand no ego-shadow need fall—reminds me of the mystic's contention that compassion arises naturally when the ego gets out of the way. Contrary to the Freudian dispensation, "Where id was, ego shall be" (ego's day job being to tamp down the id's base instincts), mystics believe that when ego exits the stage, it is not our baser instincts but the beneficence embedded in human nature that shines forth unobstructed.

Only a small number of Holocaust rescuers credited religion or

God per se as a factor in what they did (16 percent, by the Oliners' count), yet many described profound spiritual intuitions. One of Monroe's rescuers, a man named Tony, said: "I see the whole world as one living body, basically. But not our world only: the whole universe. And I'm like one of the cells." He added, "Gradually by opening your eyes, you see . . . everyone is you." I heard similarly mystical-sounding perceptions from other altruists. A woman I know who does countless deeds of charity told me: "I can remember being really young, laying on the sidewalk looking up at the sky and feeling that space was filled with this palpable energy. I could feel that same energy in people, understand what was going on inside them, especially their sadness. And I just let my heart go with them." Kidney donor and philanthropist Zell Kravinsky told me poetically how, as a child, he'd always felt "a sense of eternity. Not as time-after-time, or as endless time, or as heaven graphically, vulgarly depicted, but as a dimension *alongside* of time that runs along with us. This is the registry, the resonance of our deeds; the quality of giving or retaining that's in each act. I've always felt that pressing upon me, an unboundedness in the bounded."

In Judaism, the term *hesed* ("steadfast love") refers to God's unbounded caring that never wavers—as well as what we who are made in His image are capable of reflecting. (One scholar calls hesed "the aspect of divinity which seeks to bestow love and blessings without limit.") *Agape,* an ancient Greek word for the most unlimited, unselfish, accepting form of love, was adopted by early Christians to describe humanity's proximate attainment of God's love for His creation. It is said in Genesis that He not only handcrafted each creature, but "saw that it was good." (I am charmed by one theologian's proposition that *agape* be translated as "Seeing-Good.") Key to *agape*'s character, says a Christian ethicist, is "a feel for the preciousness of all human beings."

Here compassion is synonymous with a love not meted out according to merit, but falling like spring rain on the virtuous and the sinner alike. It has potency in the world: It creates and transforms, and those whom it touches touch others. Said a student of the Hindu spiritual teacher Neem Karoli Baba, "What astounded me when I was around Maharaji wasn't that he loved everybody. After all, he was a saint, and saints are *supposed* to love everybody. What astounded me was that when I was around him, *I* loved everybody. It's the kind of love that's contagious."

I have felt it in the presence of some Givers. The heart opens wordlessly, like a flower in a hothouse (though it's hard to say exactly what "it" is—some unrestrained sense of beneficence, perhaps; for compassion is a generative force, gathering strength rather than diminishing as it propagates). The Christian futurist Teilhard de Chardin even claimed that love was a "radical energy," as real as magnetic lines of force, the pull of gravity, or the push of photons. If so, no one's yet measured it; indeed, it is almost by definition unmeasurable.* But if most of us aren't radiating unconditional love, we're at least doing our fallible, level best to care. We shouldn't be too hard on ourselves if we don't measure up to some transcendental benchmark.

The real exemplars, far from being holier-than-thou, have always claimed to be flawed human beings like anyone else. I once heard the Dalai Lama tell a questioner: "I'm still practicing. Every practitioner

---

* There was once something of an academic vogue to devise some scientific gauge, if only to give a quality viewed as imprecise and evanescent some empirical heft. Sorokin, for example, proposed a scale of five factors: *intensity* (how deep are the kindnesses we do, from social gestures like giving up a bus seat to real personal sacrifice); *extensivity* (from basic self-esteem to romantic devotion to the love of all); *duration* (from a single deed to "great apostles of love discharging their love mission for decades"); *adequacy* (does our compassion actually achieve the goal of helping?); and *purity* (from "the thinnest trickle in a muddy current of selfish aspirations" to a "divine love" devoid of any ulterior motive).

is constantly fighting their inner enemies: attachment, hatred, pride, anger. So you see, I am not very holy!" One Holocaust rescuer, a German who was sent to a concentration camp for helping Jews (and who, amazingly, managed to continue his rescue activities from inside by bribing guards), joked that his morals were "only slightly better than those of an average American congressman." A woman named Margo, who as a consequence of her Resistance activities had been imprisoned six times, had lost contact with her young children, and had seen her fiance killed, said: "I have my good sides and my disagreeable sides. I can be a bitch, and I can be nice. I'm nothing special." The LADs, too, scored high in the quality of "modesty" (defined in the study as "humble and self-effacing, though not necessarily lacking in self-esteem"). Zell Kravinsky told me he still rates himself as "missing the courage to be good . . . to push through to the moral life." Harold Mintz, expressing discomfort with what he called "that compassion label" said: "I have good days and bad ones—you should see me get pissed off in traffic." It may be that this awareness of their own humanness makes it possible for them to so fully accept others. Rather than putting altruism on a pedestal as an unattainable ideal, we might just take them at their word.

*P*erhaps because altruism falls into a no-man's-land between our perfectly ordinary humanity and what sometimes appears to transcend it, it has been a battleground betwen spirituality and science; the former interested in the moral perfectability of man—what we might be—and the latter in a factual assessment of what kind of creature-among-creatures we actually are. Is other-centeredness, not thinking of ourselves, a form of salvation or, as secularists have tended to regard it, an invitation to self-denial and self-delusion—to bloodless piety, or even bloody messianism?

"Altruism's dark side needs to be held clearly in view," writes biologist Elliott Sober, "if we are to understand the moral dimensions of altruism and also its evolutionary and psychological character." He notes that self-sacrificing behavior on behalf of one's own group "can promote within-group niceness, but it also can promote between-group nastiness."

I was recently invited to a conference, billed as a dialogue between spirituality and science, where altruism proved to be the skirmish line. The event was flush with Givers—clergy who ministered to the poor, health care workers, advocates for the marginalized, many of them members of the "faith-based community." One speaker asked us to contemplate what would happen if all the faith-based volunteers were to disappear tomorrow. Society, he said, would grind to a halt: Who would be around to empty the bedpans of Alzheimer's patients, to staff the soup kitchens, the suicide hot lines, the drug outreach programs, the orphanages, the hospices?

The atmosphere at the gathering was genteel, but I could hear the subterranean rumble of plate tectonics along cultural fault lines. The audience sat politely as evolutionary biologists proposed that altruism might be accounted for by "misplaced nepotism," and religion itself by "a persistent cultural virus." They listened as speakers characterized their spiritual faith as "a byproduct of mental neural modules." Finally a tall, elderly, beanpole-thin man in a worn blue blazer, a philosopher-scientist able to quote both Darwinian chapter and bibical verse, took the stage. "I have a quarrel with the biologists," he said in a measured cadence. His hands gripped the podium. "They claim we are forced to describe ourselves in terms that are *alien* to our *intuition*." A native Coloradan, he gave the impression of a slow-talking town sheriff who'd stood by as a bunch of rowdies made crude moves on the town beauty until he'd had enough of their shenanigans. His laptop was loaded with PowerPoint bullets, and he was ready for a showdown.

"All these theories designed to take the altruist out of altruism," he fumed, reciting them in a litany as they projected on a screen. "'Tacit, pseudo-altruistic reputation-seeking out-reproduces enlightened selfishness!' Conscience," he drawled, "the still small voice that tells us how far we can go in *serving our own interest and get away with it.* Or how about this one: Thou shalt give the *impression* thou lovest thy neighbor as thyself! Well, those clever, *sneaky* Good Samaritans." He put a jocular lilt in his voice, but each word was slathered with sarcasm, his mouth pursed tight. "If Darwin is irrelevant to the understanding of solid geometry," he snapped, "why should he be relevant to the moral life?"

Though he was mostly shooting up a straw man, I caught his drift: These evolutionary biologists, trying to steal us blind of our nobility of spirit, drying up the well with their *malocchio,* their reductionist evil eye. Meanwhile, a biologist onstage had been listening with increasing impatience to one more Bible quote than he could stand. He burst out, his face flushed: "The Flat Earth was taken off the table! Reasonable people took the God Hypothesis off the table, too. If you want to put it back on, be my guest, but if you're here as a scientist, then play by the rules!"

I could sympathize with them both. At risk from the scientist's point of view was a reversion to superstition and wishful thinking (to say nothing of "creation science" mandated in biology class). At stake for the religionists was the holiness of compassion itself. For if altruism is *not* holy, then neither are the saints who are said to reflect the infinitude of God's love. What then becomes of that kindness that eludes all caveats, standing forever outside the container of petty human preference? The scientists, from this view, were like the denizens of Flatland, seeing the saint as an odd data point; while the religionists saw a point of light, expanding in ever-widening gyre—an uncontestable zone of contact between our plane and a sphere beyond all dimension. With all their quantifying and qualifying, the scientists were crimping compassion itself, setting upper limits on a Love that is, by definition, an illimitable asymptote.

And so it went, with the most theological lightning called down upon any insinuation that altruism could not be "pure"; while the scientists rejoindered there was no degree of it unmixed with selfish motives.

It was left to a tiny wizened rabbi to sort it all out. He slowly mounted the stage, the very image of the unworldly religious scholar, his tuxedo jacket shiny from wear, the ends of his forked beard as yellowed as if he'd trailed them in his chicken soup at dinner. It had fallen to Rabbi Adin Steinsaltz, author of innumerable volumes of commentary on the Babylonian Talmud, master of countless languages, leader among survivors of unspeakable persecution, to offer a guide for the compassionately perplexed; a path for the rest of us.

"Look," he said in his old-country Russian accent, "electricity goes in both directions, positive and negative, that's why it works, yes? About seventy times a moment, back and forth. So you could say that in every deed of love, there is also some selfishness. They are not mutually exclusive."

"It's the *problematique* of being a human being," he mused aloud. "We're practically divine on one side, and on the other side, this—this *kink* of hellish intention. The two parts come together to create a human being, a kind of angel put into the body of a gorilla! Look around you. It shouldn't be so astonishing that it works. Just do the best you can, and let the Creator who made this system in the first place take care of it." He twinkled. "After all, He's also somewhat responsible for it." He was offering an honorable compromise, a bit of rabbinical tradecraft: When faced with two irreconcilable views, choose both.

But is there no such thing, a questioner entreated him, as an unmixed motive? The man's careful articulation was at odds with his trembling voice, as if the question were a burning brand. "Rabbi, sometimes a person can happen on pure grace even if he doesn't intend it. Isn't it possible that someone can be so lost in love of God, in *agape*, " he said, asking for a reinstatement of the immaculate, "that

199

he forgets himself entirely, acts out of pure love, isn't even *aware* that he's done good?"

The rabbi didn't miss a beat. "It may happen that the first time, he isn't aware of it; but by the second time, he knows all about it. And by the *third* time, probably everybody else knows, too!" He waited until the cleansing laughter, the sense of relief at the popping of piety, had subsided. "Completely selfless deeds are completely impossible deeds," he said gently. "A person may spend so much time preparing to do the perfect deed, he'll die before he does it! People shouldn't allow all sorts of noble intentions to interfere with the doing of good."

As he came off the stage, his wispy hair pasted down on his extravagantly furrowed forehead, he looked like some *shtetl* Merlin, five hundred years young. When I approached him, he greeted me with such expectant delight, such free-floating risibility, that I laughed before I knew what I was going to say.

"So," I blurted out, "if someone is trying to become more compassionate, is there some practice, some prayer in Judaism that helps?" The question seemed inane before it left my lips, but he savored it with an enigmatic half smile. He was laughing at me, at himself, along with God. He leaned in. "Just pray for grace. Pray for God to show you the way to do good. Pray sincerely, and he will reveal it to you."

He looked at me out of the corner of his eye, appraisingly. "You know, just join the crowd."

And I realized: The Givers *are* a crowd, an embracing congregation. You could say we're all in the pews, even if we're beyond the pale. Whether we know it or not, the whole crowd of us, friends, family, strangers, enemies; mixed-up and wise, caring and craving; striving to do better than mundanity even as we cling to the status quo; opening our hearts, locking them tight, then opening them again when someone twirls the right combination, that sudden easeful click.

Judaism talks about the thirty-six Lamed Vav, the unknown Just Persons who, according to the Talmud, are required for the survival of the world. Without them, it is said, the Holocaust would have marked the death of humanity itself. The rescuers, says one writer, "saved the concept of the human being as capable of goodness."

When those who stood by as the Holocaust unfolded were interviewed decades later, researchers noted a sense of "poignant isolation, viewing themselves as individuals who were alone and helpless: 'But what could I do to help, I, just one person alone against the Nazis?'"

But they were not alone; they only thought they were.

Rescuers touched others, and not just their embattled fellow-conspirators, the paper-forgers and the people smugglers, but the bakers who sometimes silently portioned out more than the due ration, the farmers who wordlessly sold them cheaper vegetables, the occasional bureaucrat who turned a blind eye. They were too few and too far between, but thousands took tiny risks to affirm their humanity—risks that, without the rescuers, they might not have taken at all.

Every time there's a publicized kidney donation, hospitals field dozens of calls from people who say they're willing to do the same. Recently, a woman exhausted by years of dialysis posted a request for a kidney on an Internet bulletin board: "I never wanted to have to do this. Would anyone be willing to be tested?" She *got* eight hundred responses. "My first thought was 'poor girl,'" said the forty-six-year-old West Virginia woman who eventually gave her a kidney. "I knew this would be more involved than letting someone borrow my pickup, but I really didn't see it as being anything big."

On the East Coast in summer, around dusk, you'll see a solitary firefly flick on like a miniature evening star; and then, as your eyes adjust, myriad, an airborne processional: *blink-blink* in your yard, *on-off-on* at your neighbor's place, luminous semaphores in mysterious sync, green signal flares shimmering in code; and soon, all through town, this tango of light, choreographed by some cohesive intelligence. So it is with the Givers.

So it is with us all. We signal each other, set each other off, turn on each other's inborn luminosity. If we are less than kind, it may be that we feel for each other so irresistibly, with such shocking abruptness, that sometimes, below the threshold of awareness, some inner circuit breaker shuts down the heart before it can take the full jolt. But just look, really look, at somebody, anybody; laying down your defenses, not thinking for a beat about yourself, and there: the quick leap of tender flame, a little aureole of light. The knowledge is primal: wired in our brain, curled in our genes, thrumming in our nerves. Save each other, fail each other, hurt each other, help each other, it is there: *Seeing-Good,* always there, just waiting for us to notice.

9

THE ELIXIR OF FORGIVENESS

I was angry with my friend:
I told my wrath,
my wrath did end.
I was angry with my foe:
I told it not,
my wrath did grow.
—*William Blake*
Songs of Innocence and Experience

*M*y ex-Partner had been my enemy for eighteen years, give or
take a few yellowing calendar pages. He was, as far as I could
tell, my worst (and maybe only) enemy, archvillain in a business saga
of trust betrayed, idealism tarnished, and some poor schlub's labors
lost (mine). I'll spare you the details (trust me, more than you want
to know), but they would rate a turgid Victorian subtitle, say,
"Wherein I Am Utterly Ruined," with its taste of ashes on the tongue.
The man's perfidy had swept me and my family into a whirlwind of
trouble. The affair had sickened me body and soul, plunged me into
a dungeon of debt. Worse, it had broken my heart.

It wasn't supposed to be that way (is it ever?). We'd set out to create a do-good company whose mission statement was peace, love, and understanding. The business plan was progressive to the nth: flattened hierarchies and stakeholder employees, with yoga breaks and maternity leaves for all. Our venture was going to save the world; instead it had morphed into a snakepit.

I'd seen it coming from around Day Two, I suppose. Little things, like the symbolism of our second business briefing, held as he sat on a mahogany throne in a hotel lobby, having his wingtips buffed by a bent-over shoeshine man. He'd half-listened, eyes focused on the middle distance, as I stood making my case like a feudal petitioner. He'd glanced frequently at his watch. In that *tableau vivant* of power relations, I'd glimpsed the moving finger writing my severance check. (I'd lasted longer than the guy just down the totem pole, whom the Partner had once summoned to the men's room for his meeting with the seated crown.) Still, I'd given it my all and everything, shouldering the day-to-day and night-to-night of what grew into a dysfunctional, teetering multimillion-dollar business. Dazzled by the venture's endlessly spun potential, bamboozled by the Partner's charming-boy fecklessness, I'd stayed on until he'd taken the best and left the rest.

It took me years to sift through the wreckage, but I couldn't: Pick yourself up, dust yourself off, get over it. Somehow, I couldn't. The Japanese have an expression for that feeling of grievance unredressed: *The belly is not satisfied.* It seemed a clear case of virtue versus villainy, Man versus Weasel. I got on with my life, but my hatred of the Partner lingered, like a bare bulb dangling in the soul's basement, casting crazy shadows.

I tried all the spiritual home remedies. I told myself my plunge to the bottom had taught me Important Life Lessons; that my betrayer had done me a favor: I'd gone on to better things. I chewed over the notion that meanspiritedness is its own punishment; that when you hurt another, you hurt yourself: instant karma. It was no good. My aggrievedness sat like some prehistoric bug in a drop of petrified sap, its baleful gaze one for the ages.

I'd sometimes catch myself idly planning a competitive venture to blow my nemesis out of the water. I'd dropped a disparaging word in the ear of a mutual business acquaintance in hopes of sinking his next deal. I imagined what I'd do if I ran into him on the street, flinging myself headlong on all six foot two of him, grinding his self-satisfied smile into the pavement. Thus doth resentment bring us low. Maybe I had a right to be angry, but I sensed I was paying a daily tithe to the Church of Mine Enemy, enmeshing myself in the big dumb cycle of retribution that already blights the planet. The question was: How could I stop?

I do try to be large-minded in my life; the tenacity of this thing was a little baffling. We all have some tendency to archive slights, indexing them for easy reference. We bank the smoldering fire of resentment so its embers need just a few twigs to kindle back into flame. More than likely, right now you can conjure up some big, painful humiliation. Such memories have a weird persistence; they leap all too readily to hand. The expression "nursing a grudge" is apt. We keep it on life support, just to have the brain-dead comfort of its company. To say nothing of revenge: Whether in the heat of the moment or as the proverbial dish served cold, we imagine how sweet it would be (though we suspect it'd leave a bitter aftertaste).

Is there some evolutionary circuit that craves a settling of scores? It *would* behoove a primate to remember who had harmed it, to feel aversion to the ape who had kicked it a few rungs down the dominance ladder, keeping on a hair trigger any chance to regain its status. Primates address social dilemmas through reciprocity: returning good for good, but also bad for bad, mandating a close accounting of favors and harms. Apes have been observed waiting for weeks or months before finding an opportunity to retaliate against a rival. Like us, they seem to have an implacable recall for insults and a strong instinct to right the scales.

"It's your amygdala talking," a neurobiologist told me, referring to the ancient, almond-sized brain structure that primes our fight-or-flight responses. The amygdala is key (along with the nearby hippocampus) to the storage of long-term memory of emotional trauma. It is the likely home office of Grudge Enterprises and its wholly owned subsidiary, Revenge Unlimited. It has recently been discovered that the amygdala is hardwired to the brain's center of higher reasoning, the neocortex, as well as to the visual cortex, suggesting that it is the culprit in our all-too-vivid recall of past slights, and an unindicted co-conspirator in the plotting of payback. Whatever the cause, surveys in several countries show that some 90 percent of men (and over 80 percent of women) have had "fantasies about killing people they don't like, especially romantic rivals, stepparents, and people who have humiliated them in public."

A grudge, then, is no run-of-the-mill thought sprinting briefly through the mind. It digs in for the long haul, setting up housekeeping in a well-fortified bunker. It locks out the offending party, but also locks us into a spiral of mistrust. We construct such a redoubt at our own peril; the maintenance costs are exorbitant. "In those who harbor such thoughts as 'he reviled me, he beat me, he overpowered me, he robbed me,'" says the *Dhammapada,* "anger is never stilled."

Didn't I know it: Forgiving my enemy seemed like a primordial spiritual challenge. But I'd read about people who had faced it under far direr circumstances. Tibetan lama Garchen Rinpoche had been jailed and tortured by the Chinese for twenty years yet had somehow, improbably, only strengthened his powers of forgiveness. "Ordinarily, if your enemy harms you, you will feel anger," he said. "This makes your mind like water frozen into ice by the cold. In order to melt it, we need sunlight, which is the cultivation of compassion."

I knew it was past time to let the sunshine in. The day came when I thought: *Oh, the hell with it.* I hadn't set eyes on my ex-Partner since the last *century.* The Berlin Wall had crumbled into chunks of graffiti-sprayed concrete; the Pope had apologized for anti-Semitism and kissed the Chief Rabbi's cheek; whole warring subcontinents had made peace. Yet I kept upholding my grievance like those ancient Stylites who would devotionally hold up one arm as if waiting to be called on until it withered away. I *had* to forgive my enemy. But I knew I'd need his help.

I sat down and wrote him a letter: "Dear——, Scrolling through my mental PDA, your name still comes up in red letters. I'd like to strive for some forgiveness, after all this time. Would you be willing to join me in an experiment in reconciliation? Who knows, it might be for the greater good."

I was a little surprised when he promptly wrote back: "I am sorry to hear that you still harbor resentment toward me. I certainly feel nothing of the sort toward you. I would welcome the opportunity to see you. Time is a sparse commodity these days, but I would be happy to meet for a couple of hours. Kind Regards."

His letter positively glowed with decency. What was he up to? Clearly, he wasn't going to acknowledge what had transpired. Translation of his "sorry to hear": "Whatever *you* think happened, didn't." Had he vetted this *billet-doux* with his lawyer? Still, I'd asked him, and he'd offered (making clear his time, as ever, was more precious than rubies). It would be small of me not to take him up on it.

As I planned my trip, I mulled it all over. If I forgave him without getting an apology, would I just be excusing his misdeeds? "Forgiving the unrepentant," says a Japanese proverb, "is like drawing pictures on water." It's so much easier when someone shows contrition *(now go in peace, my son, and sin no more)*, but what if he never did? I realized it wouldn't matter. I was persuaded by a remark I once heard the Archbishop Desmond Tutu make: "To forgive is the highest form of self-interest. I need to forgive you so that my anger and resentment and lust for revenge don't corrode my being." I *was* corroding in my prison of ill-feeling. If I depended on my enemy to say he was sorry, then he was my jailer. I resolved that no matter what happened between us, I would filch the key and set myself free.

A few months later, I showed up at my enemy's fortress, a small, sandblasted brick office building set in a stand of trees by an ambling city creek. "He said noon," his assistant told me, "but . . ." *(sigh of affectionate exasperation for the Great Man who signs your checks)* ". . . with *him* you never know."

Finally, the ex-Partner strode in. I felt a surge of adrenaline. He seemed a little heavier, his trademark lupine look gone a little soft. But at last I was face to face with the bad hombre who'd stolen my water, left me to the buzzards, and rode off with his saddlebags jingling with gold—*our* gold.

We sat across a table from each other. I'd invited a mutual friend, a seasoned mediator, to give us some basic ground rules. I could talk as long as I liked; my adversary would listen. Then we'd switch. Finally, if we wished, we could talk together. Our friend would sit there, "holding the space." She asked us to take a few minutes in silence, then say a few words. I remembered I had resolved to ask him something that wasn't purely hostage to the past. And I was genuinely curious: Why had he agreed to meet with me?

"Because I knew it was important to you," he replied, "and I believe in healing. If I could make things better, I decided I would do it. To see what I could do for you. To strengthen my own understanding."

His answer—a *perfect* answer—threw me. He'd always been adept at dissimulating, talking the talk, a master at disarming in order to later stab you in the back. But if he were such an ogre, why was he even sitting here? After all this time, with all my painstakingly stock-piled bitterness, I was suddenly on the verge of tears.

"What I want to do," I said, my voice shaking a little, "is just tell you my side of the story."

As I spilled it all out, he listened, nodding occasionally: the shambles his hubris had made of everyone's lives, the fallout of his broken promises for me and the people I loved. When I'd become ill, he'd dismissed me with a pittance. But it had been his lack of caring that was most wounding. Without so much as a get-well card or a thanks for the memories, he'd acted as if I had fallen off the edge of the earth.

As I talked and he took it in, I saw flickers of empathy in his eyes, glints of comprehension, not a spark of malice. But I detected something else: a blankness, as if it wasn't all quite registering. I was suddenly hit with an unwelcome thought: What if all of it, so utterly consequential to me, had been just a blip on his radar? What if he hadn't lost any sleep over it because it hadn't much mattered? What if—and this would be most humiliating—he didn't even remember?

When his turn came to speak, he said as much. He did recollect some promises were made, but he couldn't quite place the details. He recalled I'd fallen ill, but not that he'd used the opportunity to drop-kick me into the end zone. He was surprised to hear I'd been hospitalized not twenty minutes from his house. Whatever I'd been through had gone largely unnoticed; he'd had his own problems.

These he laid out, talking in ellipses about an "enterprise mis-aligned with purpose" and "bad advisors" and "a certain naïveté about the business," as if some malign imp had set about undermining the venture. Because of this occult force, "misunderstandings took place" and "things didn't work out as intended." It was hard to tell whether he admitted even to himself that he had used people until he used them up. When it came to his broken commitments, he talked about "the entrepreneur's reluctance to get pinned down to entangling agreements"; his callousness became "not having the right emotional skill-set." He lamented his debts and the relentless squeeze-plays by his investors.

But as he elaborated his travails, he seemed to circle closer to the heart of the matter, describing the desperation he'd felt to make the business succeed. "I felt I needed a life raft. That I'd sink if I didn't take care of myself. I had my family to think about." When he talked about feeling like the Little Dutch Boy with his finger in the dike, I found myself involuntarily nodding. I'd often used the same analogy; I had no idea he'd felt the same way. "A person has an image of himself," he went on, "as gentle, kind, and good. But others perceive him as arrogant, narcissistic." He sighed almost inaudibly. "And then you find there *are* things about you that are shitty and insensitive."

This rang a bell. If I were honest with myself, hadn't I also pushed people too hard, though I would have claimed in the name of the greater good. When he talked about his own life—growing up feeling "invisible, always keeping the back door open, so I'd be able to get out when my family got too crazy"—even though he'd been raised as the privileged scion of old money, I knew the feeling.

Now and again, he'd come back to the issues between us. "It was hard to give you the consideration you may well have deserved. Besides," he hastened to add, "there was a certain lack of insistence on your part."

"You're saying that it was up to me to keep you from stealing my lunch money?"

He looked embarrassed. "Well, no, that wouldn't be right."

Then for the first time since we'd met, he seemed to really think about it. Abruptly, he began to talk about what it had felt like to come back from the Vietnam war, disillusioned and traumatized. "I still feel anger at all the lies. But the most hurtful thing was the feeling of betrayal." He paused. His eyes softened a little. "I can see how this would feel for you," he said, "that kind of betrayed innocence. It sears the soul."

Tears sprang to my eyes. I was speechless; this *was* how I felt. He'd reached deep down into his own feelings and pulled out a big handful of mine. That I was visibly moved seemed to draw him out further. "Look, I agree that you were not treated well. I didn't appreciate your efforts. I feel badly. I wish I'd done a better job. " I looked at him, saying nothing. "Okay," he sighed. "If it helps for me to say it, I will: You probably *were* strung along."

He paused again. Then, out of nowhere, it came.

"And I'm sorry," he said.

The words could have been hollow, perfunctory. But they weren't. And suddenly, it felt as if a stage set on which I'd been performing a long-running play began to recede on invisible casters, the house-lights coming up, the audience stirring, retrieving their coats, starting to file out. I looked again into the face of the man I'd made my personal demon. It seemed more open, warmer, more careworn; it seemed like the face of an ordinary person, sometimes crappy, sometimes kind, contending with his own problems just like everyone. I felt what would have been unthinkable a few hours before, a sense of empathy, and more: a sort of soaring liberation I could only call forgiveness.

As we left the charmed zone of intimacy, chatting about politics, kids, people we used to know, the feeling persisted. We shook hands, briefly hugged. I thanked him for his time. "There's always time for this," he said softly. He left to get back to work; the business, he disclosed, wasn't doing so well. I hadn't missed any pot of gold, just decades of typhoon-class migraines.

As I took a cab to the train station, I began to think about my own role in the mess. Don't the soft-boiled idealists screw things up as badly as the hard-boiled pragmatists? Hadn't I also been hell-bent on success, inconsiderate, overwhelmed, out of my depth? How much, for that matter, had I ever thought about *him*? I had been the talent; he was just the moneyman who signed the checks, the supernumerary who underwrote *my* globe-straddling contributions. I wondered how I'd missed the clues: my enemy, myself. We had been two young men out to conquer the known universe, using each other, and, God help us, brothers under the skin.

*I*n the days that followed, I was a little bewildered to find that my grudge seemed to have evaporated, its malignant miasms lifted. I could no longer understand how I'd allowed such a ludicrous state of mind to take root in the first place. I'd planted a hard little acorn of resentment, fallen asleep, and awakened in the shadow of a towering, moss-draped oak. Where had my enmity gone? It seemed to have dispersed, the whole sparkling memory palace of it vanished like an elaborate, colorful sand painting now swept into a pile of gray dust.

True, I'd upped the odds of success by prepping a little for our meeting. I'd asked the advice of an international negotiator who was passing through town, a woman who'd gotten even Rwandan Hutus and Tutsis to sit down and forgive each other in the wake of genocidal horror. I'd been embarrassed to bother her with my petty grievance, but she'd waved off my objections. It's *always* the same story, she'd told me, whether broken friendships, marriages on the rocks, businesses gone sour, or war's grim remains of the day. The heart shuts down, encapsulates the injury. There's the denial of the other's human decency; the refusal to empathize; the memory button set on endless replay; the cosseting of grudges; the craving for revenge. The solution—to acknowledge your own pain, put yourself in the enemy's place, and try to let go—was wrenching, painstaking, but it was the only way out of the box.

She had assigned me a simple exercise. First, to lay out all my grievances, focusing more on my emotions than any litany of circumstance. I was surprised to find that much of my discontent stemmed from blaming myself. I'd felt deeply ashamed: I'd been a fool, a tool, a footstool of someone else's ambitions. I'd felt guilty that I'd dragged my family across the country for a fistful of funny money. I could also see that the intricate ways I'd been disappointed, all of which had seemed so unerringly personal, aimed straight at my heart, were just archetypal human pathos. Seduced, betrayed, abandoned? Reeling from your losses? Heart stuck in a rut? Welcome to Life 101.

She had also asked me to imagine my ex-Partner's state of mind and heart, then express his hopes and fears as if they were my own. I was amazed how closely my guesses were confirmed by what he'd later told me: "I'm afraid to fail. I don't want to be seen as wrong," I'd written in this hat-switching exercise. "I feel I'm generous and fair. I'm afraid to give away part of my business. My family depends on me." The list had generated unexpected sympathies. Besides, with a few judicious tweaks, it could've been my own.

S till, I didn't quite understand what had happened between us. He'd apologized, and I had accepted. But what *is* this epiphany called forgiveness? The field of psychology has tended to ignore it, treating it more like a religious mystery play than a therapeutic modality. It is found in the indexes of few clinical texts. Freud, in all his writings on healing the mind, hardly gave it a mention.

Lately, though, there's been something of a renaissance. The pace of scientific research on forgiveness has so quickened that over forty laboratories around the world are now drilling down to mine for ore. Social scientists talk of "grudge theory" and "forgiveness transactions," applying "game theoretic analyses" to the dynamics of apology. Evidence indicates that forgiveness increases self-esteem (that magic word) and decreases anxiety. In one trial, men in a drug and alcohol treatment program who trained in forgiveness showed significantly less depression. And there are implications for physical health: While holding a grudge fuels anger and resentment, producing damaging stress hormones (cardiac patients who blame others for their initial heart attack are more likely to have reinfarctions), positive emotions like forgiveness lead to lowered heart rate and reduced blood pressure.

A new therapeutic subspecialty, forgiveness counseling, is making a bid for legitimacy, with volumes of theory and burgeoning self-help books in tow: three steps to forgiveness, five steps, ten steps (one method calls for *nineteen* steps). A certain hyperbole has already crept in: One therapist trumpets forgiveness as "as important to the treatment of emotional and mental disorders as the discovery of sulfa drugs and penicillin have been to the treatment of infectious diseases." And there is the inevitable controversy. Some clergy warn of a shallow secular dispensation, a forgiveness stripped of its most challenging moral dimensions, while some psychologists accuse *them* of guarding an exclusive religious franchise.

Some of the confusion may pertain to different degrees of forgiveness. At its most basic, forgiveness is an act of self-healing. I would rather have been hung by my thumbs than let bygones be bygones until I realized how much my burden of resentment was hurting *me*. Forgiveness begins with acknowledging one's own pain, shame, and sense of failure; healing the shattered sense of self-worth; grieving the loss of faith in other people. To liberate ourselves from a hurt inflicted by another takes the psychological courage to open an old wound, evoke a painful memory, pull up a tangled skein of issues we'd rather keep under wraps.

Many mental health counselors believe that this focus on personal healing should be where forgiveness begins and ends. In a recent poll of the profession, 66 percent said they "do not endorse activities that acknowledge and address the significance of the offender" and do not encourage empathy toward them. "The majority of respondents," concluded the survey, "appear to view forgiveness as a gift primarily to the self alone." One researcher quotes a woman who simply said, "Forgiving means to write the person off."

Though understandable—why *not* x-out the creepazoid who messed with your life?—I wonder if without striving to find empathy for the offender, healing is really possible. President Jimmy Carter once defined forgiveness as "putting yourself in the position of the other person and wiping away any sort of resentment or antagonism you feel toward them." Observes one clinician: "To forgive, one must have the capacity to identify with others and view them as more than simply extensions of oneself. One must be able to feel a modicum of social interest, a willingness to admit a personal role in relationship dysfunctions, and a genuine concern and empathy for others." Psychologist Heinz Kohut points out that a person who is too self-centered may be incapable of forgiving at all: The offending party is not seen as an individual in his own right, but as "a flaw in a narcissistically perceived reality." There can be no I-Thou when the Thou is subtracted from the equation.

One leading forgiveness researcher, Robert Enright, believes that without this Thou in the picture, forgiveness is radically incomplete. Enright founded the University of Wisconsin's Human Development Study Group in 1985, inaugurating the most extensive scientific investigation of forgiveness to date. He observed that a person may abandon a grudge, only to be left with "detached indifference, writing off the offender as morally incompetent . . . and not worthy of our time." In that case, he says, rather than forgiveness, we "end up replacing resentment with alienation." After a study of the existing psychological literature (along with the beliefs and practices of the world's religions), he concluded there is a deeper level of forgiveness, a kind of spiritual transformation he calls "a willed change of heart." He encourages his clients to strive for a "new stance . . . [of] compassion, generosity, and even love" toward the offender.

It raises hackles among some social workers, who tell of domestic abuse victims counseled to forgive a perpetrator only to suffer new injury at his hands. Forgiveness horror stories make the rounds. Writes one clinician: "Some counselors have worked, as I have, with parents and grandparents who 'forgave' the behavior of drug-addicted youth, resulting in not only failure to treat the addiction, but, in some cases, the murder of the 'forgiver.'" At the very least, they caution, letting go of vindictive feelings can mean relinquishing necessary self-respect and needed self-protection.

Some kind of warning label seems well advised against what could become a forgiveness fundamentalism, or just a mishandled new tool on the therapeutic utility belt. But a preponderance of time-tested wisdom points to the power of forgiveness to restore relationships, to heal communities, even to kickstart something akin to unconditional love—love that is not dependent on the other person conforming to our expectations or being instrumental to our needs.

This sort of forgiveness is a form of mutual healing. Desmond Tutu speaks of reconciliation as a human necessity: "It is important that I do all I can to restore relationship. Because without relationship, I am nothing, I will shrivel." One social worker goes so far as to suggest that "forgiver and forgiven need each other" and that without acknowledging their "interdependence," an "injustice can be committed through unilateral forgiveness." Another researcher claims to have found in cases of deep reconciliation something that, for a person on a spiritual path, would be a pearl of great price:

"Every individual I interviewed said that nothing could be unforgivable again."

S ome years back, in a younger, crazier time, I discovered through someone's slip of the tongue that a good friend had had a brief affair with my girlfriend while I was away on a months-long business trip. It felt like a serrated steak knife between the shoulder blades. With icy-cold voice, I declared our relationships null and void. I refused to talk to either one of them. It seemed an unforgivable breach of trust.

But to my amazement, they refused to accept my edict of banishment. My girlfriend called every other day, sending roses and handwritten letters and notes of apology. My friend, stricken, told me, "I'm just not willing to lose your friendship. Tell me what I have to do." He didn't wait for an answer but contrived various tokens of apology and expressions of remorse. Though I'd turned to stone, they kept up their campaign of almost daily erosion. I could see both of them were genuinely suffering. I was secretly surprised to realize how much they really did love me. After a while, I couldn't hold fast to my sense of outrage. To remain adamant was making me feel small, even cruel. They had so empathized with me that their pain about the pain they'd caused me had made *me* feel for *them.*

And of course, underneath it all, I loved them, too. Putting aside that I was the aggrieved party and looking at the situation objectively, I could even understand how it had happened. Loneliness is a powerful thing, and sex is . . . well, *sex,* an elemental force that rampages through our lives, eyes ablaze, bending even history to its will.

Eventually, I relented. I forgave them. Our relationships were restored, and more—they grew mysteriously stronger in the broken places. My friend became, in the fullness of time, my best friend. My girlfriend and I affirmed a deeper, less contingent love; though we separated years later, we remain close. There had been an annealing in fire. I know that if I had clung to my first wounded impulse, my life would have been incomparably poorer. And was I not oddly indebted to them for revealing a love less dependent on happy circumstance; a love, in the end, beyond betrayal?

Besides, I really had to wonder: What was it about being the injured party that was so paradoxically seductive? In the early days of Internet spam, marketeers discovered that people would readily open any e-mail whose title line read "I'm So Sorry," proving that most of us feel somebody somewhere owes us an apology. I could recall other times I was unequivocally wronged, unfurling my white sail of innocence even as my own vessel, heavy with its cargo of shortcomings, rode low in the water. I had to acknowledge the truism that we judge most harshly those who embody our unadmitted failings. Had I ever in my life cheated on a romantic partner? *(Yes.)* Had I ever acted on a selfish desire and hurt another in the process? *(Oh, yes.)* Had my friends, then, been my tormentors or my scapegoats? Christ's words on the cross, "Forgive them, for they know not what they do," is compassion's holy formula. We all miss the mark in our blindness, ensnared by ego and self-deception; miss it more than we care to acknowledge.

Thinking now of my business nemesis, it seems that none of it was personal. Wrapped in his own private fogbank, he'd hardly even *seen* me. An old Buddhist fable: A ferryman is taking a rich nobleman across a river. It is a misty night; he can see barely ten feet ahead. Suddenly, another boat glides out of the murk and rams into his prow, spilling his finely dressed fare into the water. The ferryman is furious: A rival has decided to spoil his good fortune. Cursing, enraged, he lifts his pole, readying himself to strike his adversary as the other craft sweeps past, only to see—an unmoored, empty boat.

Maybe it's possible to forgive others' trespasses by realizing how blindly they harm us. Like empty boats, adrift on their own currents, colliding with us by happenstance, they're not quite all there; and neither, if we can admit it, are we.

*U*nless we are solitary anchorites, cartoon hermits with beards grown down to our toes, we live in relationship, which guarantees we will be hurt by others and inevitably will hurt them. Forgiveness, the binding of wounds, is indispensable to our lives together. To accept our own hurt, taking it in rather than projecting it out, distills the healing elixir.

Unresolved emotional pain is the great contagion of our time—of all time. This does not deny the struggle for justice: There *is* a world out there, and it cries out for rectification. But those who cannot sense the pain of the one who wounds them will dispense, under the banner of righteousness, a misshapen justice, and create yet more enduring wrongs. I could be deep in goody-two-shoes territory, but I suspect the final extension of forgiveness is just as Lao Tzu said: "It is the way of the Tao to recompense injury with kindness." The spiritual consensus is too wide to ignore. As Rabbi Pinhas once boasted of a favored disciple, "My Raphael knows how to love the most wicked evil-doers!" The other day at lunch, I even got the message from my fortune cookie: "The way to get rid of an enemy," counseled the Peking Noodle Company, "is to make a friend."

I've concluded, at least in theory, edging toward practice, the same. I'm persuaded that the theologian Paul Tillich put forth an ideal worth striving for: "Forgiveness," he wrote, "means reconciliation in spite of estrangement; it means reunion in spite of hostility; it means acceptance of those who are unacceptable; and it means reception of those who are rejected. Forgiveness is unconditional, or it is not forgiveness at all."

I'm inspired, but it's still lofty enough to give me vertigo. We have all experienced that hardness of heart that makes reconciliation seem unattainable. Yes, I've always wanted to glimpse the good flame burning bright in even the dim and the wicked and Lord, judge not, judge not. But I find it a mighty tall order for a heart that often comes up short. I still get miffed when an acquaintance passes me in the market without a warm enough hello. I know people for whom a simple social snub has fueled a lifetime of rancor. To forge my own minor act of forgiveness had taken decades.

And aren't there some choice specimens we *should* place beyond the pale? The ones who yank our chains or just plain creep us out; those paragons who've tromped on our sensitive insteps without a murmur of apology; who've screwed us in the past and, given half a chance, would stick it to us again, this time with a little more torque? And what about the rotten people, the cold-blooded calculators and hot-blooded haters, the ones we shun, abjure, justifiably loathe? In the Greek New Testament, the term used for compassion toward one who has wronged us is *splanchnizomai,* from the word for intestines (to pour out one's insides: forgiveness is gutwrenching work). Sometimes it just feels impossible.

But now and again, we hear of people who have forgiven the unforgivable, extending themselves to the perpetrators of unspeakable crimes. How do they keep their hearts open amid the buffetings of true malice? I wasn't sure I could imagine it. I was about to find out.

10

LOVING THE MONSTER

What shall we make of our darkness?
—*Blaise Pascal*

t's a four-hour drive from Atlanta to the Telfair State Prison down a lonesome stretch of I-75, which slices through central Georgia like a straight-razor cut. I put the tuner on scan and, just as I pass the Pinetucky Church of God, catch a burst of pure southern-gothic, some ballad about a dying preacher who "a-laid his bloodstained Bible right in that hooker's hand." Years of long-distance driving have made me appreciate any oases in the staticky desert of rural bandwidth, where the choice is either Black Sabbath oldies or the Good Book's greatest hits, and the tale of Mary and Joseph at the inn becomes "the Bethlehem Motel Six *refused* to take their *credit card!*" Down here, it's all tower-of-power gospel, every other word Saviour, sin, repent, Heaven, Hell, or ActNowWithoutDelay.

I play a mental game, slugging in my own translations for the more overwrought sermonizing. When the preacher shouts, "Friends, I wouldn't live a day without Jesus," I think, *without compassion,* for what else was he, and amen to that. "Repent!" becomes *take a frank and fearless inventory,* and I try: The truth is, I'm whistling in the wind, a little nervous I'm on my way to meet a cold-blooded killer.

The murder had shocked the down-at-heel Atlanta neighborhood of Vine City. Residents there were no strangers to crime, but the victim had been an angel. Forty-three-year-old Patricia Nuckles had come up from those very streets, gone away to college and then returned to her roots, working as a librarian, tutoring kids, doing charity work in her spare time. Trish, as everyone knew her, had had an unusual upbringing: an African-American woman raised by a white couple, Hector and Susie Black, who'd moved down in the sixties to do grassroots civil rights organizing. There, in the Deep South, trying to quench the flames of hatred while others fanned them higher, the Blacks, their three other daughters, and Trish had formed an unlikely, fiercely devoted family.

Trish's cousin Michelle had been the first to hear she was dead. She had been half-watching a newsbreak about a homeless crack addict who had burglarized a home and murdered the owner, a drearily familiar tableau of flashing police cruisers, yellow crime-scene tape, and a beat reporter striving for gravitas. *I know that place,* Michelle thought, then realized with a ripple of horror that it was Trish's house. Not long after, police caught thirty-two-year-old Ivan Simpson hiding at his mother's place. "What type of animal could have done that, killed her the way he did?" Michelle asks me. "Trish would literally give you the clothes off her back. She helped the homeless, too; she would have helped *him* if he'd asked."

The terrible pathos of good woman brutally slain, of a family shattered by a monster in human skin, made the case a prosecutorial slam dunk. When Simpson pleaded guilty, the DA shifted his focus to getting the death penalty. As the crime's terrible chronicle was read into the court record, Hector Black, who had driven down from the Tennessee farm he'd bought after all the kids were grown, felt thankful his partial deafness made some of the account inaudible. He could

222

hardly bear to glance at the powerfully built black man, head down and shoulders drooping, who sat in the docket.

The defense attorney recounted how Ivan Simpson had been born in a mental hospital to a severely disturbed mother. His life had been a nightmare of violence and deprivation. When it came Hector's turn to read his prepared victim impact statement, his feelings were in turmoil. Standing with his sport jacket thrown over his bib overalls, he told the court of his joy when Trish had come into his family.

"Although she was not our child by any claims of birth," Hector told the judge, "she was our child by every claim of love." Over thirty-five years, he had watched her bloom from the thin, neglected child of a neighborhood alcoholic who often forgot to feed her into a woman intent on making the world a better place. He opened his briefcase and took out his favorite picture of Trish as a beaming eight-year-old, telling the court of the mortal dark that had swallowed their lives; of his feelings of abandonment by a God whose eye, he'd once believed, was always on the sparrow.

Such statements are usually a platform for crime victims to hammer home the enormity of their loss and demand the maximum penalty, but Hector had a starkly different purpose. "I know that love does not seek revenge," he told the court. "We do not want a life for a life." Facing the startled judge, he read the words he had written to the murderer. "I don't hate you, though I hate with all my soul what you did." Then summoning a reserve of will, Hector turned around to speak the last lines directly to the prisoner. "My wish from my heart is that God would grant all of us peace who have been so terribly wounded by this murder—including you, Ivan Simpson."

Hector remembers the moment. "It was almost like I was grabbed to turn around and look at him. He lifted his head, and our eyes met. Tears were just streaming down his face, such a look of . . . oh, God, like a soul in hell. It was one of those rare moments, when the raw wounds strip away all pretense or falseness."

As he was being led away, Simpson asked to speak. Turning to face the family, he said, "I am so sorry for the pain I have caused. I am so sorry." Even the court's victim representative, accustomed to stony silence, false contrition, or even cruel mockery from the accused, told Hector she felt a sense of awe. "This is something we rarely see, genuine remorse." Either that, I think, or world-class method acting, angling for a Clemency Emmy. Simpson was sentenced to life without parole.

*T*he Telfair Prison guard towers rise miragelike in the swampy sunlight, like giant mushroom caps on gray concrete stalks. Behind them, low, boxy buildings warehouse some thirteen hundred violent prisoners, a third of them doing life without parole. The assistant warden, a whippet-thin bleached blonde in her fifties, agrees to take me on a quick tour of purgatory.

We walk the path outside the yard, passing knots of marble-eyed men with time and blood on their hands who pause in their furtive talk as we approach. A young man with a shaved head saunters by, an enormous blue swastika tattooed on his skull. "It's good they got rid of the weight room," she says with asperity. "These guys were bulking up so they could pound each other to a pulp."

There are hundreds upon hundreds of terrible crimes contained within these walls, she tells me, and she pretty much knows them all. My curiosity morbidly piqued, I ask her to describe a few. She glances at me sharply, quizzically. "Isn't Ivan's crime monstrous enough?"

She leads me to a fluorescent-lit room, its walls decorated with fake flower wreaths and a pastoral painting of hunters and hounds chasing down a fox. Four brass ceiling fans whisk the soupy air. I'm seated at a conference table with twelve chairs, like a jury room. "He's probably going to cry," the warden says dourly. She puts a roll of toilet paper on the table, implying Kleenex would be too good.

Ivan Simpson is led into the room wearing a prison-issue white jumpsuit with an oddly stylish-looking blue collar. I expected a glowering, manipulative sociopath, his sulfurous soul burnt to cinder; or some feral con man, behind whose mask I would spot the hard gleam of cunning. I am unprepared for this man with an abject air of guilelessness, speaking in soft, country cadences.

When I ask him about his childhood, he tells me of the morning his mother, a schizophrenic who had been in and out of mental hospitals since he was born, had awakened him, his four-year-old sister LaToya, his brother Chuck, and two other siblings for an early outing to the local park. He'd felt excited and happy. They were at the edge of the swimming pool when his mother, raving that they were all "a threat to God," scooped them up and plunged into the water, trying to drown them like a litter of unwanted kittens. His sister LaToya died before his eyes. Ivan managed to thrash free and pull his brother Chuck to safety while the others struggled from her grasp.

Ivan was adopted by his great-aunt. He recites his ghetto coming-of-age story in an emotionless monotone. Hotwiring cars at fifteen. Moved up to "B-an'-E," breaking and entering, earning a two-year prison stint. Then the revelation of crack cocaine—"just a few minutes of everything's-at-ease." He'd supported his habit through "property crimes, lying, and manipulating," sometimes stealing his aunt's rent money, watching as she lost her house, her car, and her job to the monkey on his back. The crack, he says, "seemed to take away all my caring for other people."

Had he ever really cared? I ask him. "Oh, I grew up in a loving atmosphere," he says quietly in his slow, heartful drawl. "My adoptive mom, Marie, she raised me good. She loved us, just loved us." A tear squeezes from his eye and meanders down his cheek. "I never had thoughts about hurting nobody."

Despairing over his addiction, he had tried to kill himself several times before being admitted to a treatment center. Clean for a few years, he'd been given a car and a furnished three-bedroom house by a woman at a local church, where he, his common-law wife, and son lived in exchange for simple upkeep. It had been a stroke of inconceivable luck, but soon he was addicted again. He picked his gift-house clean of anything he could fence and wound up back on the street. He'd finally moved back to Marie's and gotten off his habit again. But one night, walking to the convenience store to buy cigarettes, he ran into his old dealer, who offered him a rock of crack. Soon high and craving more, he impulsively decided to do a burglary. Chance led him to Trish Nuckles's darkened house and the crime that had unfolded like a Greek tragedy.

When Trish had unexpectedly walked in on him, he'd knocked her down and tied her up. After that, he remembers having a strangely cordial-sounding conversation. Trish, trying to calm him down, had asked him about himself. He'd said he was hungry. She had urged him to take some cooked chicken and ham and sodas from the fridge. Typically concerned, she even told him, as he was leaving with her computer and stereo under his arm, that he should try to get some help. He promised he would, adding he would just use her car to drop off the stolen goods and leave it parked where she could find it, next to the Chinese restaurant up the street.

He remembers thinking she was a nice person; even remembers telling her to be sure to install some outside floodlights and put her lamps on timers to deter future burglaries. "And then I just left." I can hear the relief in his voice. "Just *left.*" For a moment, he is back at that crossroads, as if he could turn around and walk the other way; as if the story could end right there, with just another B-and-E. His cellie hears him in his sleep sometimes saying, "I'm leaving, Trish, I'm leaving."

Instead, Ivan scored some more crack. As he sat in Trish's car smoking it, he was startled to hear a voice, ghastly cold and glacially clear: *Go back and kill her.* He looked over at the passenger seat; the voice had issued from thin air. He recreates his hallucinatory dialogue.

"I said, 'I ain't gonna kill that lady. She didn't see my face. Her glasses fell off. She can't ID me.' "

You go back now and kill that lady, said the voice. *You go back and kill her.*

Ivan knew then he was remonstrating with a demon; a demon, he says, "name of Legion." He smoked more crack, then returned to the house. "Legion want me to kill you," he told the still-bound and now terrified Trish. He remembers her asking why, after he'd been "so nice up to now," her begging him to just take her car. He told her he wanted to have sex. She said he'd have to kill her first.

"The only thing I remember," Ivan claims, "is watching myself . . . strangle her. That's . . . that's all I remember. Standing above. Watching." Now a stately cortege of teardrops rolls down his cheeks. He swears he'd never been violent before, in all his years of crime. "I don't know why she had to die," he mutters disconsolately, "or I should say—why I took her life."

For Jesus had commanded the evil spirit to come out of the man. Many times it had seized him, and though he was chained hand and foot and kept under guard, he had broken his chains and had been driven by the demon into solitary places.

Jesus asked him, "What is your name?"

"Legion," he replied, because many demons had gone into him. (Luke 8:29)

The ranks of the possessed—by personal demons of defeat and dysfunction—*are* legion in the world. Ivan Simpson had had what psychiatrists call a "command hallucination"; crack, which addicts call Kryptonite, is notorious for them. But isn't most crime perpetrated under some malign influence: drugs or alcohol; or a haze of rage, a pall of misery, a flash of jealousy; the sharp spur of desperation; the vise-grip of vengeance? I am revulsed by Ivan's crime, by his vile massacre of an innocent. Yet I think of a prayer by the Dalai Lama: "Those who, maddened by the demons of delusion, commit violent negative actions that destroy both themselves and others, should be the object of our compassion." Navajo tribal healers who treat modern mental illnesses, like the violent flashbacks of soldiers returned from war, call it all *nayee*—"monster." "What is the essence of the cycle of violence," writes a Navajo lawyer, "in which children who are abused or neglected become offenders themselves? *Nayee*. Antisocial personality disorder? *Nayee*." Just as Hector's mother had been "told" to kill his little sister, Ivan, in some awful restaging (a psychologist would call it repetition-compulsion) had been ordered by a phantom to snuff out a blameless young woman's life.

*H*ow could I hate this man who had suffered so much as a child?" Hector had wondered in his diary after the day in court, "someone so tormented by what he had done?" He had been unable to sleep that night. For the first time since the ordeal began, the coils that had wrapped themselves around his heart, crushing every fragile bone of hope, had loosened a little. He knew he'd done the right thing to oppose the death penalty. But there was something else, something he hadn't expected. "I knew then that I'd forgiven him," he says, the echo of surprise still in his voice. "And though I found it an awful stretch to think I could be concerned about the man who'd destroyed Trish, I also knew I had to write to him, encourage him that his life wasn't over."

Hector had stayed up until dawn trying to find a way to put his new feelings on paper. "The thought of being in prison for the rest of your life," he wrote Ivan Simpson, "must be very hard. But it doesn't have to be the end. You can still find ways to help people who need help. You can be a force for peace and for light in dark surroundings. Patricia tried to make the world a better place. We should also try. If you will let me, I would like to keep writing to you. It would mean a lot to me to hear from you, especially knowing how hard it is for you to do this. Please try." He signed it, "A Brokenhearted Father."

Ivan tells me that after his arrest, he had only one purpose at his trial: to die. "I felt like for what I did, I deserved to go. I done took someone's life. Even though my dying wouldn't make up for it, why should I still be here?" He had told his lawyers, over their objections, to plead guilty. He'd wanted justice to take its course, straight to the electric chair. When they told him about Hector's opposition to the death penalty, he was baffled.

"Come on! How can someone not want me to die, and I just took his daughter's life? And Hector, how can he get up in court and say he hated what I did, but he doesn't hate *me*?" He looks at me wonderingly. "Eyes can tell you a lot about a person. I saw his eyes, and he was for real. And, at first, I really didn't want that forgiveness. Fact, right now, up until this point, I ain't really forgave myself for what I did."

His voice catches only slightly. His head sinks in shame. He is stern as he weeps. He will not permit himself the concupiscence of a sob. His tears will fall of their own accord, subject to the law of gravity, like raindrops trailing down a windowpane. I strive to withhold my empathy, as if allowing myself to feel anything would be collusion, would betray the life he took. It's not easy to do, as I sit with a man forever condemned to dry his own tears.

Hector continued writing Ivan, sometimes as often as weekly, the correspondence growing into a thick sheaf. He sent Ivan a letter with a leaf of scented geranium, but the censors confiscated it as contraband. He regaled him with the quotidian doings on his farm; the struggle to keep the grass in the orchard under control after heavy rains; chasing a neighbor's escaped cows. ("Pesky things never go in the direction you want. I ran them with my little riding mower in top gear like some kind of cowboy, whooping and hollering to scare them some; otherwise they just look up at you with those big eyes of theirs and won't budge.")

Hector told Ivan about his skateboarding grandson and the teenage kids from the halfway house he invites out to climb around his property's waterfalls and savor a few unfettered hours. And Ivan wrote back in a scrawled pastiche of block letters and cursive about "the thorn in my side," about how the hardened inmates "think I'm crazy because I cry some nights about what I did." He described persuading a despondent man who had killed his own children not to hang himself, and breaking up fights and arguments between people "who literally want to see blood." He was trying every day, he said, to do good.

"The hardness I have against myself," he wrote Hector, "is a sort of strength to help others that I draw from. I used to pray for myself, but I realize it's not about me. From the moment I came to realize the hurt, pain, and grief I caused. I can pray for others now. It's hard going, giving up anger, jealousy, lies, and pride. But I am trying."

"Sometimes," Hector tells me, "I doubt myself. Are you crazy, writing to the man who killed your daughter? What kind of strange bird am I? I do have to wrestle with my feelings." But somehow, improbably, he'd grown to care deeply for a man struggling in the grip of damnation.

*W*hat had happened to create such an overturning? Hector's plea for clemency had been on moral and intellectual grounds. But even with his Quaker philosophy and his big heart, he had hated Ivan's guts. "When I found out Trish was raped, especially," he says quietly, "I tried to demonize him. I felt like he had power over me, like someone was shoving my face in the mud. I had these horrible pictures in my head of the murder; I just couldn't shake it."

But something had caused him to feel a mercy toward his daughter's murderer that transcended any abstract principle. When Hector saw Ivan on the docket, facing a sentence of death, in a courtroom "filled with our family, folks from our church, and he all alone, nobody there for him," he had felt something shift. St. Paul said that higher morality is "written on the heart," not in the canon. Studies have shown that belligerents in war will feel sympathy when shown a picture of an enemy soldier in pain. When photos of a frightened, bedraggled Saddam Hussein being dragged from his spider-hole were beamed around the world, many people expressed oddly ambivalent sentiments for the Beast of Baghdad. "I felt pity to see this man destroyed," a Vatican cardinal was quoted. "Seeing him like this, a man in his tragedy, despite all the heavy blame he bears, I had a sense of compassion for him."

Is this what had occurred in Hector's heart that day in the courtroom? Aquinas contended that love is a "natural law" grounded in God's very design of His creatures. Maybe it was the mirror neurons themselves, murmuring their litany, *you in me, me in you.* "I suspect brain structures for nurturant behavior fall in a rough range of candidacy," a biologist once told me. "Helpless, defenseless, weak, the underdog."

It is perhaps easier to be magnanimous when we have the upper hand, gazing down on a human being prostrate in defeat. But religious doctrines often enjoin their followers to imagine even a superior enemy as weak and fallen, trumping the mind's logic with that of the heart. It takes a discerning eye to see vulnerability behind the fright mask of those who oppress us. Martin Luther King used to portray his racist adversaries as broken people, living in spiritual exile, in need of a forgiveness only the oppressed could grant them. He inspired among his followers a paradoxical sense of empowerment: It was only they, the victims, who could heal the damaged souls of their enemies, by moving them to mercy and leading them out of hatred's wilderness.

There is an intellectual component to understanding the fruitless cycle of revenge, and a moral one to the willed extension of humanity to a hateful other. But compassion goes beyond moral decision-making. It is an irresistible force, breaking down the thickest fortress walls that separate us from each other. Psychologist Pumla Gobodo-Madzikela, a member of the South African Truth and Reconciliation Commission (TRC), had taken it upon herself to interview the jailed former security chief of the apartheid regime, Eugene de Kock. Chief planner and sometime triggerman in the government's brutal shadow war, de Kock had been the mastermind of the infamous Vlakplaas "death farm" where the worst killings and tortures had taken place. He had by his own hand murdered and maimed. For the horrors he had visited on so many, he had become known to the public by the so-briquet "Prime Evil." Madzikela's prison interviews had begun as a detached study of a specimen of inhuman detritus through a psychological microscope.

Convicted as a common criminal on murder charges, de Kock had surprised everyone by asking to meet the widows of three black policemen who had been killed by a bomb he himself had planted. Madzikela was further astonished when one of the women told her after the meeting, "I couldn't control my tears. I could hear him, but I was overwhelmed by emotion, and I was just nodding, as a way of saying yes, I forgive you. I hope that when he sees our tears, he knows that they are not only tears for our husbands, but tears for him as well." The widow's response went beyond empathy; she had offered de Kock a priceless gift, a reentry into the human community: "I would like to hold him by the hand," she said, "and show him that there is a future, and that he can still change."

Madzikela's own friends criticized her for the equivalent of sitting down on a first-name basis with Hitler. She herself was shocked as a rapport grew uninvited. She had been "dumbfounded," she says, to discover that she and de Kock shared the same birthday: "I had to steady myself just to consider what it meant to share something so personal with a man whom many would consider a mass murderer." But meeting with de Kock, so close she could sometimes feel her skin crawl, she saw in spite of herself a man whose remorse was so deep he was wearing "an intolerable shirt of flame." She found over time her revulsion was challenged by the suffering of the human being sitting before her, leaving her deeply conflicted—consumed, she writes, by a "fear of stepping into the shoes of a murderer through empathy." She was taken by surprise by her own conclusions.

In her book, *A Man Died That Night,* she writes, "Empathy reaches out to the other and says: 'I can feel the pain you feel for having caused me pain.' . . .[T]here is something in the other that is felt to be part of the self, and something in the self that is felt to belong to the other."

You in me, me in you. "I know it's a cliché," Hector had told me, "but deep down I'm not that different from Ivan Simpson. I really believe we each have a capacity for evil as well as good. What kind of person would I have been if I'd been born into his circumstances?"

Somehow, Hector's open heart is having an inexorable effect. More than penitence, Ivan is absorbing into his charred soul Hector's unpretentious lovingkindness. When Hector sent him a small money order, Ivan was amazed. "How *can* he, I'm wondering? Where was his hate at? 'Cause I have to tell the truth, if the shoe was on the other foot, if someone took a loved one from me, I couldn't send them nothing. But *he* goes, 'Here's ten dollars.' He asks me to use it to buy something I need, some stamps or a candy bar. It just felt funny, it really did, for this man—I'm gonna have to say it—for him to love me. And I really believe he loves me. Even when I couldn't love myself. When I look around and wonder, is there really some love left, or care, or kindness, here he is."

Theologian Paul Tillich wrote that "God's forgiveness is independent of anything we do, even of self-accusation and self-humiliation." But Ivan is the lowest of the low. You could say I was sitting across a table from an irredeemable monstrosity, another iteration of Prime Evil, a man who had killed a sweet young woman out of sheer depravity and then—there is no delicate way to put this—returned to ghoulishly rape her body. No one is going to make him a *cause célèbre* or a symbol of the pressing need for penal reform.

But I could not help but see in him what Hector did: a person possessed not by demons, but by an unmistakable spirit of human worth he struggles daily to reclaim. That Hector's love is a force working on the very substance of Ivan's heart, I cannot doubt. "For real," Ivan intones when he talks about Hector's forgiveness, with a mingled note of awe and bewilderment. "For *real.*"

"Like you say all the time," he wrote Hector recently in his childlike hand, "somewhere a seed has been planted, and then with water, pruning, and love, it can grow and blossom."

*D*own a few twisty back roads and deep in a Tennessee holler, there's a sign that reads, "Entering Spring Creek Sanctuary: Animals and Plants Protected." Hector's house is a little farther on, a modest affair concealed in a green jumble of vegetative exuberance. When I walk up the path, his big dog doesn't let out a hint of a bark at the stranger, but trots up to amiably nuzzle my hand.

Hector's farm grows everything from chestnuts to cherries, but it's the blueberries that are running riot this season, the fields spread with an azure impasto as far as the eye can see. A big carton of fresh blueberries sits in the living room. There's blueberry wine, blueberry preserves, blueberry muffins, and thick blueberry juice dark as indigo, at once sweet and tart, steamed right from the fruit. Homemade, all of it, as are the exotic plant jellies set on the dinner table by his wife, Susie, who trundles around the kitchen with cheery efficiency despite being wheelchair-bound from rheumatoid arthritis. She's sixty-seven to Hector's seventy-eight, and I tease him about robbing the cradle. He's heard it a million times, but laughs good-naturedly. They have a stand at the farmers' market every week with the Quakerish motto, "Plain But Delightful."

Hector on first impression is just a tall, snowy-haired farmer in Liberty brand overalls with tarnished brass buttons, a folksy sort who calls his combination fax-printer a *watchamajiggit,* uses *okey-dokey* as his preferred assent, and reserves *humdinger* as an accolade for a stellar occasion. He's an atypical local—his degree, from Harvard no less, is in social anthropology—but he'd gone to agricultural school just before World War II and is clearly at home with anything that issues from the dirt.

"If it bears fruits or nuts," he says cheerfully, "I'm interested in it." He raises exotic plants as a member of the intrepidly named North American Fruit Explorers. As we walk through his nursery, he offers me a calamondin, a tiny fruit with a sour inside and sweet skin. There's jujube from China and Russian *ananaznaya,* a succulent hardy kiwi that grows like a grape, looks like a plum, and tastes like a pineapple. His current passion is autumn olive from the Himalayas. "The USDA's really interested in this one," he tells me. "Seventeen times more lycopene than tomatoes. Just loaded with antioxidants. *And* it's nitrogen-fixing." He's scoured the planet for new varieties, cadging those with the best features of size and taste. A gaggle of Russian plant biologists came through recently, conveying in thick Slavic accents their admiration, along with a certain covetousness.

All they needed to do was ask. Hector's an open hand. He'll likely just give away most of his blueberry crop this year. I suggest that with his 280 acres he could make a real go of it, get his organic certification ("too expensive," he snorts), mount a grander operation than a few Mason jars with blurry labels printed on his inkjet.

"If I had any sense," he shrugs, "I suppose that's what I *would* do." But it doesn't seem to be the point. He looks to be just getting by. He sold eighty acres to a community land trust at a no-interest steal. I get the impression his stewardship of the land is where his heart is; that, and the experimental secret garden he hopes will yield something of use to the world.

Hector is just a Grade A Giver. He grew up in a family of them. His aunt Mollie inherited a pot of money, gave it all away to charity, and went back to her day job. His mother was so generous with her table during the Depression that the hobos used to mark the house with chalk. He is another with that quality the sociologist Sorokin called "generativity": something in him which likes fostering and the provision of sustenance. "You just like taking care of things," I tell him mock-accusingly. "People, plants, the dirt under your toes . . ." He considers this, then nods. "I never looked at it that way, but maybe that's about right."

He talks about Trish, remembering "this little kid with impetigo sores on her legs from lack of sanitation and nutrition who was like a starved plant. She absorbed all the love you could give her, then just bloomed." Trish had passed that same love along, he says, taking in a young girl from the neighborhood and seeing her through college and marriage.

"When she died, I was in darkness," Hector says. His voice is ruminative, far off. "Susie reminds me that the first night, I was wild, crying, saying, 'I'd like to kill that bastard!' I don't have any answer why forgiveness happened. It was like a hand pulled me out."

His eyes mist. "I wanted to find something good in all the horror. I'm one of these people who doesn't believe in accidents. Though I do have a hard time figuring out what the hell happened and why this guy Ivan's in my life now." Then he laughs, and the laugh shocks me with its uproariousness, a burst of cosmic humor to shoo off any lurking grief-buzzards.

/ t *is* surpassing strange. The purpose of the justice system in capital cases, after all, is vengeance. Either the killer is himself killed, terminating his tenure on the same earth his victims' loved ones must walk; or else he is buried alive where they will never have to know he still exists. Either way, victims are offered the grail-cup of final closure.

I once attended a meeting of a group called Parents of Murdered Children (POMC). Around the circle of a dozen mothers and fathers of varying ages, races, and backgrounds come together to cope with the ultimate tragedy, the current of outrage ran deep—at the "slime-bucket killers," at the "donut-eating detectives" who couldn't catch them, at the "injustice system" that couldn't convict them, or hold them, or execute them.

The stories they told were heartrending. So were their lives. The past haunted them, the wound still as fresh as yesterday. They told of being subject to "backflashes" and "grief bursts." One woman proffered the thin consolation that "you do get numb after a while, but you're never the same again, because a part of you has been torn away." Legal retribution held out the only hope of peace from torment.

But for many that peace seemed more elusive the longer they sought it. I was struck by a woman who had brought along a white plastic bag filled with memorabilia about her daughter and her case. She carried it everywhere. "They call me the Bag Lady," she said acridly, her mouth a tight slash. Her daughter had been killed—"at the age of twenty-seven years, five months, eight days, twelve hours, and four minutes old"—in a hit-and-run, on Christmas Eve, while making a charity delivery of food. The Bag Lady thinks she knows who did it. She has collected Ziplocs of paint chips from the cars of potential suspects, collated boxes full of evidence, from the coroner's report to mortician's notes. She may yet have the triumph of justice long denied, but meanwhile, it's eating her alive.

"I'm more full of rage than a seven-foot, 350-pound man," she said as she tugged from her bag of sorrows a framed picture of a beautiful long-haired young woman and passed it around the circle. "I was one of the best Christians you'd ever meet, but now I'm like a pit bull on steroids. This has made me a bitter, angry person. I know some people who are my targets *shouldn't* be, but . . ." She trailed off. She has loosed a covey of Furies, and now they pursued her with the same pitilessness she reserved for the killer who still eluded their talons.

An elegant British woman of about seventy with swept-back gray hair, a blue shawl over her floral dress, smiled at her. "Well, I may not be a pit bull," she said, her diction gentle and precise, "but I *am* a British bulldog." Her son had been kicked to death by three men outside a bar, and the wheels of justice were grinding exceeding slow. She'd been complacent about the legal system, she said. "Now I tell them, 'I'm sorry I'm not easy to deal with, but that is of *no consequence.*'" She looked over at the Bag Lady. "I might want some of those rage drugs you talk about next time I go in there." I got the impression of a crew of diligent carpenters constructing something that, with each turn of the screw, became too deeply joined to ever dismantle.

No one can judge how another deals with the most tragic of losses and certainly not whether they ever choose to forgive. Notes one clergyman, "We sometimes speak of forgiveness as though it were some sort of coin you can reach into your pocket and hand someone. There is no 'cheap and easy grace.'"

And Hector's decision has not led to any cut-rate closure. Ivan has become, from within his entombment, a vital presence in his life. Rather than consigning him to state-sponsored nonexistence, Hector has chosen to receive his letters, think about him, care about him. To forgive someone who has eclipsed the very sun of joy—to gaze into his soul and find some indwelling virtue, no matter how besmirched— seems a form of spiritual heroism few could muster. Hector claims that he is the one being healed. "I just can't imagine that I would be the person I am if I had not forgiven," he says, "if I hadn't continued to write to him. In recognizing his humanity, I found my own again."

And granted it to another. It has been said it is not the wrong-doer's repentance that creates forgiveness, but the victim's forgiveness that creates repentance. This is where forgiveness enters a realm of paradox and panacea; becomes a mysterious gift offered to one who does not merit it; becomes the essence of compassion itself.

*I*n a famous scene in Victor Hugo's *Les Misérables,* Jean Valjean, a desperate man just released from nineteen years in prison for stealing a loaf of bread, is taken in by a kindly bishop. The cynical ex-con repays his hospitality by stealing the church silverware in the dead of night. But when Valjean is caught by the gendarmes, with the cutlery in his sack, the bishop lies that he had given it to him as a gift, pressing upon him two more silver candlesticks. Valjean, whom the dungeon had turned into Prisoner #24601, a brute incapable of imagining a world with any kindness, feels his humanity reawakened by this single gesture and begins a new life of virtuous service to others.

But what could Ivan Simpson possibly give back?

"Oh, I have a chance to give a lot," he tells me. "I'm in a place where a lot of people are going through pressure, having flare-ups. I try to point out stuff to them, keep 'em out of trouble, maybe just that day. I believe if each man just sat down and not dwell on his past, but look over his life to see what he started, the envy and strife, and how his attitude is making him now, it would humble him. I learned this: A soft answer to anybody'll turn away wrath. Sometimes you can hear two people yelling at each other, tensions are building. If one of them answers in not a harsh way, the other's going to stop. 'Cause you gotta have wood to make a fire burn. Without enough wood, the fire ain't gonna burn. I try to point these out to—"

Suddenly, I burst out laughing, some admixture of irony and delight. I can't help myself: Ivan, like Hector, has become a *peacemaker.*

Silent Simpson, the men in the yard call him; Quiet Ivan. Ivan, the crackhead killer, making this harsh world of murderers and madmen, within its razor-wire circumference, a better place to live.

The assistant warden and a guard sit on the couch, leaning forward, listening in, expressionless. I don't want them to think I'm being conned, chatting and laughing with the man as if I've forgotten who he is, what he's done, the lives he's blighted. But I can no longer hold, any more than can Hector, to a strict taxonomy of inhumanity.

I feel the urge a few times to comfort Ivan, though I know it is not for me to offer dispensation. I get a glimpse of how some of the survivors must feel: as if to show the slightest softening would betray the lost loved one. How would *she* feel to see me smile with her murderer, consorting with the bringer of her death? Would I not be, in some people's eyes, negating her life?

But . . . the sweetness that steals over Ivan's face when he talks about Hector. It's almost unendurable. Could it be this man will quietly punish himself to his dying breath? Every day, Ivan says, he reads Psalm 88, a song of abandonment and of impossible faith.

> *O Lord, God of my salvation, when, at night, I cry out in your presence,*
>
> *let my prayer come before you; incline your ear to my cry.*
>
> *I am counted among those who go down to the Pit; I am like those who have no help . . .*
>
> *You have caused my companions to shun me; you have made me a thing of horror to them. I am shut in so that I cannot escape . . .*
>
> *Are your wonders known in the darkness, or your saving help in the land of forgetfulness?*

"It's when David thought the Lord had forsook him," Ivan explains, "but he was just trying to show him that he's always there." It strikes me as unutterably sad, but Ivan insists, "That's a *good* song, a song of hope."

I ask him what hopes he could have. "There's another passage says be of good courage and wait on the Lord," he says in his deliberate way. "I didn't know whether it meant to wait on him, like, he'll show up so don't rush, or wait on him like a waiter or waitress. So I try to do both. I wait for him, and I try to serve him by helping." But how could he help, in lifelong lockdown, with his faith at once puerile and profound? "I pray," he says simply, "for inmates, for officers, for everybody. I try not to pray for myself. That goes back to the life I've taken. I know Miss Patricia did touch a lot of lives. I believe if I ask for someone else, he'll help them. And if I can get to see that, see it manifest a little, that's good."

Trish used to help the homeless, I say. She might have even helped *him*.

He hangs his head forlornly at this; and I feel badly, too. I almost regret my glimpse of this man's private suffering, because now it will haunt me. I have been unexpectedly pierced. Weeks and months after I return home, his sorrowing face, those indelibly stricken eyes, rise in my mind. If I possessed the right spiritual implement and the skills to use it, I would choose to excise some portion of his anguish.

Ivan says nothing for a while, then brightens a little. "Hector just got some more of his crops in. I think some peaches now. He took them to the farmers' market. He got a bunch of them." Hector's sent him pictures of the trees and plants on his property, and Ivan exults to him, "I never knew plum trees blossom. My favorite bloom is the water lily. If you could see my face right now, you'd see I'm smiling out of joy for the beauty. I bet Susie can make some good blueberry pies from all the berries in the field."

He ends every letter with "I ask your forgiveness."

I ask Ivan if he thinks about the future. He's quiet for a minute. "I'm going to live out my natural life in prison. So I have to treat this as my home and do what I can to make my home a peaceful place. My future is to speak right or just walk right, try to be an example if I can.

241

If I can. Encourage someone no matter where they at. That's just how I look at it."

He stands up and juts out his hand. It's cool and dry, the grip light, tentative, not making contact. He expects no warmth from the clasp, no friendship. I rein in any urge to offer solace, even to hug him, but I know he senses it; though I've tried to strictly ration my sympathies, it's no use. Though Ivan Simpson is by any normal measure a monster, a ghoul, he is also a figure of deep pathos and—it sounds almost obscene to say it—of improbable hope.

*A*s Hector and I hike up a hill—me panting, he barely winded— he recites a running inventory of the critters he's spotted on his property: river otter, deer, muskrats, mink; scarlet tanager, indigo bunting, mourning doves, whippoorwills, great blue heron, vultures; even the bald eagle's coming back, he says. We come to a stand of dawn redwood trees that marks Trish's gravesite. "These used to cover all of North America," he says. "They were thought to be extinct until they were found in 1946 in northern China. They'll grow to be ninety feet or more." He seems uncommonly happy about it.

The grave is a homespun affair, outlined with hand-laid rocks and covered with pink and red impatiens, aka Busy Lizzy, which bloom all summer long. The simple headstone reads: "All the darkness in the world cannot extinguish the light of a single candle."

It would be glib to say that light is growing. But though Hector may be "a strange bird," as he puts it, he's part of a flock of others like him who have managed to fill the mortal void of loss with living compassion. I'd expected them to be a gaggle of church ladies in deep denial, bringing hot soup and hand-knit socks to hardened cons who laughed up their sleeves at them the minute they left. Instead, I've found people who, by repaying humanity for inhumanity, heartfulness for heartlessness, have become, without setting out to be, agents of social healing.

There's Jennifer Bishop, whose pregnant sister was murdered in 1990 by a teenage thrill-killer from a wealthy family. The Ivy League–bound honor student and athlete, now serving three life sentences, has never explained or apologized, let alone asked for forgiveness. "I'm not doing it for him; I'm doing it for me," she says. "I've heard it said, 'Hating is like drinking poison and expecting the other person to die.' It's not going to kill them; it's going to kill you." Her sister's last act, she tells me, had been to write "I love you" on the floor with a finger dipped in her own blood. "I'm not going to second-guess the power and sacredness of that message," says Jennifer. "We need to be about the business of loving, of trying to solve our problems, and making society a less violent place."

Jennifer has been a leader of Murder Victims Families for Human Rights, a group that has grown from a small number of victims' families bearing witness against the death penalty to an activist organization of over five thousand members. Hector has become one of them. So has the mother of Emmet Till, the young black man whose lynching in 1950s Mississippi awakened the nation to the horrors of racism; and the son of James Byrd, whose gruesome 1998 death by dragging in East Texas reminded it of the virulence of hate unquenched. Members have been accused of being, as one puts it, "either not good enough or too good to be true." They've been told to their faces by capital punishment supporters that they are betraying their dead loved ones. (One member recalls being invited to talk to an audience of bereaved who, alerted to her viewpoint, had held aloft miniature nooses all through her talk.)

But the group is part of a larger movement, a society-wide, even worldwide search for a justice that heals. The quest to balance justice and compassion is one of historic provenance: On one side stand those who counsel restoration, restitution, and absolution; on the other, those who favor some variation of the eye-for-an-eye tradition of what is known as the Talionic Code (from the word *retaliation*). In

the Jewish *Sefirot,* the Tree of Life, the branch of justice (*din*) is balanced on the opposite side by compassion (*rahamim*). Hassidic tradition says that God himself struggles to tip the balance to overcome
his trait of judgment (*midat ha'din*). Indeed, in many traditional cultures, the justice system is weighted heavily toward compassion.
Leading Navajo jurist Robert Yazzie points out that his people's word
for justice, usually translated as "reparation," is actually a verb
meaning to "enter into a respectful discussion of the hurt" or "to be
made whole." Navajo law focuses less on punishment and more on
healing and reintegration with the group, working to restore relationships between offender, victim, families, neighbors, and community.

Programs of reconciliation that bring together victims and offenders—usually matching those in different states not linked to the
same crime—are becoming common. For some offenders, it is the
first time they have understood the impact their deed has had on the
lives of real people. "I knew I had hurt my family and friends who
trusted me, yet I never considered the wider effects," writes one prisoner who took part in the program. "I was so caught up in the actual
event that brought me to prison that I hadn't even thought of reconciliation. These classes opened my eyes to the world, the way we're
all connected. I will never be the same. Maybe one day, I'll get to tell
my victim's family, 'I'm sorry,' face-to face."

We live in a world where's there's a lot to say "I'm sorry" for. The
Archbishop Desmond Tutu helped found South Africa's Truth
and Reconciliation Commission so that everyone could finally apolo-
gize to each other. Some have criticized the Commission as an extreme application of the principal of Christian mercy, allowing
wrongdoers to escape punishment through public confession, placing
the reweaving of the social fabric above rightful justice.

Others see it as a continuation of a radical experiment in mercy begun two thousand years ago and continued in fits and starts ever since. When Peter asks Jesus how many times he should forgive, Jesus rabbinically answers the question with a question: How many times do you think? Peter, deciding it would be wise to exceed the three times mandated by Pharisaic law, answers tentatively, "Up to seven times?" to which the holy Teacher responds, "I tell you, not seven times but seventy-seven times."

Far from being cheap grace, seventy-seven times takes everything, and more. Once Tutu had to sit and listen to a police torturer who had killed a man and used the grisly photos to intimidate his next victims. "He said of the man's death, 'It leaves me cold.' Then he told the person's name, and I nearly fainted. This was a friend of mine. And I put my head down on the table and wept. What could have eaten at the vitals of this man's humanity?" Only one perspective had gotten him through it all, Tutu explained: "When you are dehumanized, inexorably, I am dehumanized. If I want to enhance my humanity, then whether I like it or not, I must enhance yours."

Enhancing humanity's no cakewalk. But from what I've seen, it's not just for spiritual professionals or prodigies of conscience. I suspect it will be written into some future history that, after eras of assuming only real saints could ever get the hang of it, it was in our time that the doctrine of forgiveness finally took hold—took hold because it had to—from individuals forgiving individuals to entire peoples reconciling with those who warred against them. (For aren't all wars waged by parents of murdered children, children of murdered parents, brothers and sisters of murdered sisters and brothers?)

I wonder if we aren't seeing prefigurations of an age when the binding of wounds takes precedence over the binding of captives; the beginning of a new covenant to heal the damage done by not caring passionately enough what happens to each other. I get the feeling history has written only the first provisional lines of that story. If we can stick around awhile, it's going to be a page-turner.

11

ANOTHER LITTLE PEACE OF THE HEART

He maketh wars to cease unto the end of the earth;
he breaketh the bow, and cutteth the spear in sunder;
he burneth the chariot in the fire.
—*Psalm 46: 8–10*

A story I am ashamed to tell: When I was in the third grade, my younger sister broke my favorite toy. I yelled at her, she screamed back, and then, to my surprise, she launched herself at me in a fury, scratching me hard on the arm. My reaction was blind, unthinking; I raked my own nails down her forearm, making furrows that, to my shock, began to ooze blood. I was punished, but nothing cut so deeply as the guilt I'd felt at her pain.

I've wondered from time to time what happened in this primitive, instinctual tit for tat, a variant of any playground fight. Some kid pinches you, and you pinch them back: *There, now* you *know how it feels!* The word revenge doesn't quite cover it; in an odd way, it's more like enforced empathy, a need to make the other feel, first-hand and in rough proportion, the suffering they caused us.

"Revengefulness is that passion which ariseth from an expectation or imagination of making him that hath hurt us to find his own action hurtful to himself," wrote Thomas Hobbes in *Human Nature*. Put simply: See how *you* like it. From there, it's not such a leap from the dynamics of schoolyard rivalry to the logic of clan warfare: *Here's* what it felt like when you dishonored my family, terrified my child, killed my brother. Carried to its extreme, it is the twisted reasoning of warfare itself: *This* is what it is like to have your church destroyed, your crops burned, your city ruined; *now* do you understand?

On a typical day on the planet some fifty conflicts rage, from armed clashes of massed troops to guerilla skirmishes, civil uprisings, and border incursions, most of them classified as "low-intensity" (though scarcely so for the forty thousand whose lives they claim daily). The differences between sides—religious dogmas, nominal ethnicities—are often so tragically trivial, they only affirm the combatants' commonality. Even the most "just" wars seem heartbreakingly preventable had the victors in a previous conflict been kinder to the defeated, who rose up to become aggressors in the next. Despite their specifics, the basic narratives of territory, ideology, and historical grievance are so standard, all that's required is to fill in the blanks with the countries' names.

If we really want to heal our world, we'd better find an antidote beyond the topical remedies of truces and treaties. If war is an infection in the human system, its cure must lie in strengthening what it most directly attacks: compassion itself. If war deadens sympathy for the "enemy's" suffering, only compassion can restore it. If enmity sharply draws a bayonet-sharp distinction between self and other, only empathy can cross that line *(you in me, me in you)*. If strife builds up impenetrable armor (emotional; literal), then compassion calls for mutual vulnerability. If fighting is justified by some historic grudge, forgiveness destroys its rationale. If war is the repayment of blood debts, peacemaking assumes the infinite debt of love.

But how do we get there from here? We may all be in this together, but when I pick up the paper, I want to throw in the towel. Every official road to peace has a dotted white line running down the middle of it, like a perforation that says Just Tear Here.

*P*alestinians and Israelis must be the planet's unhappiest cousins, keeping the small house they cohabit in such constant uproar that it threatens to drag down the neighborhood. As of this writing, there have been an average of a hundred combined dead each month of the *intifada*. The grisly scorekeeping—Cain Kills Abel, film at eleven—makes me wonder if the leaders are statesmen or soccer hooligans armed with bombs, guns, and rocket launchers. From an aerial view, the ancient sibling rivalry between the children of Sarah and the children of Hagar——*Just get over it! No, you get over it!*—looks like a pointless dustup in a sandbox. But it's also a tinderbox that could set the world afire.

Here every square inch of soil is claimed by great narratives both congruent and contentious. Here God is said to have been last seen face-to-face—the One whose angels broke bread in desert tents, whose only Son was crucified and rose, whose last Prophet ascended heavenward on a white stallion. Underfoot are ancient bones cubits deep, every step a genuflection to the past. The living feel upon them the watchful eyes of ancestors whose begats go back to the Beginning of It All. Would that the Holy Land were not just hallowed ground, but a seedbed for the peace that passeth understanding.

That isn't the latest bulletin from Bethlehem, but there is news behind the news, and it comes down to this: three teenage girls sitting, knees nearly touching, their ancient enmity for now foresworn, trying to make a little peace of the heart. Amal, an eighteen-year-old West

Bank fundamentalist with streaked blonde hair and the face of a Modigliani madonna is telling an Israeli girl that Muhammad was the last Prophet and the Koran the final Book.

"God gave us all the land. He orders us into *jihad*—not just war, but holy war."

Rachel, a fair-skinned, heavyset Israeli girl in blue jeans, flushes deeply. "By Jewish law, all Israel is for the Jews. By Muslim law, it's all for the Arabs. The only way possible to fulfill these laws is by killing millions of people!"

Fatima, a dark, curly-haired Palestinian born in Israel, is caught in between. "I feel lost. I'm half-half. I can imagine the little child who saw her daddy shot by soldiers in Jenin *and* the Israeli kid whose mommy was blown up on a bus. My father was killed. Everyone I know has lost their cousins. I'm sick of these mean leaders who only want their place in history. Stop hurting each other, that's all I can think of."

The three are part of a group of some thirty girls* flown from an eternal war zone to a borrowed lakeside estate deep in the heart of rural New Jersey. Under the auspices of a program called Building Bridges for Peace (part of a larger organization called Seeking Common Ground), they will live together for two weeks, sleeping in one big room on air mattresses, their relationships a microcosm of internecine strife and a litmus for any hope of resolving it.

"I feel like I live in the middle of a stupid world," Rachel tells Amal and Fatima. "All that's important to me is you, and you. We're destined to live together in the same place at the end of the day. If I don't know you, it's easy to hate you. If I look in your eyes, I can't. "

Amal shrugs elaborately. "When we're here, who knows, maybe we're friends. When we return, you are my enemy again. My heart is filled with hatred for Jews." She says it bluntly, coolly, planting her flag. But I detect a wistfulness, the barest hope that her burden—of

---

* Some of their names have been changed.

poisonous rancor, of history's dolorous weight—might somehow be lifted from her shoulders.

"History," wrote James Joyce, "is a nightmare from which we're trying to awake." This is no high school civics debate, and Rachel's "stupid world" is no typical teenage plaint. There are Israelis here who one day soon will be girl soldiers carrying rifles that could be pointed at Amal—at sad Amal, whose uncle was arrested, released, and soon after shot dead in his home by soldiers; haunted Amal, who will never forget; vengeful Amal, who admires the *shaheed,* the suicide bombers; hard-hearted Amal, who has come here a hater but may secretly hope she can learn how to love.

A child of the second *intifada,* Amal has never met Jews who don't wear fatigues and combat boots. "She's one of the generation that 'did not know Joseph,'" says Melodye Feldman, the preternaturally calm American social worker who founded the programs. Melodye grew up as one of only three Jews in her Florida grade school. She remembers one of her friends groping the top of her head to feel for horns; remembers being jumped, kicked, thrown into puddles, coming home to her parents and sobbing, "If only they knew me, they would like me."

It could be the motto of her program. She has been bringing together Israeli and Palestinian teenagers for the past ten years with no other agenda than to place them in fertile soil for compassion, give them water and sunlight, and hope they grow. Melodye, who had been an Orthodox Jew and staunch anti-Palestinian until visiting East Jerusalem in 1989, was inspired to act after seeing firsthand the mounting despair among the youth of both sides. Meeting sometimes in secret with Palestinian counterparts, she proposed a program whose only goal was to shatter the stereotypes of the Enemy. "I didn't know what I was doing," she admits freely. "I just wanted to do something to give young people some hope." She designed a camp-style retreat for young women that would use every tool of empathy she could think up, cadge, or improvise. What resulted is a sort of living lab for peacemaking, its protocols honed through trial and error.

At the first Building Bridges program some girls, in close quarters with their adversaries for the first time in their lives, were desperate to leave, but Melodye had shrewdly confiscated their tickets and passports. "You're not your nationality here," she told them. "You're not your ideology, your religion, your history. All that counts is who you are as a person." The Palestinians had staged a demonstration, refusing to share tents with the Israelis. But then a freak storm blew in, full of Old Testament thunder and Koranic lightning. "They all got in tents together fast," says Melodye, "and snuggled up during the night."

The next morning, one Palestinian girl confided how soldiers had come to her home, beat her family, and discovering they were mistaken, left without apology or offer of medical care. Using a technique known as "compassionate listening," Melodye asked a Jewish girl to repeat the story in the first person, then describe the emotions it had made her feel—terror, anger, revenge, sadness. The Palestinian girl burst into tears. "My enemy heard me!" The Israeli girl wept with her, and they became fast friends. Melodye, a cheerful, unflappable forty-five-year-old whose sharp eyes, set in a soft, open face, convey that little escapes her attention, knew she was onto something. "As the saying goes, God gave us two ears and one mouth," she says, and so created a program devoted to just listening.

There hasn't lately been much listening in the Middle East. Even if the two sides had been so inclined, the background noise—the shouted slogans, the crackle of small-arms fire, the explosion of bombs in the market, the grinding of tank treads—muffles the dialogue. The kids are children of war, Melodye says. They've known little but stress and trauma, life in a garrison state, an occupied town, a refugee camp. Many have never met anyone from the opposing side. They are dispatched to her program by their respective communities, thinking they will champion their cause to the enemy's face.

Instead, they wind up literally taking their enemy's pulse: The first thing Melodye has them do is gently grasp each other's wrists. "They've never touched their 'enemy'; they have no idea what they feel like. Then suddenly it's like, 'Oh, warm! I feel blood beating!'"

A few of the kids have been to other programs—"youth diplomatic corps," one put it a little sarcastically—the kind where issues are debated and coexistence extolled. But Melodye doesn't want them to coexist; she wants them to care about each other. She's insistent on keeping it personal. *Fine,* she tells them, *keep your hate, if you must, but now just touch her hand, her face, look in her eyes, speak your heart.* These are kids who have yet to pick up weapons, but their minds are locked and loaded, ready to go off half-cocked. "Here, you just give those stares that could kill," Melodye tells them. "When you get back, you could do much worse. This could be your last chance to know the other side, their hopes, their dreams, what they're really feeling."

Melodye will try anything, silly stuff, to get them to drop their canned historical laments and encounter each other as people. They make life masks out of plaster, molding the wet goop over each other's faces, tracing the unknown contours. She gets them to form a soft machine by connecting to each other with motions and sounds, or sit in a circle singing nonsense songs, patting their own legs and those of their neighbors in a blur of rhythm. At their first meeting, staff members, mostly Palestinian and Israeli kids who've been through the program, loop rope "handcuffs" around the girls' wrists, entangling them in binational pairs, challenging them to get free of each other when tugging on one end only pulls the other end tighter. They're from a part of the world where symbols count, and the games are rich with metaphor. The singing, the touching, the laughter help them, when they sit in small circles and the hard ugly things are dragged into the light, to see each other without the suffocation of blanket judgments.

I chat with a Palestinian girl wearing a T-shirt with a cartoon gun shooting a little flag that says "Bang," knowing that when she returns home, the bullets will be real. "I had all these boys who wanted to marry me," she tells me. "One said if I didn't, he would bomb himself." I'm shocked, but she just giggles: Strapping on a suicide jacket if they can't win a heart is a common boast-cum-threat of lovesick West Bank suitors. Her fiancé is with the Palestinian intelligence service; his job is to ferret out the *ameel*, the collaborators—find them, report them, maybe hurt them. She doesn't want to reveal much more, but kids on both sides talk of violence with stunning casualness. For her, the *intifada* is always and everywhere; for the Israelis, it's wondering about the next bus bomb, worrying if, as citizen-soldiers, they'll be sent across the green line into the occupied territories.

*B*ut at this camp there are no dividing lines but the ones the girls brought with them and carry inside. I eavesdrop as they talk their teenage flotsam and jetsam of shoe styles and skin care, boys and CDs; girls who on both sides are every hue from freckled white to dark olive, who by their ancient genome are virtual half sisters. I find it hard to comprehend how deeply Other they are to each other.

"An enemy," wrote psychologist Karen Horney, "is an economical way to form an identity." Economical, but surely not cheap, with its costs amortized in collective tragedy. The Israelis are raised hearing about the horrors of the Holocaust and their state's David-and-Goliath victories over Arab foes bent on their annihilation. "We're shown the old family photos and it's 'Hitler got her, Hitler got him,'" Rachel tells me. "Every year on Holocaust Day, survivors lecture in the classrooms. One history final exam is mostly about the Holocaust. And then we all join the army."

The Palestinians grow up hearing about the *Nakba*, the Catastrophe of 1948, when according to dueling versions of history, they fled or were driven from their hereditary lands as Arab armies marched into battle against the Zionist Jews creating a nation in their midst. In the wake of utter defeat, living as refugees for generations, a stateless people in their own diaspora, they have taken guerilla commandos and suicide bombers for heroic role models.

"See, after fifty years of occupation, chaos, and resistance," sighs one of the Palestinian staffers, "we're all fucked up. To live as a refugee, it's the same as being subhuman. We're going to need years of national therapy. The whole Middle East needs therapy!"

Therapists have taken a keen interest in the conflict as a case study in how war and hatred take root in the human psyche and how they might be extirpated. Each side in the conflict, says Israeli psychiatrist Yitzhak Mendelsohn, sees itself as a victim of history struggling to survive in a hostile world, with the other side as the ultimate threat to its existence. Individual biography is woven into a collective narrative of woundedness—what he calls a "dependence on negative memory. People get hooked into a potent resentment that primes them for revenge and escalation. Hate becomes a way to create the illusion of power."

Mendelsohn, a quick, intense man with a neat black goatee, comes to his specialty in "ethnic national conflicts" from an intimate perspective: Grievously wounded in a Palestinian terrorist attack on a restaurant ("I got two bullets and needed twenty-five units of blood"), he is a self-described "victim without hatred." He is, he says quietly, "personally familiar with the psychological obstacles to peace." The task of reconciliation, he believes, is to break down the "symbolic scars that bind people to the group" and offer "some larger sense of 'we' to replace the victim identity."

Melodye has her own diagnosis. "Nations are stuck in a developmental phase approximating an adolescent identity crisis," she says, "refusing to compromise, seeing everything in black and white." It's hard to argue the point: geopolitics as teenage wasteland. An adult personality can selflessly give, but the world's nationalities are grabby, cliquish, defensive, obsessed with ego-boundaries. They announce, "It's my room and I can do what I want in it," leaving a mess for others to pick up after them. They gang up on weaker kids; they're hyper-sensitive; they lash out explosively. There is a line in the *Chatu-Shataha Shastra:* "Buddhas see delusion as the enemy / And not the childish who possess it." How many posturing politicians and gung-ho generals have the courage of these coltish girls who struggle to see through delusion to reality's shades of gray—and beyond, to life's true colors?

These kids who could soon be gazing down gun barrels at each other are just teenage girls with half-articulated thoughts and in-choate longings, still safety-pinning their identities to fit: One minute they're mouthing the slogans of the *intifada* or proclaiming the tenets of Zionism; the next they're tooling around doing figure eights on the pink Schwinn they found in the garage or teaching each other American country-swing steps.

"First they need to define the box they've placed themselves in," Melodye says, "then they can step outside it." In an early session, they're asked to list, in order, their most defining characteristics. A Jewish girl says, "Family, friends, music, Jewish religion"; another says, "Being from the city, being a high school student, clothes, travel." Other Jewish kids put "human being" first, or the environ-ment, or love of animals. But for most of the Palestinians, the list is more circumscribed: *Arab, Palestinian, Muslim, colonized, refugee.* It is the template of oppression, of a people defying erasure by carving a collective face in granite. If each side is living in an identity-jail, the Israelis' is medium security, the Palestinians' more like twenty-three-hour lockdown.

"Self-esteem is in large measure a function of the esteem accorded to groups of which one is a member," writes one social psychologist. As a result, he notes, "The sources of ethnic conflict reside, above all, in the struggle for relative group worth." It reminds me of a T-shirt I saw on a marcher in one of New York's ethnic parades: "It ain't where you at, it's where you from." (*No,* I wanted to say. *It is where you at. And here is a recipe for peace: 1) Cut pride into bite-sized pieces; 2) chew; 3) swallow.*)

This is not to argue against ethnicity, which is in any case a fact on the ground. In a homogenizing global society, with the unique wisdom of entire cultures being lost as surely as languages themselves are going extinct almost weekly, we need a counterweight against punch-card citizenship in a corporate McWorld. But without the translucent overlay of a common human identity, real peace is a mirage on the horizon.

"We're all of us brainwashed," Fatima, the Israeli-Palestinian, says to the circle. "We accuse each other with these phrases, but don't know what they mean. We want freedom? What is it? Words someone told you to say, not really coming from your heart. Seriously, where did you get all that stuff?"

"What do you think causes war?" Melodye asks them.

"History," says one.

"Injustice," says an Arab girl in a headscarf.

"Religion . . . leaders . . . misunderstanding," offer others.

"We do," says Fatima. There's a silence as it sinks in. "All of us. Without people buying into it, it wouldn't happen."

As the days go on, identities become more fluid. One minute they are pouring salt into each other's wounds, the next probing them as tenderly as private-duty nurses. They talk it through, feel it through, first in anguish, then in relief: "I don't want to kill *you.*" "Well, *I* don't want to kill you, either!" I hear ululation drifting in from the sunporch used by the Palestinian delegation, the yearning, keening vocals of Arab pop music mingling with sinuous Israeli rock from the dining room.

One night, they are told the story of the Seal Wife: A seal-woman is courted by a man from the shore. After they marry, he hides her sealskin in a chest. They have children. She forgets all about her free-swimming, aquatic life. But one day the woman unlocks the chest. She realizes her true identity has been concealed from her. Her life has been a lie. What should she do? Mixed groups of Palestinian and Israeli kids are asked to come up with different solutions. First, though, they must argue it through with each other.

"How about she decides to leave her husband and go back to the sea?"

"But she shouldn't leave her *children.*"

"She was just hypnotized by her husband; she's not in love with him!"

"That's not the children's fault!"

"Okay, how about she leaves with them and takes them to the edge of the ocean, but as she's going into the water, she realizes the children will drown and she turns back—"

"—yes, yes, that's better—"

"—but she says to her husband, 'No more lies!'"

One group has the Seal Woman fetch sealskins for her family "so they can all live as humans during the week and seals on the weekend." Great approbation from the audience at this clever dual-species menage. In another version, the woman gives the man an ultimatum: If he really loves her, he must join her and the children as a seal-man. "The man gives up everything for the woman—poetic!" yells a girl to general merriment.

What if, the story cleverly poses, you were a creature who could magically slip in and out of different skins, inhabit multiple domains? The alluring image of such freedom seems to exhilarate them. They are giddy with life's possibilities, who they will be still up for grabs, their fate open and beckoning.

The next morning, they make a list defining their mutual identity as women. They catalogue their strengths: giving birth, raising and educating children. "Women are more patient, smarter, and more tolerant," one declaims, to wide assent. They enumerate their common challenges: discouraged from working outside the home, treated as sex objects, blamed for divorce and even for not having more male children. And they make a list of why it's women who are best able to make peace: more open to making sacrifices, more skilled at negotiating, more willing to be flexible. Their great strength, they agree, is that they don't need to be "strong."

They're having a great time, but this isn't just Camp Runamoka, telling stories by the campfire, eating s'mores and singing "Where Have All the Flowers Gone?" Their ability to resolve their blood feud is a field test for peace on earth. If these girls can't find a way to love each other, what then? I find myself walking around with a lump in my throat, thinking how it has fallen to them to do what their foolish leaders will not.

*T*he next day, paper bags labeled with the toughest hot-button issues are put in the center of the room, and each girl is asked to write down a phrase that best expresses her feelings about it. The responses are scrawled in magic marker on big white pieces of paper and posted on the walls.

Under "Zionism," an Israeli has written, "idealists who fought to come back to their country," and a Palestinian, "an evil organization that wants to kill all the Arabs in the world."

Under "Palestine," a Palestinian has written, "a dream that will come true, my homeland forever, my soul," and an Israeli has scrawled, "hostile territory, a danger for my existence."

Under "suicide bomber," the Israelis write "a killer" and "a dead murderer"; and the Palestinians, "a blessed person," "a winner in the next world," and, chillingly, "what I hope to be."

The kids shuffle from poster to poster, subdued, disbelieving. Now it's all been shoved out into the open, every threat and calumny; their faces are ashen at this secret ballot of fear. I can hear everyone's heart thud in the silence; it's suddenly a roomful of hunted rabbits.

"I see these words and I feel scared and angry and want to leave," says one Israeli girl.

Tears tremble on eyelashes, overspilling rims of reddening eyes as they attempt to smile through the pain, as if to spare others, or cling to their sinking hopes. A passed Kleenex box quickly empties.

"It hurts so much that each of us has deep hatred for the other. It's like you've been sleeping in the same room with a person who wants to get rid of you." My notes don't say whether this was spoken by a Palestinian or an Israeli; it's irrelevant.

The dire mood is fleetingly broken by the town's Funny Bunny Ice Cream truck careening around the corner outside, blaring its tinny recording of the Disney anthem, "It's a Small World After All." A few kids who recognize it laugh at the irony, but it's not a small world, not at all. It's a vast one, and they're lost in it.

As the tears dry, they're more curt, defended; they put on their game faces. "I feel proud to be Arab, proud to write these words about *jihad* and *shaheed*," says Amal defiantly. They trot out their litanies of grievance, their sullen prejudices. But they also seem to recognize something momentous is occurring. For once in their young lives, the truth has been laid bare, a force to be reckoned with—unpredictable, frightening, liberating. "These words on paper are our biggest fears," says Fatima. "They're what we're hiding behind our laughing faces, being dishonest one to the other. I want to learn about them from you."

Later, they are asked to build a bridge out of arts and crafts supplies. As they sort through popsicle sticks and pipe cleaners, Rachel and Fatima tell Amal, "We're here to listen to anything you want to say." But Amal shakes her head. She doesn't want to talk. "I just want to draw a bridge," she says tersely. "A bridge that's been broken."

It sometimes seems the bridge has been broken since time began.

What are the root causes of war, of millenia of hatred and strife? Those who study conflict look at everything from politics and economics, history and religion, child-rearing methods and marriage customs. But some point to a key human (and for that matter, primate) emotion that, in individuals and nations alike, seems to drive the cycles of violence: humiliation. "People would often rather die than live with such a sense of shame," writes one psychologist. "Even considerations of self-interest become irrelevant." The need for recognition, to be heard and seen, is universal. The Nazis cunningly appealed to restoring German pride after the crushing settlement imposed by the victors of World War I. In 2001, a nameless man—was it in the streets of Cairo, Karachi, Jakarta, Damascus?—cried out from among a crowd that cheered 9/11: "You Americans think we are nobody, like you are the only human beings," he said. "Now you have heard us. Now you know we, too, are men!"

Shame is a wound to the very sense of self. Palestinians speak of the daily humiliations of border crossings ("We're herded into a chute like cattle," one girl tells me bitterly), of grinding poverty and strutting Occupation soldiers. One girl tells me how her father died in an ambulance held up for four hours at an Israeli checkpoint outside Jenin even as his heart gave out. He was forty-seven. "I had thoughts about becoming a bomber," she says. "But I realized when I came to this camp last year that there was nothing worse than to lose my life to make others die. The responsibility for this suffering, it's not Jew or Arab; it's this circle of history, of violence with no beginning or end."

Humiliation is surely not just the province of the Arabs. "For Jews in general and Israelis in particular," says a writer in the Jewish magazine *Tikkun,* "there is a lasting form of shame associated with having been vulnerable and victimized during the Holocaust . . . a determination 'never again' to be subject to such humiliation as to be helpless prey to a ruthless predator."

*T*he Holocaust Museum is a marble building like others in the nation's capital, a massive stone cube devoid of postmodernist histrionics, built to last for as long as history shall endure. As I walk through the entrance, passing a sculpture of a deconstructed black swastika, its arms twisting to the sky, I see a quote by President Jimmy Carter carved into the wall: "We must harness the outrage of our memories to stamp out oppression . . ." In the company of the Palestinian and Israeli girls, bussed down for an all-day field trip, it strikes me as a very Middle Eastern sentiment: Isn't this what the Palestinian *shaheeds* think they are doing? And the far right-wing Israeli settlers? All over the world, there is no problem harnessing outrage; the problem is keeping hold of the reins.

A perky museum guide highlights the exhibits she feels are "pretty neat—check them out"; the atrium, she suggests, is "a fabulous place to take pictures." But the museum is not designed as a tourist trap; it is a funnel into moral blackness. To walk its corridors is to follow the saga of a civilization's premeditated murder of compassion itself. First the Nazi book-burnings, harbingers that failed to kindle the world's alarm. Then the artificial creation of stark ethnic divisions: here the lurid charts of racial mug-shots; there a poster promulgating laws against "racial defilement" and a glass case full of "scientific" meters of curious design: calipers to measure skulls, and eye- and hair-selection guides in handheld compacts for white-gowned nurses to classify children for extinction. I read through a 1934 document from the managing director of the effort that dutifully pledges "to provide the physician of our German body politic with the material for his examination . . . of whether diseased conditions must be cured by corrective interventions."

The visitor's claustrophobia grows as exhibits show all cultural institutions—art, music, theater, medicine—suborned in service of the deranged hygiene of ethnocentrism. In his 1906 book *Folkways,* W. G. Sumner catalogued the ubiquity of the self-versus-other distinctions made by tribal cultures the world over. "Each group nourishes its own pride and vanity, boasts itself superior, exalts its own divinities, and looks with contempt on outsiders."* There are only a few insidious steps to regarding the other as subhuman; astonishing, unthinkable, but to anthropologists, sickeningly familiar. Sumner notes in a later work that nearly all the tribes he had studied called themselves by names that meant simply " 'men,' 'the only men,' or 'men of men'; that is, 'We are men, the rest are something else' . . ." Modern anthropologists point to the Amazonian Yanomamo, whose fierceness seems to derive in part "from their belief that they were the first, finest and most refined form of man to inhabit the earth, and that all other peoples are a degeneration from their pure stock." Among the headhunting Amazonian Mundurucu, rival tribes were linguistically lumped with game animals, providing a conceptual frame to overcome the natural aversion humans have, along with all other creatures, to methodically killing their own kind.

The Holocaust Museum corridors narrow as Hitler's power grows and the tapes of crowds *Sieg Heil*ing themselves hoarse grow louder, engulfing the visitor in a gathering dark. The museum's architects have designed passages that dead-end in cul-de-sacs, emplaced red-and-white-striped barricades. You don't know where you're going until you get there, and even then, you're not sure you haven't been treading a no-exit circle. One exhibit tells the saga of the Lodz ghetto, sealed in April 1940, trapping 164,000 Jews behind bricks and barbed wire, forcing them to live with "overcrowding, starvation, disease, and the stench of raw sewage," the first of four hundred ghettos created to wall off the millions.

---

* In a poll taken in Kosovo in 1997, two years before the genocidal "ethnic cleansing," Serbs and Albanians living in that province were asked to chose which words they thought most accurately described themselves and each other as a group. When it came to themselves, the Albanians selected adjectives like "hospitable, peaceful, courageous, clean, honest, intelligent, united, and hard-working." The Serbs characterized themselves nearly identically. But Serbs described Albanians as "united, those who hate other nations, treacherous, backward, rough, hard-working, exclusive of other nations, and selfish." And, predictably, the Albanians chose virtually the same words to describe the Serbs. With ghastly consequences, both groups lay claim to laudable traits for their own identities, while threatening traits are projected outward.

From there, you traverse a wooden catwalk and embark on a journey into Hades: a railcar with a thin shaft of light falling onto a blood-red wooden floor. Pathetic piles of abandoned luggage, hand mirrors, hairbrushes, and toothbrushes. The malignant efficiencies of industrialized murder: canisters of Zyklon-B; a narrow bunk from one of the Auschwitz barracks where skeletal prisoners were stacked like pieces of cordwood awaiting the fire. Relics of Dr. Joseph Mengele's infamous Block 10, where the most gruesome medical experiments were performed; photos of sterilized children, of bodies disassembled like department-store manikins. A line from Elie Wiesel: "Never shall I forget the little faces of the children whose bodies I saw turned into wreaths of smoke beneath a silent blue sky . . ."

I see one girl who'd proclaimed herself a would-be *jihadi* in tears. An Israeli, overcome, sags against the shoulder of a Palestinian friend, who clasps her tight. I see others walking slowly, arms around each other's waists.

The museum is a temple of doom, a place of stone and metal where the only forgiving material is the wood of the railway transports and the hard slats where the damned slept on top of each other. When it opens out at last into the muted, sifting sunlight of the white marble Hall of Remembrance, I finally break down and weep. When I emerge, I see Amal and two of the more militant Palestinian girls in checked kaffiyeh photographing each other as they sign the visitors' book in Arabic. I feel touched.

Yet there is something odd as they mug for the camera, flashing their V-signs. A whisper goes through the bus on the ride home, building to an agitated buzz. An Israeli who reads Arabic says the girls wrote something terrible, something unthinkable. What they had inscribed, in large, curlicuing letters, was: "Death to All Jews."

By the time they get back to camp, all the girls are in an uproar. They gather in knots to scream and to cry, beside themselves.

"It's none of your business what I write!" shouts Amal. She claims it's freedom of speech. "The guard told me to write what I felt, and this is what I feel. If Jews went through all this suffering, why do they make us suffer, too? *I've* suffered. I get to say it."

"So now it's public!" a Jewish girl yells back. "It proves you want to hurt us, to exterminate us! I can't believe I spend a week with you, and now I know you want me dead."

"Don't you feel sad at the piles of bodies, the millions who died?" another Israeli demands, in tears. "For a few hours, you couldn't just leave off your suffering and feel ours?"

But this is just the point. A quiet, lissome Palestinian who has barely spoken all week shouts: "We've seen bodies, too! What do you expect? We go through hell because of you. A ninety-year-old Holocaust survivor at least has had some happiness now, for himself, for his children. I don't know how much longer I can go on. One day when I'm sick and tired of all this, I might blow myself up!"

A shocked gasp goes through the room. It takes me by surprise, too, though it shouldn't have: Many Palestinians saw in the museum not the sorrowful history of the Jews, but a mirror of their own plight. They did not, *could* not empathize; the pain of the other only reminded them of their own.

"Ghettos, checkpoints, identity cards, this is my reality back home," one told me. "A camp with barbed wire, surrounded by soldiers, the streets filled with sewage. My dad grew up in a refugee camp, and then me. I saw *me* in that museum—me every day, not fifty years ago. I can't compare it to medical experiments and extermination. But I felt defensive: This is happening to us, too."

Amal will bend only this far: "I should have written death to all Israelis, not death to all Jews." One of the Israelis spits out, "You expect to be treated as a human being, but you don't act like one. You don't *deserve* human rights!"

Amal's eyes go hard and glossy, her face immobile as a basilisk. The lowest blow, for them, for anyone, has been struck. "It's the Israeli soldiers," she says, her voice finally breaking a little, "who shout at you, 'You don't deserve to be treated as human.'"

hoah. Nakba. My people's historical disaster is more horrible than yours; its wounds fresher, its losses more enduring, its anguish more palpable, its injustice a sharper blade. But is there no end to it, each tragedy planting the seeds of the next? The Serbs who oppressed the Muslims in the ethnic cleansing of the late 1990s felt *they* had been oppressed by the Muslim Ottoman Turks, the injury of their defeat still throbbing after six hundred years. The unhealed wound is the psychoanalytic nubbin of the problem; everything else, the fighting and the oppression, can seem like mostly acting out. The whole planet wired with big red sticks of dynamite like an old Warner Brothers cartoon, the close-packed explosive of unassuaged anguish, a fuse waiting for the right matchstick of a hatred only kindness can snuff out.

"If we could read the secret history of our enemies," wrote Henry Wadsworth Longfellow, "we should see sorrow and suffering enough to disarm all hostility." But in many places around the world, this equation is forbidden to have an equals sign. "The Jewish community would be up in arms," says Melodye, if someone dared to compare one people's ultimate tragedy of genocide with another's of exile and oppression. "They would be called a self-hating Jew, anti-Israel."

In May 2004, Israel's justice minister, himself a Hungarian-born Holocaust survivor, criticized a plan to demolish Palestinian homes in Gaza. As quoted in a *New York Times* story headlined "Offering Empathy," he told Israeli radio: "I did think, when I saw a picture on the TV of an old woman on all fours in the ruins of her home looking under some floor tiles for her medicines—I did think, 'What would I say if it were my grandmother?'" His remarks created a wave of national outrage. Scolded a fellow cabinet minister: "Any analogy, even hinted at . . . has no place in any form."

Primo Levi writes with grim eloquence in *The Drowned and the Saved* of the pain seared into collective memory: "The injury cannot be healed; it extends through time, and the Furies, in whose existence we are forced to believe . . . deny peace to the tormented." But it must be healed, lest the injury be transmitted down through generations, forever blighting new lives. There is hardly time to wait for national policies and official proclamations. What's needed are private edicts of empathy, little peaces of the heart. The work couldn't be harder, or more humbling: the hearing and telling of the world's most painful stories; the emotional truths that are too hot to handle alone.

I watch as Rachel and Amal attempt to mirror each other's feelings in front of the group, trying to neutralize even a scintilla of the elemental toxin. Their body language says it all. Arms folded, legs crossed, heads turned to the side, barely glancing at each other, they are stoic, removed, their looks searing. They repeat each other's words with smirks and rolling eyes. They interject their own opinions, Rachel taking a moral position, citing history and ethics; Amal an emotional one, claiming the Jews are blind to the suffering under their noses.

It seems as if there can be no meeting ground, for nobody's pain is dispensable, not even for a second. The conversation advances a few notches—"We need to point to the tragedy for humanity," a Palestinian suggests—but I notice something happening that is beyond words. Even in the midst of their outrage, the kids, Israeli and Palestinian alike, are treating Amal not with ostracism, but with an outpouring of affection. She had done her worst, walked up and detonated her nail-bomb of hate-speech in a supreme shrine to memory, and yet they refuse not to love her. She pretends not to notice at first, or to care, but when Rachel, leading a game, asks Amal to come play, I see a quick flash of relief. She hesitates only a moment before joining in.

The next day has been scheduled on the calendar as a day of silence. Before it officially begins, Rachel approaches Amal, who wears a black T-shirt spelling Mustard in jagged yellow letters. "Look, I know I will never fully understand your pain," she says awkwardly, her tone struggling against formality, "but I'm sorry for what happened to you in your life. I might seem only angry at you, but I was hurt, too. I know you wrote those words because you thought no one knew your suffering." Amal, gazing into the middle distance, finally nods with the smallest of smiles. Rachel tells me later: "All that day, we communicated with looks and hands. And when I could turn to her with words, we were talking again about this and that."

Rachel later wrote a short story that is, for an Israeli, a traitorous heresy, comparing the Hebrew concept of *milhemet hakodes,* the holy struggle to preserve one's humanity against all that seeks to erase it, with the "holy war" of jihad. Could these vile acts, she wondered, stem from the same desperate drive of a people to assert a sense of self-worth?

"People call me a moral relativist for seeing both sides," says Melodye. "They pat me on the head and say I'm naïve for thinking I can make peace this way. But I know that even the smallest steps are good. I tell them it's messy work here on the ground, but one by one, people really do change; and those who do, change others. It may take generations, but real peace will come."

In small ways, it already has. One of the Palestinian staff, Muna, confides to me, "I used to completely deny the Jews' suffering. Then I became close to an Israeli and realized, all this horror happened just fifty years ago. Their parents are orphans. They're all in recovery." Her sense of empathy had come to her unexpectedly. Muna's brother is still, after years, in Israeli administrative detention. A former athlete, he has nerve damage in his wrists, which she claims came from a prison beating and from "being stretched" in interrogation.

"Years ago, when I came here, I was ready to blame," she says. "I was prepared to respond to being attacked, but when you see they're actually listening, saying, 'I'm really sorry you go through this,' it shocks you. It was my first contact with Israelis other than the guards at the checkpoints, the soldiers who hurt my family. It left a stamp on me, inside of me." She became friendly with one Israeli girl. "I realized we were both sixteen-year-olds who can't live without fear, both of us. Why can't I invite her to my home—*why?*

"My hopes and dreams for a country haven't changed," she adds.

"We need a homeland. I won't forget my suffering. But I'm willing to forgive the minute that suffering is recognized. We're looking toward the fruit; not us, but later, thirty years ahead, for our children."

More than four hundred girls have crossed Melodye's bridges for peace. All have been changed in some way, some more visibly than others. There have been Israeli girls who resolved to endure the social stigma of not serving in the army. Some have become peace activists. One Palestinian is now a leading environmentalist, enlisting people on both sides to save the fragile desert ecosystem they all share; another, to the ire of the fundamentalists in her community, has become a feminist.

R'wan, a Palestinian staff member with blue hair, a pierced tongue, and a tattoo of a Chinese ideogram she says means "Love, Woman, Friendship," first came as a stone-thrower in the Bethlehem *intifada*—a "hardcore militant," she says. But she was touched when, months later, an Israeli who had been her archnemesis at camp was the first to call her when her school was bombed, even before any of her Palestinian friends.

"I have to take it from my society for this," R'wan says, "for saying that I love Israelis." She would cry when an Israeli bus was bombed, while her cousins cheered. "I had to worry if I went back with new ideas I'd never be accepted in our society, even in my own family. Peacemakers are so rejected in our community." She's studying to be a schoolteacher, hoping to reconcile the alternate-reality curricula, the warring maps imposed on the same geography. In some Middle Eastern schools, the scurrilous forgery of the *Protocols of the Elders of Zion* is still read as nonfiction. Palestinians are taught that Jews secretly run the world. Jews believe the Palestinians aim to complete Hitler's unfinished project. Each people defines itself as a victim of hatred and oppression, a refugee and an outcast. I once passed one of those impossibly specialized stores you find on New York's Lower East Side whose sign said it sold only "non-reverse image mirrors." I know the perfect place to open a franchise.

But now the girls have taken out their vanity mirrors. After their day of silence, the schedule calls for a "spa night." Their only instructions are to spoil each other, pamper each other, make each other feel special. Once again, there's laughter as they massage each other's hands and feet. I flash back to my time with the bonobos: social grooming behavior; female alliance. They are subverting war and hatred and death with red toenail polish. Tentatively, but with growing courage, these children are doing what their childish leaders are afraid to do: open their unguarded hearts.

*T*ime is growing short. Soon they will be going home. Now it's in earnest, their heads bent toward each other, the talk urgent, intimate. Suddenly they're on fire to say everything and anything.

"We haven't finished the job we started," Amal tells me. I detect an unexpectedly wistful note in her voice. The signs still leer menacingly from the wall: Settler: "someone in my family I love"; "someone who deserves to be killed." Israel: "place I love"; "place I hate." But the enmity has flickered on and off like a worn-out lightbulb filament. Curtains have parted, letting in shafts of natural light. What they say they want in their circle today is so ingenuous: "I hope to have a best friend here, to visit each other when we get back, to meet each other's family." When a Palestinian says, "I only hate soldiers who kill my neighbors," one militant Israeli, a middle-class kid in a horse-camp T-shirt, allows, "If someone was doing this to me, I might hate them, too." One girl, the nationality doesn't matter, tells me incredulously, "I wanted them to know I have pain, too, but that's exactly what they're telling me!" Can the chain of violence be weakened, link by human link, until it finally snaps?

The final night is a gala feast, a kosher shindig thrown by a local Jewish organization: homemade *gefülte* fish and matzoh ball soup, pot roast and roast chicken, potato kugel and carrot *tsimmes* with little marshmallows. An elderly man in a toupee, one of the organization's board members, approaches a cluster of Israeli and Palestinian girls that includes Amal. He introduces himself as a Holocaust survivor and, pointing to the Palestinian girls, counts jocularly: "One, two, three, four—after this week, I'll bet we have four less suicide bombers."

Amal's face drains of blood. The room grows still. "You think we're all *terrorists*?" She looks as though she will faint. Then her eyes flash back to life, and something shocking occurs. Amal the warrior, Amal the stoic, Amal who has carried her hard ball of pain like some priceless heirloom—Amal cries. The invisible chalice of tears she has balanced without spilling a drop falls, breaks into a thousand shards, splashes out all its contents. Amal cries, and she can't seem to stop.

And the girls gather around Amal, their own angry one who had secretly gotten used to being treated like just herself; who had opened just a little in the sun of their affection; who had begun to sense what it might feel like to be sprung from identity-jail. All of them, Jews and Muslims and Christians, Palestinians and Americans and Israelis, surround her, telling her, *You are* not *a terrorist, you are* not *the enemy; we* know *you, you are* Amal. The man, too, stricken, apologizes for having missed what was essential but invisible to the eye. And Amal's smile, that fugitive always running, always hiding, darts back in for a moment.

"Soon she's returning to the *intifada*," says Melodye. "They all are." But one of the militant Palestinian kids, the one who had talked about blowing herself up, has approached her quietly, surreptitiously, about training as staff. "She's recognized that what she's been taught in books, what the media has portrayed, what both sides want them to believe about the other, it's all false. She told me, 'You can't make borders to keep people's hearts from meeting.' She says she wants to be a force for change."

They all will be, in their own way. These children belong to families, and families to clans, and clans to villages, and villages to nations. Have these two weeks implanted an antivirus of compassion that will spread slowly through their own societies? There's no telling how far the tentative words of peace they have spoken to each other here will reverberate. In the desert air, voices carry.

That past week there'd been little signs of hope back home. Israel had released five hundred prisoners. On the Palestinian side, a shaky truce, a *hudna* of no bombings, had held for two months straight. But I don't know that any of this was a greater achievement than Rachel and Fatima and Amal's bridge. They finally did finish it, a span of green popsicle sticks over which walk three resolute, Day-glo pipe cleaner figures. Amal has pressed her blue paint–saturated hand onto the construction paper, joining their palm prints of pink and purple. Like the hands outlined in ochre on the cave walls of Lascaux, bearing witness to people thirty-five thousand years distant, theirs is a primeval act of self-declaration: *My blood is your blood. I, too, am human.*

J oseph Sebarenzi knows what it is like to struggle to affirm his humanity. Or so I'd been told. A friend had suggested I look him up if I were ever in Washington, D.C., saying only he was a Rwandan refugee with some stories to tell. But when I call to confirm our two o'clock meeting, Joseph tells me in a soft voice he's had a few friends over that afternoon and they're running late. Might I come by closer to suppertime?

I only have a few hours before my train, I tell him, insistent. I really need him to fit me in. True, I'd scheduled our meeting on short notice—as an afterthought, really—but I'm hard-pressed to understand how he would prefer hanging out with his buddies to a chance to speak on the record.

When I ring the buzzer in the lobby, he doesn't buzz back but comes down to greet me. Impossibly tall and gracile in the Tutsi way, he refuses my hand and with a broad smile bends from his lofty height to give me a hug. When we enter his apartment, he introduces me as "my friend" and gestures to an imposing man with gold teeth and a dull yellow sport jacket. "Please meet His Majesty." I think he's joshing until the big man offers his card, embossed with a simple "His Majesty King Kigeli V of Rwanda." Another man in the pink clerical shirt of an Anglican priest gets up from the couch to shake my hand. He turns out to be Rwanda's archbishop. I'm mortified to realize Joseph has interrupted a long-planned, high-level meeting to see me, too polite to refuse.

Joseph's face has a sweetness to it that belies his bitter life story. He was born in the 1960s during the first civil war and remembers having to flee into the bush with his parents. In 1990, the nightmare began all over again. The dominant Hutu tribe had acceded to power and set out to destroy their hereditary enemies, the Tutsi, once and for all.

The Hutu leaders took a page from the dogeared playbook of Hitler and Stalin, Pol Pot and Milosevic. First came the society-wide propaganda campaign through the radio, newspapers, and leaflets. "They would make ugly proverbs about us," Joseph recalls. "Like, 'If you invite a Tutsi to be a guest in your home and give him the living room to sleep in, by morning he'll be in your bed.'" The Tutsi were soon forced to carry Identicards. "A card with 'Tutsi' stamped on it meant 'enemy.' You'd interview for a job, all the requirements were met, but there was a policy of quotas. I had a sociology degree, but I couldn't be hired." (Social theorists call this process "badging": An in-group finds ways to distinguish itself from an out-group, whether through genetic traits like skin pigment, stature, hair texture, and facial features; or artificial signifiers of clothing, adornment, headgear, tattoos; or manners, rituals, etiquette, speech patterns. "Irrational beliefs serve the purpose far better than rational ones," one anthropologist has noted. "They are easier to produce.")

Soon enough, cards and quotas were supplemented by an official campaign of bizarre racial slurs. "They called us *inyenzi*. It means 'cockroach.' You see," Joseph says with a sad smile, "a cockroach is an insect found everywhere; you try to kill them and kill them, but you're never finished." The word grated ceaselessly from every radio in the country: *Inyenzi, inyenzi,* or sometimes just "snake," free-associating the Tutsis' tall, thin stature with a symbol of evil.

First empathy, then compassion, and finally all sense of human commonality withered under the incessant barrage of racial propaganda. It amazed him, Joseph recalls, how the words wormed their way into his own brain, making him ashamed of how he looked, of the way he walked, the Tutsi's long, graceful stride. "It can shape your mind until you no longer admire even the beauty of the woman you want to marry," he tells me, shaking his head.

Seeing the handwriting on the wall, he sent his wife and infant son away and, after he was jailed and then released, fled the country. A month later, the genocide began. The virus spread fast, replicating its malignant memes through the pamphlets and broadcasts that inflamed the Hutu populace to turn upon Tutsi neighbors who had once been their friends, even murdering their own Tutsi wives and half-Tutsi children. (The radio exhortations so fanned the deadly grass-fires that a pop singer whose malicious melodies had dominated the airwaves would be among the first war criminals brought to trial in Rwanda.)

Between April and July 1994, as many as a million people were massacred, mostly hacked to death with machetes. Joseph's father and mother, who had insisted they could weather the new crisis until suddenly the roadblocks and killers were everywhere, perished along with his seven sisters and brothers, and many of his nephews, nieces, and cousins. "It is a pain that is difficult to describe," Joseph says, his eyes welling up. After a long minute of silence, he says almost apologetically, "I cannot find a word to express that."

In the aftermath of the war, Joseph returned to help in reconstruction, creating an assistance association for the survivors. He was eventually elected to parliament. Many Tutsi, he says, wanted him to avenge their abuse from his new position of power. "Friends would tell me, this guy or that guy should be arrested. Sometimes I would refuse; other times I would say, 'Yes, I'll arrest them,' and then do nothing. I had friendships with Hutus, but I had to keep this secret, or I would be seen as a traitor.

"From talking to them, I knew that the Hutus who'd participated felt guilty. They had killed and killed, they told me, out of fear the Tutsi would come back and kill *them*. I didn't want revenge. I knew their sense of guilt could make them more dangerous in the future.

"Besides," Joseph says, "I had no courage to arrest the Hutu people in my village."

I'm puzzled—he certainly seems like a brave man. Then I realize he's using the word in the French sense: He didn't have the *coeur,* the heart for it.

"Yes," he agrees, "I had no feeling, no power inside me, to hurt these people back."

Helping to translate between imprisoned Hutus and their Tutsi captors, he could see they were in "the same situation of dehumanization as we Tutsi had been. And one day," he says with some amazement, "I ran across the man who had been the mayor of my village, who had been very active in the genocide. He was probably the one who oversaw the killing of my family! I remembered how I used to see him in the village, official, powerful, beautifully dressed. Now I saw him in a prison camp, suffering, in rags, reduced to nothing. And I instantly felt sorry. I had some money in my pocket and I gave it to him." An ambiguous smile plays around Joseph's lips. "I really don't know why I did that."

In 1997, to everyone's surprise, Joseph was elected as a compromise candidate for Speaker of the Parliament, the country's third most powerful post. He argued staunchly for a policy of reconciliation. "I made a speech that said if there was revenge, the virus would never stop. We are all already victims. I can't bring back my family. I didn't want it to be that the one who's powerful today overcomes the weak one, because then tomorrow it will be reversed all over again. Our children and grandchildren would be killed. So I do this for my grandchildren. I told the Hutus that I hadn't come to hurt them, that they shouldn't cry; but they all cried anyway, even though it's considered bad for a man to do so!

"I live for the idea to not pay back evil," Joseph says earnestly. "When I returned to my home village, I hugged the people who I knew had helped to kill my family." I must look a little dumbfounded. "You see, after the genocide," he explains, "it was a time of anger. I was thinking all the time, How do I care for my life, but also take care of others who are suffering? I saw that both were the same thing. The anger and resentment I felt toward those others was killing *my* body. *I* could have a heart attack and die."

More than that, it had dawned on him that the survivors had a great and difficult duty. "I realized reconciliation maybe doesn't come first from the perpetrators, but the victims," he says thoughtfully. "Maybe victims must take the first step. They should help the oppressors to move from guilt to apology to reconciliation." He seems surprised when I mention that this was one of Martin Luther King's great doctrines: the paradoxical power of the oppressed to restore the oppressor's blighted humanity. "This is good," he says with his big smile. "I like this. I am glad I am not alone in my crazy ideas."

*J*oseph and Melodye and a smattering of Middle Eastern teenagers do not a mass movement make. They are ordinary people who decided to take the ideals of the great social prophets and apply them right here, right now. They are trying to grasp hold of a peace beyond religion, ethnicity, and politics, one that can be manually fashioned with their own two hands.

"I don't want my opinion attached to some stupid political leader or to any country," seventeen-year-old Fatima told me at the peace camp. "I'm an Arab, yes, but I feel like I'm a world citizen. I've seen people change if I just listen to them, even when what they're saying are the hardest things to hear. Everyone around me says I should get real," she says, rolling her eyes. "That I haven't seen the way this world is. But I'm going to keep my water clear of anything that could poison it. I think that innocence is realism, too."

She's not the only one. When the United Nations General Assembly proclaimed an "International Decade for a Culture of Peace and Nonviolence for the Children of the World" in 2000, a hundred nations became signatories. Thousands of local, national, and international organizations have now formally joined a global movement for building, from the ground up, societies based on peace, starting with the hearts and minds of their own kids.

It is a typical U.N. manifesto, full of dromedary phrases made by committee: "sustainable development . . . transparency . . . tolerance . . . solidarity . . . harmony . . . meeting the needs of the people"; the highflown diplomatic equivalent of *yadda-yadda-yadda*. It is also nothing less than a first-draft blueprint for a compassionate world.

"In the past," read a summary, "the struggle for human rights and justice has often been violent. But violence reproduces the culture of war—authoritarian, hierarchical . . . and above all, mobilized to destroy 'the enemy.' Now we must build a culture of peace . . . to liberate the oppressor as well as the oppressed." From that standpoint, it is a revolutionary broadside filled with incendiary (and one hopes, *anti-incendiary*) ideas. A formal declaration of interdependence, perhaps; a founding charter for a Sane New World.

Once King Solomon dreamed that God appeared to him and

offered to grant his fondest wish. Solomon asked only, "Give, then, Your servant a listening heart." Can something as simple as listening and being heard liberate the world? And would it be too much to agree, once and for all, that the heart is the country to which we all belong, and love the only state we owe our allegiance?

12

THE BELOVED COMMUNITY

Grandfather
Look at our brokenness.
We know that we are the ones
Who are the divided
And we are the ones
Who must come back together.
—*Ojibway Prayer*

. . . The end is the creation of the Beloved Community
. . . It is this love that will bring about miracles
in the hearts of men.
—*Martin Luther King*

I happened to come to New York a few days after the world blew apart, into a stricken city of the walking wounded. A charnel breeze, burnt and bitter, blew through the ghost town of TriBeCa, making the lungs and the heart ache. Like everyone, I couldn't sleep; I'd snap on CNN at three in the morning, nod off with it still murmuring. Below my window, ad hoc choirs of passersby serenaded firemen at the station house next door, its bricks festooned with Missing posters, homemade floral wreaths, and kids' crayon drawings of skyscrapers blooming with flame and cherry ladder trucks zooming to the rescue. I watched friends straggle back toward faith, or lose it.

U2's bittersweet ode to love, loss, and bravery, "Beautiful Day" dominated the airwaves. Beneath tragedy's skin, there were invisible sinews of tenderness. Even my most tough-minded friends seemed surprised at how catastrophe had catalyzed a sense of mutual belonging; had reawakened—on the street, in offices, cabs, and elevators—some instinct to be better, to love more. Despite the news testifying to an ineradicable streak of human brutishness, you could feel what anthropologist Stephen Gould called "the victorious weight of innumerable little kindnesses." It became impossible to relegate compassion to mere sentiment, to a poignant lump in the throat or a one-off act of charity. It was as basic as air.

But things gradually drifted, in fits and starts, back to normal. "Everyone was wide open," observed a friend, "but then they crusted over again." As the months passed, there were fewer uncalled-for hugs, tears, and smiles. Down went the "Our Grief Is Not a Cry for War" placards on Union Square; up went the velvet ropes that let some in and kept most out. Subway riders no longer wedged their bodies into a closing door so stragglers wouldn't be left behind. New York's patented *get-outta-my-way-I'm-going-places* street pushiness made a comeback. "People loved that tender we're-in-this-together feeling, however awful the cause," said my friend, a lifelong Manhattanite. "But they couldn't quite hang onto it."

How to understand this mysterious force at once fundamental and fugitive, emerging in crisis as our natural endowment, only to be crowded out by our pressing little agendas. To say nothing of our national ones: These days, the notion of building a more compassionate world takes a backseat to the dictates of security. It is a time of the hard-eyed realists. The secretary of defense sardonically quotes Al

Capone: "You will get more with a kind word and a gun than with a kind word alone." The peacemakers have been banished to the kids' table with the rest of the utopians. It is said we've crossed an historic threshold, from an interregnum of innocence to a new age of terror.

I don't believe it. Yes, there is awful public tragedy, wrenching private sorrow, the dire clangor of arms. Plague-dogs of rage and cynicism roam the planet's nameless back alleys (and some name-brand front offices, too). And we are *not* safe. I read it in the *Times;* I can read it in Thucydides. It is a long battle, this struggle between love and hate. But to live in a climate of fear, with its color-coded thermometer readings, means that men with box cutters, bullets, and bombs sit above us like kings. The hermetic paradox still holds: In the poison is the medicine. Hatred summons forth its unconquerable opposite. Still, if love is ever to triumph, it's not just knocking the haters off their thrones. What we need is a regime change of the heart.

That somber week in September, I'd adopted a group of stranded young Romanian actors, letting them crash on the couch. To escape the black hole of the moment, I took them to the Metropolitan, bought them their first-ever sushi. Waiflike kids who'd grown up under Ceausescu's vile dictatorship, they were mad for the Bard, spinning out lines from *A Midsummer Night's Dream* that swung from glum to giddy. When one girl got lost in the subway, a boy yelled in his Romanian-accented Elizabethan English, "So quick bright things come to confusion!" When depression stole over our itinerant band of players, another declaimed, "Turn melancholy forth to funerals: the pale companion is not for our pomp." In a funereal time, I was grateful beyond words for their company.

We walked toward the Site, its force of gravity pulling us south until we were halted at the barricade by terse Irish cops and narrow-eyed young soldiers with M-1 carbines. The gatekeepers looked shell-shocked; behind them, grim truths were being excavated by the hour. The sky above was a mottled bruise from the lingering miasm of vaporized glass and steel and bone; fused elements new to Earth sifted down from the plume over Ground Zero. One of my young friends softly intoned a stanza that was swallowed up by the rumble of a passing derrick. When we got home, I asked him what he'd said, and he wrote in my notebook in neat, schoolish penmanship: *Swift as a shadow, short as any dream / Brief as lightning in the collied night / and ere a man hath power to say "Behold!" / the jaws of darkness do devour it up.*

There seemed to be nothing to do but mourn and leave the cleanup to the uniformed municipal employees who now straddled the truncated skyline. I felt useless, but I couldn't imagine what I could do—what help I could be to the guys scooping up the horrific wreckage with cranes and dump trucks. I was unaware that behind the barricades something—something heartening, even wondrous— had escaped the jaws of darkness entirely.

Its epicenter was St. Paul's Chapel of Trinity Church, an eighteenth-century architectural gem at the foot of the towers that had survived miraculously unscathed ("standing defiant," in the mayor's phrase). A team of young parishioners and clergy had immediately reopened the chapel, and the entire world had flooded in. The Site had attracted Givers from every compass point (disaster experts call this the "convergence phenomenon"), some with official sanction, others fast-talking their way through police lines, all intent on supporting the rescue workers. Those city crews faced a disheartening task, searching around the clock for survivors in what was turning out to be a mass grave. But out of the cauldron of despair arose something beyond the ubiquity of death: a community based on, in the words of one volunteer, "trying to outdo one another in the showing of love."

It wasn't until I met Courtney Cowart that I understood the re-demptive secret overshadowed by the bellicose actors who have since held center stage. An attractive thirty-five-year-old theologian whose career path had taken her through professional ballet to studies in existential philosophy to TV advertising before finding her calling, she'd been in a church office a few blocks from the towers when the planes hit. She'd heard the percussive roar of a hundred floors pancaking, endured a sudden dark night as her building's ventilation system sucked in the black soot. She had made her way out through the chaos, managing to shepherd some visiting monks and clergy to safety before the second tower fell and she had to run for her life. "I was one of those gray ghosts coming up Fifth Avenue covered in ash," she tells me over breakfast in a Greek greasy spoon. It had been a near-death experience, she says, one that had kindled an overwhelming desire "to walk back into the enormity of the void" and somehow be of help.

The church's corporate types, she says, had seemed bureaucratically paralyzed and virtually incommunicado. Instead, a makeshift community of helpers sprang up of its own accord, like proverbial grass blades poking through pavement, and the ensuing stories are legendary: giant vats of Cajun food cooked up by a crew that materialized from New Orleans, truckloads of brand-new boots donated to workers whose own had virtually melted off in the smoldering pit. Under the auspices of the chapel's Reverend Lyndon Harris, and with Courtney as newly minted chief of staff, what had begun as a ragtag collection of food and aid stands planted amid knee-deep debris became a twenty-four-hour, all-volunteer support operation for the men and women digging through the rubble.

But there was a story behind the story, she says, that only those who were there really know—a mystery, a revelation of something so marvelous that many who witnessed it are still grappling with its impact. Ten thousand volunteers of every political stripe, income level, race and sexual persuasion, of every religion and no religion, had transubstantiated tragedy into an ad hoc affirmation of humanity's indestructible goodness of heart.

It was a defining event for those who experienced it, a harrowing of their old ground of belief and the planting of new, still-unknown seeds. Joseph Bradley, a hardhat crane operator who had helped build the World Trade Center when he was twenty-two, had volunteered to help pull up the wreckage. Like so many workers at the Site, he had been overwhelmed by the carnage, sinking to the curb after his first night under the savagely bright arc lamps, his head cradled in his hands. "That's when the Salvation Army kids appeared," he remembers, "in their sneakers with their pink hair and their belly buttons showing and bandannas tied around their faces. They came with water and cold towels and took my boots off and put dry socks on my feet.

"And then, when I got to Houston Street, a bunch more of these kids, all pierced and tattooed with multicolored hair, had made a little makeshift stage. They started to cheer as we came out, and that was it for me. I never identified with those people before, but I started crying, and I cried for four blocks. I can't tell you—I was taken so off guard.

"I got home and saw my wife, who asked, 'Joe, are you okay?' 'Sure!' I said. You know, the bravado came back. But she said, 'Are you sure? Go look in the mirror.' There I was with my filthy dirty face and just two clean lines down from my eyes." His voice quavers just slightly. "You become like a child after you get banged around a bit."

A community of love was the last thing anyone had expected to find in the mouth of Hell. Douglas Brown, a monastic prior, had stood upon the still-smoking Pile and imagined he was standing on a new Golgotha. The awesome devastation, he said, was "like a place of crucifixion." To him fell the soul-crushing task of blessing human remains as the heat of the wreckage coursed up through his shoes and the naked, ruined, crazily canted gothic arches from the tower's first floor seemed to mock all churches and sacraments.

One day, he saw a small, aged fireman digging through a slope of debris, searching with his comrades for his missing son, who had last been seen trying to rescue people in the collapsing South Tower. A week later, Brown saw a news photo of the same fireman tenderly carrying a body from the pile. He prayed that the man had found what he had been seeking.

"It struck me then, on the spot, that what I was seeing, acted out in front of me, was all that Jesus said about the shepherd who leaves the ninety-nine of his flock and goes looking for the one who is lost. This obsessive commitment not to leave anybody behind, even though it was clear no one would ever be found alive; that they still needed to be found, they needed to be cherished and honored."

The firemen's sacrifices formed the inspiration for many at St. Paul's. Said one volunteer: "Once the planes hit, the guys who went up to the top floor knew they weren't coming out, but they actually gave up their lives to try to save someone else. You can't put a price on that. That was what really made me want to go down there. I didn't care what I had to do, if they asked me to get down on the street and lick it with my tongue. I felt like I had to try in my own way to help. And whatever it took, that's what we did."

St. Paul's, with its gold-encrusted altar and fourteen sparkling cut-glass chandeliers, was the church of the eminent and powerful. George Washington had once bowed his head in his own reserved pew. The altarpiece—Mount Sinai wreathed in clouds and lightning—was the work of Pierre L'Enfant, designer of the nation's capital. It was Wall Street's chapel, where titans of American finance had searched their souls, seeking benediction (and maybe absolution) for the keenness of their enterprise. Now it became a church dedicated only to the fruits of compassion. In place of stations of the cross, the enactment of Christ's tortured journey, there were instead what one called "stations of compassion" that grew to include gourmet meals and clothing, massage therapists and grief counselors. Everything was donated in a spirit the people who were there still remark upon. "Everybody who walked in that door experienced the same amount of love," recalls one volunteer. "It didn't matter who they were. It was so unconditional and so overpowering. And when you were there, you knew that every creature in that room was loved as much as you were—and you were loved more than anybody. I mean, there was no quantity to it."

Food was given out "like Communion, with this love and goodwill that humbled you, this phenomenal trust and generosity that made you feel embarrassed, almost humiliated." Few of us, it seems, feel deserving of uncontingent goodness, yet here it was in flagrant abundance. Maybe it was embarrassing to know, really know, that it had been there all along, free for the taking, and the giving. Martin Cowart, a fifty-year-old TriBeCa restaurateur, was recruited by his cousin Courtney to run the food service. "People helped each other because there was nothing else *to* do," he says. "The emotional need was so great that it was almost like madness, a human madness of giving and receiving to each other no matter what that was. It was such a strong current, you could not resist it."

Martin's no sentimentalist. Only blocks away was the charred hulk of the bank where he'd once worked as a numbers-juggling financial wizard. He'd traded his pinstripe for downtown hipster black in his second career as a restaurateur, keeping his shrewdness intact, along with a certain mistrust required to navigate the viciously competitive New York food trade. His last venture, a fledgling shabby-chic neighborhood coffeehouse that couldn't withstand Starbucks, had just lost its lease. Then the planes tore into the towers, and his life changed forever. "I learned that what mattered most was not being important, but belonging." He snorts at the angels-with-dirty-faces irony of it. "Wonderful way to live, huh?"

It was, but he felt part of only a select few who were privy to it. The small miracle that became known by the shorthand Nine-Twelve was taking place behind a sort of Damask Curtain. The church hierarchy had been dubious about the St. Paul's operation from the start, about opening the gates and unlocking the doors to a possibly fragile eighteenth-century architectural treasure. Father Harris had just gone ahead and done it. Things seemed to be spinning out of control. There was talk of just shutting it down. Even as the growing role of "the little church that stood" became a big story, officials questioned the unorthodox goings-on. "Some of them didn't really think it was 'the business of the church,' " recalls Courtney. Managing the news spin became an ecclesiastical concern. One reporter, a religion editor for a Texas paper planning a dulcet puff piece, got more than she bargained for. A volunteer remembers watching as she interviewed a fireman slumped on break in a seat by the church door:

"He said to her, 'Do you know what I do every day in the Pit?' And she said, 'No.' And he said, 'Well, I spend most of every day on my hands and knees, digging with my bare hands for body parts.' And she was totally stunned. And then he went on to describe in the most vivid language the darkness and the suffering and the death of the Pit, really laying it on her. Suddenly his whole demeanor changed, and he stood ramrod straight, sucked in a whole chestful of air, and said, 'And then I get to come here.'

"Standing in place, pointing at every concession around all of St. Paul's, he said, 'Lady, I come in that door dirty, covered with blood, angry, pissed off, and they hug me. They welcome me like I'm a real person. They treat me like a human being. And then after they hug me, they feed me, they massage me, they counsel me, and I sit here and listen to incredible music.'

"He said to her, 'I'll bet you're a Roman Catholic.' She said yes. He said, 'So am I. But I come here every day not just for the hugs and the food. This is where God is. And these are my people. This is my new family. It's the greatest sense of God's presence I have ever known.' " Many who were there commented how shared suffering had engendered a sense of wholeness, even joy, a profound paradox one summed up cryptically as, "Most pain, best time."

"For me, it was hearing the story of a person who lost a loved one, every single day," says Martin Cowart. "I felt this deep, deep sense of human pain that I don't remember I had ever felt. I think the common denominator is the breakdown of your ego to a place of vulnerability. We are brought up to think we all want to be happy and comfortable and *up* and that's what we're programmed to go for. And I don't think anybody in their right mind would want to go for the other. But when you have been put there, you become aware that you can relate to others who have been there as well. Hearing firemen talking about finding bodies the night before and feeling the pain they were going through. And it wasn't morbid. It was just . . . connected."

With that connection, all barriers seemed to tumble. Jews from a nearby synagogue helped celebrate the Eucharist. A clergyman laughs at the memory: " 'You did the what?' I asked them. 'Yep,' they said. 'We did. This is our church, too.' It was a full service chapel for everybody. Even the atheists were happy."

Another parishioner remembers being deeply affected as a rabbi stood at the pulpit to deliver a memorial sermon. "He said, 'The crucifix is one of the most beautiful symbols of mankind because it points straight to heaven and across to each other. Now is the time to strengthen that 'across.' " In the Church of Nine-Twelve, "across" became the only hierarchy. New York's notorious codes of class and signifiers of status disintegrated. "When somebody asks what do you do and I say sanitation worker," says Tony Palimeri, "I always have in the back of my mind that they might be saying, 'But you're a *garbage man.*' But everybody was so great. They didn't care what I did. They didn't care I was heavy. What they cared about was me as a person. Nobody had any agenda. No one was trying to outshine anyone. Just people coming together saying, 'You help me. I'll help you. We'll help each other.' And I started to learn a little bit about people; that we all need each other."

Mary Morris, assistant to the dean of the seminary and wife of an Episcopal priest, recalls her astonishment as the staid institution's pecking order turned upside down. "I saw a bishop cleaning toilets at St. Paul's while a sanitation worker was preaching! Every time I went down there, and I encountered somebody I would never ever have spoken to in my real life, it's like my soul went up in love. Our facades were stripped. It was like it pushed Mary Morris, egocentric human being, aside. What Nine-Twelve taught me, absolutely concretely, is we're all in it together and we're all the same. And when you are equal, there are endless possibilities of communion and community."

Each person in their own way felt they were bearing witness to something unprecedented, some proof positive that a less troubled world was possible, one where simple compassion made the carnage splayed at their feet seem a vestige of some bygone dark age. Was the experience at St. Paul's a freak exception in troubled times, a temporary resurrection of what theologians call "the primitive church"—or a homing beacon of the future?

"Up until that point, universal love was theoretical for me," says Courtney Cowart. "I'd only read about the idea, and then it appeared in our midst, this microcosm of the Kingdom on Earth made visible. Then it was gone, vanished, with only the people who were there knowing how real it was—and still is." To her, the story of the little church that stood was not a symbol of defiance or evidence of the indomitability of a faithful nation. It was the filling of a space that had been hollow. It was a harbinger, a living prophecy of the caring society to come.

It was what Martin Luther King had glimpsed one day in the spring of 1966, after the March to Montgomery, as he gazed out over several thousand homeward-bound marchers who had been delayed at the airport. Amazed and touched as he looked out over the crowd, King wrote in *Where Do We Go from Here*: "As I stood with them and saw white and Negro, nuns and priests, ministers and rabbis, labor organizers, lawyers, doctors, housemaids and shopworkers brimming with vitality and enjoying a rare comradeship, I knew I was seeing a microcosm of the mankind of the future. . . ."

For Cowart, Nine-Twelve had changed everything. What she had seen was more than what the Church could be, but what the *world* could be. "I realized I would not be able to go back to arguing over altar linens," she says wryly. Whatever she'd thought was important, her rising career as a theologian, was reshaped in the crucible of 9/11. That September, she had been thrilled to have lunchtime colloquies with the archbishop of Canterbury. Now, she spends two hours each day feeding lunch to "Mr. Pierre," the paralyzed, speechless father of a Trinidadian friend. "I didn't know where the treasure was," she says. "In God's economy, you put the other first. That's what makes us thrive and feel most joyous." Wasn't this, after all, the original impetus behind every church and synagogue and mosque and temple: an affirmation that compassion *is* a contagion, its flame leaping heart to heart, blazing without being consumed, like the miraculous desert bush?

I've heard other anecdotes of this mysterious conflagration that fires souls, melding them together. My friend Svetlana (not her real name) had grown up in the old Soviet Union, where joining the Young Pioneers was obligatory and college students were expected to volunteer to serve the state. One summer, she and a few other young women were put in charge of a rustic retreat for forty hard-luck, abandoned kids, mostly preteen victims of child abuse.

"We were scared at first," Svetlana remembers. "We'd been dumped at this place in the woods with all these screwed-up kids, no training, no teaching materials, no structure: good old Communism! What did we know?" But then, she says, "The strangest thing happened. We fell in love with them, the most helpless kind of love. These kids were such a mess, so needy, that it just drew it out of us. Maybe it was our maternal instincts waking up with a bang, but we were *drunk* on unconditional love, and they felt it; they began to change, too, under the influence of this power."

Where did it come from? Svetlana's not one for cloying sentimentality—she has, if anything, a certain Russian dolor—but she fills for a moment with a kind of wonder, smiling at the memory. "We found out we could easily teach them all their school subjects, all the ones they'd been miserably failing at, and they just soaked it up like sponges. I'm convinced we could have given them advanced calculus, and they would have learned it from us, under the force of this love. Honestly, it's something I've never felt before or since. As the summer ended, I found myself wishing I could adopt them all. It was devastating to leave this community we'd all made."

*M*any scientists remain skeptical that there could be such a thing as a truly caring community. Some seem to find almost a glee in wiping the *moue* of self-satisfied virtue from the do-gooder's face, in stifling the trill of the pie-eyed optimist. "No hint of genuine charity ameliorates our vision of society once sentimentalism has been laid aside," wrote biologist Michael Ghiselin in a famously acerbic passage. "The economy of nature is competitive from beginning to end . . . What passes for cooperation turns out to be a mixture of opportunism and exploitation . . ."

Science is a dirty job, and someone's got to do it, but—those sharp little teeth, rending at our most cherished beliefs. It's a view that doesn't conduce to sunlit idealism, but maybe that's the point. Pipe-dreams about what society *could* be based on wishful thinking about human nature has nearly driven civilization's eighteen-wheel rig right off the scenic overlook ("scientific socialism," anyone? the Year Zero? or for that matter, "trickle-down economics"?). Now is not the time to squeeze our eyes shut and clap real hard for Tinkerbell.

But we sense that the picture Ghiselin and his ilk are showing us is only the torn-off corner of a much larger one. While those who sourly assess our possibilities have looked in one direction, some scientists are starting to look in another. A recent Emory University study showed that when players of a game called Prisoner's Dilemma decided to trust each other and cooperate rather than betray each other for gain (as the game allows and even encourages), a part of the brain associated with feelings of joy lit up. Forget "greed is good": Social cooperation has its own neurological reward-circuit, portioning out the endogenous dollops of pleasure that are evolution's good housekeeping seal of approval.

The study of such "prosocial" (as opposed to antisocial) feelings is so new, it's still possible for scientists to put emotions on the map that hitherto hadn't been named. Jon Haidt (that's "height," not "hate"), a professor of cognitive psychology at the University of Virginia, wasn't setting out to be the heart's Magellan; it's just that he'd gotten his own broken, and it hurt like hell. Miserable and mooning, Haidt had a sudden insight: "Hey, there's an actual pain here; an aching heart isn't just a metaphor." His dashed romance temporarily eclipsed by scientific curiosity, he began asking colleagues in the biology department how they would explain his feeling. The general consensus was the vagus nerve which ferries signals back and forth between heart and brain.

It made Haidt wonder about another heart sensation that had always intrigued him: that warmth in the chest (often accompanied by a "choked-up" feeling) that we get when we witness a good deed. Film critic Roger Ebert once remarked that the movie moment that most reliably floors him is when the hero performs an act of nobility and sacrifice. We all know that one, emerging into the lobby's too-bright light blinking with still-moist eyes, exchanging tremulous half smiles, enduring the skeptical looks of the action-flick crowd.

Haidt found that this response, which he dubbed "elevation," usually occurred when witnessing someone helping the downtrodden, the sick, or the weak. He quotes an interview with a woman who was driving home with three friends after a morning of volunteer work for the Salvation Army. It had been snowing hard, the flakes piled up in a thick blanket, when they'd passed an old woman trying to shovel her driveway. One of the men in the group asked to be let off. "I didn't think much of it," the woman said. "I had assumed that this guy just wanted to save the driver some effort and walk the short distance home. But when I saw him jump out of the backseat and approach the lady . . . I realized that he was offering to shovel her walk for her.

"I felt like jumping out of the car and hugging this guy," the woman reported, still surprised at her strong reaction. "I felt like singing and running, or skipping and laughing . . . I felt like saying nice things about people. Playing in the snow like a child. Telling everybody about his deed."

That this small act of kindness had a specific and disproportionate effect tipped Haidt off that a built-in biological response might be at work. The woman had experienced such a profound lifting of her spirits that she gushed about it to her roommates, who in turn clutched their hearts and smiled. Why *are* we so moved by good deeds? he wondered. A neo-Darwinian to the core, Haidt was sure that evolution must have had something in mind to install such an automatic response. Elevation also seems to be unusually contagious, often accompanied by what he academically labels "changes in the thought-action repertoire." When he asked his respondents if the feeling had made them want to do something, they described an almost overwhelming desire to "be with, love, and help other people."

Feelings of elevation also seem to foster admiration and a desire for closer affiliation with the good deed-doer. Said the woman in the snow-shoveling incident, "Although I have never seen this guy as more than just a friend, I felt a hint of romantic feeling for him at this moment." (I wonder if this attraction isn't a sign evolution is tickled by the prospect of a few more altruistic genes in the pool.)

Haidt has collected enough descriptions across cultures and through history to conclude that elevation is a universal human trait. A forty-six-year-old Japanese housewife described how she felt when she saw people volunteer to help in a natural disaster: "The heart brightens up *[akarui]* and I feel glad *[yokatta]*, relieved *[anshin]*, admiration *[sugoi]*, and respect *[sonkei]*." A primary school principal in a small village in Orissa, India, reported a feeling of joy *(ananda)* and a tingling sensation in his body when he saw people in his school step forward to defend a teacher wrongly accused of having stolen some books. Thomas Jefferson wrote to a friend about his "elevated sentiments" upon seeing "an act of charity or gratitude," describing the feeling in his chest as "dilation." (Think of the expression, "My heart swelled.")

A Unitarian parishioner told Haidt of his "tears of celebration" when his church voted unanimously to become a Welcoming Congregation (a church that officially invites homosexuals) after a gay member had stood up and publicly come out for the first time. The man described it as "a tear of receptiveness to what is good in the world, a tear that says it's okay, relax, let down your guard, there are good people in the world, there is good in people, love is real, it's in our nature." It reminded me of a comment made by one of the Nine-Twelve communicants: "I discovered the emotional magnificence of life. The joy of being human. Living that love for real. The beauty of it. The glory of it. The confirmation of it. The glee of it."

Elevation opens a picture window onto the expanse of our nature. It implies we are drawn to each other's goodness, hardwired to exult over it. The elation seems to stem, as much as anything, from sensing oneself part of some common stream of virtue—an apotheosis of *you in me, me in you;* a sort of *we in us.*

Haidt told me he uses a secret weapon in his lab studies: an *Oprah* episode he claimed was a surefire tearjerker even the flintiest heart could not resist. *Bring it on,* I told him. I popped his "induction sequence" into my DVD as soon as it arrived, settling back to watch with a certain can't-make-me-cry stoicism. It was the story of a ghetto kid whose life had been turned around by a kindly public-school music teacher. The young candidate for the thug life had instead gone on to fame as a jazz trumpeter, but he had never forgotten his crucial father figure. Years later, it influenced his unexpected decision, at the pinnacle of his career, to become a public-school teacher. As he told his story, the camera panned to his old mentor planted in the audience, head bowed, overcome with emotion.

Then Oprah surprised the young man by showing a video of *his* students thanking him for changing their lives, and, well . . . the teardrop-shaped stain on this page is not the manufacturer's watermark. Afterward I trundled over to the HeartMath equipment still set up in a corner of my living room and confirmed, as Haidt's own studies have shown, that his devilishly sappy video increases heart-rate variability. My balloon was floating in the stratosphere: I was certifiably *elevated*.

"Oh, the effect is real, all right," Haidt tells me. "One of my pet peeves is this notion that you can explain away virtue as just secret selfishness. Scientists haven't looked at it in the right spirit. We really *do* have some beautiful things in our nature."

He is particularly intrigued by elevation's "power to spread. A witness to good deeds," he writes, "[may] soon become a doer of good deeds . . . If frequent bad deeds trigger social disgust, cynicism, and hostility toward one's peers, then frequent good deeds may raise the level of compassion, love, and harmony in an entire society." I might once have taken this for a Chamber of Commerce brochure from the Wonderful Land of Oz. Now I'm not so sure.

Still, let's face it: Frequent good deeds aside, the world of frequent bad deeds is still very much with us. Hatred, too, is a contagion—and sometimes a pandemic. I found myself in the Balkans a few years back, not long after Serbia's ethnic cleansing campaign had been halted by NATO's bombardment. The war was over, but war and peace are more than the victories and defeats of armies. Even in Dubrovnik's fanciest hotel, the grim-faced maître d' seemed a vestige of the old police state, still uncertain whether to greet the guests, guard the buffet table, or round up the diners for questioning.

I was in Croatia for a conference of peace activists. That week the country had advanced to the World Cup soccer quarterfinals, and bedlam ruled. Young men ran through the cobbled streets of the Old City waving flags and pounding the roofs of passing cars. A thoughtful Serb student protest leader remarked that it had been like this when the malignant nationalism had taken hold in Belgrade. In every bar, he said, you could hear the hoarse bellowing of fight songs, see drunks tumbling into the street in hard knots, accosting passersby. There was a woozy, tingling excitement in the air. "You were expected to join in this euphoria, in everyone losing themselves in the group mind, or you were looked on with suspicion."

I've never been in a war. The idea of a whole society deciding to hoist a warm gun instead of a cold beer and turn it on their neighbors is mystifying. Hearing there was still sporadic shooting a few hours away in Mostar, I convinced a young Croat named Igor who knew the town to drive me there. We pulled into a charming city center dominated by the snaggle-toothed stone walls of old Roman ruins—or so I thought, until Igor informed me they were bombed-out buildings, this one an office complex, that one a department store, here a mosque, there a church, now gutted and tumbledown. At one point, he said, opposing forces had arrayed themselves on opposite sides of the main street and simply blasted away at each other.

The bridges of Mostar over the meandering River Neretva, once famed for their beauty, had become infamous symbols of the gulf between the Muslim and Croat quarters of a newly divided city. At the height of the conflict, if you had been a Muslim attempting to cross into a Croat area or vice versa, you stood a good chance of having your forehead drilled with a small, neat hole by a waiting sniper.

"How could they tell who was who?" I asked. Muslims here are mostly light skinned and often blue eyed; everyone looks alike. Well, Igor said, sometimes it was the ethnic giveaways: a scarf on a woman, the size and composition of family groups. But mostly, since it was a small town, people knew each other on sight. The idea confounded me: If you recognized a former neighbor who was now your newly designated enemy, then said Igor, "Maybe you just plugged him, *pam!*"

I was reminded of how, a few years ago, authorities in my town had taken a sixth-grader into custody, confiscating a select list of classmates on which he'd penciled the word *Kill* next to each name, like a to-do reminder. I live in the Columbine Shooting state; there's no such thing here as a schoolboy prank. The student told police he'd created his roster based on which kids "looked weird" to him (a boy with freckles, a girl who was too skinny). The Balkan madness seemed just as arbitrary: the sociopathy of small differences; the mind's gearbox seized up in low, stuck in some primitive sortition of good and bad, friend and enemy; its talent for abstract distinction turned, during a time of derangement, into a murder motive.

We wandered into the Muslim part of town, finding ourselves beneath a seven-story mosque, its minaret crowned with a curlicue of metal flame, the speaker system blaring a recorded *muezzin's* call to one o'clock prayer. But the people themselves were taciturn. No one wanted to talk to us, not the tough-looking young guy in the blue tracksuit, not the street sweeper pushing his contraption of a garbage can mounted on bicycle wheels. The streets were reservoirs of silence, brimming with terrible secrets.

We finally stumbled by accident across a little office with a sign that read "Human Rights." A stocky, dark-skinned man in his late forties excused himself from a meeting of Muslim and Croat young people—reconcilers in whom all hope for the future resides—and came over to talk. He wanted to explain what had happened here. Igor translated as he began the story where everyone did, with recitals of territories seized and retaken over centuries, capped by the rise of the crazymen, Tudjman and Milosevic ("an idiot lost in space and time") who used boundaries and ethnicities to fuel their megalomaniacal ambitions.

But what had really *happened?* I asked. In this city, every third marriage was a mixed one, with residents living side by side in an ethnic patchwork locals compared to stripes on a tiger skin. He shrugged: Mostar had been a symbol of harmony, a rendezvous of East and West, and so, of course, it had to be destroyed. The propaganda machine had cranked into overdrive. "Who you prayed to, where your family was originally from, suddenly became all-important. To get people to hate each other. People are not poultry," he sighed, "but they behaved that way."

He told of the night they'd come for him. "They burst into my apartment in their black ski masks, and I thought I was dead for sure. But then I suddenly recognized the one holding the AK—he was the son of a neighbor! I recognized him from his voice, his eyes. 'I know you,' I said. 'I know your father. I knew you as a child.'" The man had tried to disguise his voice by lowering it to an ominous growl. But then he'd hesitated, softened for a moment, and spared his neighbor's life.

I kept pushing for more of an answer, though I was beginning to realize there wasn't one. We'd lapsed into French by this time, his fluent, mine such as I could retrieve from the undergraduate mists.

"C'était les têtes vides," he finally sputtered. "The empty-heads! Without a brain! People in town, one after another, people you knew, people you'd *always* known, all were *tout-à-fait* empty-heads!" For some years, it seems, the Empty Heads had been the region's dominant political party.

Or perhaps it was not so much a case of empty-headedness as heads stuffed with loony ideas, minds hijacked by roving gangs of delusions, brains infected with some mutant cultural spirochete against which they had all too little resistance. "Men will die like flies for theories and exterminate each other with every instrument of destruction—for abstractions," notes an all-too-prescient 1938 paper on aggression and war. What was it Gandhi had said about your thoughts becoming your destiny? Here was a textbook example of the power of mental fixation to paint reality in any color—in this case, dead black.

The mass mind-meld was, per usual, incalculably amplified by media, fueling the descent into society-wide paranoia. Says Milos Vasic, editor of *Vreme*, the only independent magazine in Belgrade during the war: "All it took was a few years of reckless, intolerant, warmongering propaganda to create enough hate to start the fighting." To understand what happened, Vasic says, "Imagine a United States with every little TV station everywhere broadcasting Klansman David Duke. You, too, would have war in five years."

I remember a conversation with a student leader, a raven-haired woman with almond-shaped eyes, half-Bosnian, half-Serb, who belonged to an interethnic youth organization that called itself the Post-Pessimists. She told me how at the height of the war, she had been horror-struck to see Serbian television news footage of an atrocity committed by Bosnian troops. A few weeks later, sneaking across the border to visit her Bosnian relatives, she had seen the same footage again, only now it was attributed to *Serbian* troops. "For all I know," she said, "it was some old footage from World War II!" She looked at me and said, half in plea, half in declaration: "So, do we just keep our parents from killing each other, or do we change the whole human equation?"

*T*hat's easy: Change the equation.

But is there any inoculation that *could* prevent the next outbreak of this dread social pestilence, this anti-elevation that turns friends to enemies and town squares to ancient ruins? Violence is not just the doing of crazy men, who'd remain street-corner ranters if no one saluted. Real peace seems to depend on a culture's baseline immunocompetence, some self-healing system that kills hate germs dead on contact.

Columbian priest Leonel Narvaez so believes in social healing that he is leading a government-sponsored, historically unprecedented experiment in mass psychotherapy. With the goal of helping tens of thousands of ex-combatants from his country's brutal civil war reintegrate as civilians, he has organized cadres of therapists to address combat traumas that, left untreated, would inevitably trigger renewed conflict. Leonel had spent long years working in what he calls "The Kingdom of the FARC," the rural villages controlled by the insurgent *Fuerzas Armadas Revolucionarias de Colombia,* mediating between the guerillas and the government. He had grown up in the same small town as the FARC's leader, known as Tirofijo, or "Sure Shot," after his flair for killing enemies with a single bullet. They even shared the same birthday, although they couldn't be more different. The town's old people say of Tirofijo, "The desire for vengeance ate him up." Leonel, now in his late forties, has long been consumed with the desire to make the only permanent peace—the peace of the heart. "I was trying to explain to Tirofijo once that hatred and anger mostly hurt the person who experiences those feelings. Tirofijo just snapped, 'Get down from the clouds, priest!' "

But Leonel, head in the clouds, maybe, but feet surely planted on terra firma, has moved ahead with a series of bold social initiatives, founding Schools of Forgiveness and Reconciliation known by the acronym ESPERE (Spanish for "hope"), which are slowly spreading throughout the country. He doesn't plan to quit until he's turned his whole war-accursed nation into a beloved community. Though he is a strong believer in justice and human rights, he is convinced that what he simply calls "tenderness" is the ultimate antidote. "The heart is where violence is born," he says, "and so it is there where peace is reborn."

He knows that the world has had its fill of grand social engineers, the ones with the Big Ideas who pretty well screwed up the twentieth century for the rest of us. All Leonel wants to do is propagate some basic soul-healing technologies; do a little patent-busting to ensure that brotherly love and forgiveness aren't "a monopoly held by churches and priests, but indispensable elements of everyday life." His ideas may look simple in the extreme, but that simplicity is deceptive. "Against the irrationality of violence, it is necessary to propose the irrationality of forgiveness," he says slyly.

For him, it's not just about the FARC or the government or the right-wing paramilitaries. It's about the sodden meanness of the streets, the domestic violence against women and children, the police who "model aggression to the citizens," even the human rights workers who, he says, "have so much anger and hate they're also in the trap." His "reconciliation schools" represent a crucial step from peace treaties to peaceful entreaties, from truce enforcement to truth-force. He recites his classrooms' core curriculum: "I decide to move from darkness to light; I choose to forgive; I see with new eyes; I share the pain; I accept the other within me." It's a new pledge of human allegiance.

"We need new ideas of conciliation," says Leonel. "Not just techniques, because they don't get to the root." This is more than just a wistful lament from a new-age Catholic priest who wishes everyone would just be really, really nice to each other. The mayor of Bogota, a slum-ridden, deeply unruly city of eight million, has asked Leonel to help him transform it into a new urban paradigm based on mutual understanding.

"We're going to try to transplant it into civics," says Leonel excitedly. "We're proposing a citywide network of reconciliation. We're going to try to reverse the historical and cultural attitudes that say you react to violence with more violence, that you should punish a crime with a crime. It's hard even for me to believe, but now there's a bill in Congress for a new law based on restorative justice. We're training the police not to speak the way their gun speaks, but to speak with their hearts. We need a whole *culture* of reconciliation, where even people who get aggressive behind the wheel learn to drive with compassion.

"Quite possibly," he says, "someday I will run into Tirofijo again, and this time I will be the one to say, with great respect: 'Get down from the clouds, Don Manuel. Without forgiveness and without reconciliation there is no future. Not for you and not for anyone!'" His goal, he says, is to build a new city from the inside out, but I'm not sure he'll stop with Bogota. For Father Narvaez, there's no place on this whole spinning dirtball he couldn't lay a cornerstone for the shining city on the hill.

/ can't always see it, this glimmering hope becoming a reality. Nor hear it, for that matter, what with Alpha Chimp Björn rolling his orange war drum down Main Street these days, slam-banging for all he's worth. But I like to think he already senses he's a creature of the past, making a big noise while he still can. With the day fast approaching that a handful of angry, calculating people can blow up not just a restaurant but the city that lists it in its yellow pages, the good of each is tied to the good of all. What happens in our own hearts is suddenly as big as the whole world. It's true our human task is made harder by the institutionalization of hurt and harm, by an accumulated investment in the ruin of our own prospects. But we are, collectively, wiser than our leaders, kinder than our institutions, more open-hearted than all our dogmas.

On my better days, I feel I'm witnessing, across the planet, the subversive innervation of some neural net of kindness whose filaments are so fine as to be invisible (but like threads from a spider's spinnerets, more tensile than steel). It no longer seems far-fetched to

302

imagine a kind of compassion insurgency, a revolt against all the wasteful diversions of our creativity; a Good Society Movement, if you will, a self-emergent, adaptive cultural mutation. Could the sum of all the little changes be a popular uprising of the heart change that will burst forth, as did the soft revolutions of ironclad eastern Europe, seemingly out of nowhere? Is our global organism developing prosocial antibodies against the plague that has too long infected the body politic?

If you can't see it yet, it's not surprising. It's still circles within circles, networks of networks; an infiltrating social mycellium whose scope and range, once you catch a glimpse beneath the surface, are a little breathtaking. I know citizen-negotiators who have reconciled Azerbaijanis and Armenians—nationalities with centuries of murderous grudgery—using just skills of compassionate listening and bearing witness to each other's hurt. I recently met a freelance mediator who believes that parties in conflict want nothing more from each other than empathy. Marshall Rosenberg travels around the world with a guitar case and a suitcase full of silly props—a jackal puppet (to symbolize paranoid, judgmental thought and speech) and giraffe ears (to signify an ability to listen openly—giraffes having the animal kingdom's largest heart-to-body ratio). He's an utter eccentric, plainspoken and deliberate, with a mournful look that disguises the sly, slow-dawning sense of humor that has helped to reconcile Tutsis and Hutus, rival street gangs, and battling spouses.

He's seen how kindness spreads person to person, he says; seen his techniques taught in a hundred schools from Ashkelon in Israel to the Navajo nation. He shows me a sheaf of airline tickets of his upcoming travels—Santa Barbara to Switzerland, Argentina to Côte d'Ivoire. Like empathy's own Johnny Appleseed, he sings his funny little songs, tells his stories, and some kind of pay-it-forward magic just happens. He recounts it with a look of pleasant bafflement.

"I feel like there are two different worlds," he tells me, his hawk-wing eyebrows waving up, then down. "There's the world I'm living in, where every day I meet people who are doing all these wonderful things. And then there's the world of these folks," he says, gesturing to the complimentary copy of *USA Today* lying on the bedspread in his hotel room. He shakes his head. "They don't seem to connect at all."

It does seem that we suffer from a collective cognitive dissonance. We know the children are starving; the ice caps really *are* melting. We know our designer sweats are connected to designer sweatshops; our automobiles to the turbid atmosphere; the food on our table to the dwindling water table and the chemicalized soil. We sense that life in the developed world has become a desire machine cranked up to maximum RPM, spinning out a dizzying succession of induced wants for which satisfaction is supplied, scratches for itches, at fair market price—no matter the cost. We also know there's already enough to feed, clothe, house, heal, and educate everyone, without exception. It's less a shortage of resources than a short-changing of imagination: compassion being an ability to imagine—to *see*—the connection between everyone and everything, everywhere.

From that standpoint, isn't that connection love itself? Isn't it love itself that underlies all wanting? Don't we only consume the Earth in our hunger for a love already abundant in our own hearts—and waiting in each other's? And if, enriched by that love, we took less, gave more, would not our astonishment, as the Midas World we've built receded and the outlines of the Beloved Community emerged, be boundless?

*T*hat community's founding members are the ones who root for the other team, the people Martin Luther King prophesied we would become when "our loyalties . . . transcend our race, our tribe, our class, and our nation." I've met them, these traitors to any boundaries, their fidelity pledged to the human family. I know a young woman named Nadja, a Bosnian who during the siege of Sarajevo was terribly wounded by Serb shrapnel. After the war, watching a scared-looking Serb soldier weep during his televised trial—a man who might have been the very one who'd lobbed the mortar round—she wept, too. When her brother angrily scolded her, she told him: "I can't keep a separate heart, one for my friends and one for my enemies." She echoed a Burmese activist named Ka Hsaw Wa, who confided to me he has learned to feel empathy—what is called in his language *ko gin ser* ("my heart is trying to be your heart")—for the government soldiers who have attacked and tortured him and his people, even as he opposes their brutality with the nonviolent weapon of international law. He and growing numbers of others are the loyal subjects of the Country of You in Me, the Empire of Everybody.

The Yad Vashem medal reads, "Whoever saves a single life saves the world." In a time when the entire planet needs saving, maybe we're all being called to be Lamed Vav. Why only thirty-six Righteous Ones? Why not 36 million, 360 million, 3 billion and change? Beneath the daily headlines, the true state of affairs is almost laughably obvious: a world poised on the brink of self-discovery, awakening to the fact that if we are to go anywhere, we must all go there together.

13

ALL MY RELATIONS

We are caught in an inescapable network of mutuality.
—*Martin Luther King*

Truly, universally, relations stop nowhere.
—*Henry James*

I recently saw a local news story about a boy who became lost in the Colorado woods in the dead of winter. As hypothermia set in and he began to freeze to death, he saw emerging ghostlike out of the swirling snow two large elk. Feebly, he threw stones at them, shouting until his voice gave way, then lost consciousness. Early the next morning, he awoke to find himself sandwiched between the two great beasts, who had laid their warm bodies next to his through what would have been a fatal night.

Or so he told the search team when he staggered into a clearing and was rescued. They were skeptical—hallucinations are a side effect of extreme duress—until he led them back to his sleeping spot. There, in the snow, they saw the concavities made by two enormous animals, the imprint of a small boy in between.

Why would the animals bother? Why not just curl up with each other for some languorous elk-frolic through the wintry night? (Three's a crowd, and besides, in these parts people *shoot* them.) There are a million stories of our fellow creatures being kind to us for no good reason—from dogs who, with no rescue training and at risk to their own lives, rush into the flames of burning buildings to drag strangers to safety; or dolphins who nose drowning swimmers to the surface, wait for human help to arrive, then take off with an errant tip of their fin. There are inexplicable ways compassion radiates through the world; some spirit of sympathy drawn toward any distress like white cells to a pathogen. When Wordsworth spoke of "a motion and a spirit that impels all living things," was he talking about the systole and diastole of some universal heartbeat?

Mitakuye oyasin, say the Lakota: "All beings are my relatives." We are just starting to get the implications. Recently the Tumbling Creek Cave Snail, a creature so tiny it's invisible to the untrained eye, was put on the federal list of endangered species. Scientists had noticed the snails dying off in large numbers. They finally realized that not only was the Missouri cave stream where they lived polluted, but also the aquifer that supplied the stream on which animals *and* people depended. All of Nature is now the canary in the coal mine.

But is it enough to calculate the cost-benefit analysis of "preserving the environment"? Given our shaky collective plight, knowing Nature's "value" may not be enough; we may need to *love* it (that, or start looking for an evolutionary niche that's not already occupied).

Julia Butterfly Hill, notorious for the two sentinel years she spent camping atop the redwood tree she named Luna, is intimate with nature. When she lectures—pacing the stage barefoot, weeping, laughing, doing uncanny imitations of a chainsaw's splutter and the crashing of great trees onto the forest floor—she is appealing not just for the preservation of the wild, but a blind passion for it. Her over-the-top antics get on some people's nerves. Environmental activists are one thing, actual nature-lovers quite another. We don't entirely trust them: Like all lovers, they seem prone to exaggerate.

Besides, love is for people, not for plants. We know the stories of people who can open their hearts to their prize rosebush and lavish their love on Fifi but have a heart hewn of granite toward the people next door. But why should we think it's mutually exclusive? Sociologist Kristin Monroe observed that many of those who rescued Jews from the Nazis seemed to have altruistic feelings that extended "beyond the world of human beings to include all living things. Margot talked about the humanity of dogs. Lucille spoke of not harming any living thing, even spiders. Others spoke of 'the good earth' itself (Knud) or the animal and vegetable kingdoms (Tony). Life itself was something to be valued for these altruists."

Perhaps our ultimate human assignment is to extend our sense of kinship beyond family and clan and strangers to all other creatures. (We turn out to share a surprising percentage of our genome with everything from trees to fleas to manatees.) I believe Hill when she says, "I'd come to value Luna as myself, my own body. When she was cut, I felt that a loved one had been attacked." The emotion we feel toward those we love—wonderment at their uniqueness, desire to foster their complete unfolding, appreciation not for their uses and benefits but their inviolate worthiness—might be the only force potent enough, *tender* enough, to save the world.

I spent part of last winter staring at a potted amaryllis bulb someone had given me for Christmas. I was firmly in the grip of seasonal affective disorder, and this thing seemed in similar straits. It was a typical watched pot; nothing stirred. Then one day a pert green spatula extruded, then another. The longer it sat there, growing, the more baffled I felt: *So . . . an inert lump of vegetal matter, plus dirt, plus water, plus light, plus . . . what? a lattice of info-molecules? self-emergent properties of sufficiently complex matter? élan vital?* and then this slow-motion *kerplow* of impossible creativity. I thought of Dylan Thomas's line: "The force that through the green fuse drives the flower." *What* force, and what was nature thinking, making it so unnecessarily gorgeous? I wanted to call friends to rhapsodize about it, to tag it as forensic evidence of some divine immanence. Sometimes I almost caught it looking back at me, one living thing to another.

Mystics and shamans have long claimed that all of Nature has, as it were, an emotional life. Says Peruvian shaman Pablo Caesar Amaringo: "People may say that a plant has no mind . . . A plant may not talk, but there is a spirit in it that is conscious, that sees everything, which is the soul of the plant, its essence, what makes it alive." Some years back, I met a gruff, disheveled former detective and polygraph expert named Cleve Backster, an investigator of plants' secret lives. He'd had the bright idea to affix skin galvanometers, which detect changes in the electrical response associated with emotion, to the leaves of philodendrons. He noticed that when he cut the leaf of one plant, the tracings of other nearby plants spiked in what looked for all the world like a sign of distress. (The plants reacted the same way when he rigged a nearby device to kill tiny brine shrimp at random intervals.)

During my visit to HeartMath, Rollin McCraty, noting my suitably wowie-zowie response to his research, decided to administer a coup-de-grâce and reveal his ultimate Stupid Heart-Trick. He took some yogurt from the fridge and dumped it, along with its resident colony of acidophilus and bifidis bacteria, into a petri dish. He took out a tan metal box with a dial and a needle called a "portable bioresponse meter," and placed its electrodes in the dish. As expected, the needle just sat there. "We're measuring the baseline electrical activity of bacteria, which holds pretty steady," he explained. "Biophysics would say that the needle shouldn't move at all."

Then he asked me to think of a deeply disturbing emotional experience. Rummaging through memory, I had a sudden flash of my sister's death, and I was flooded with a surge of grief. At that very moment, all by itself, the needle on the meter buried itself in the red zone, then oscillated wildly back and forth. We hadn't touched anything. The box was hooked up to nothing but the yogurt (strawberry, my favorite). Nothing in the room had changed but my feelings. When I switched my mental focus back to my surroundings, the needle went still.

"Okay," McCraty said, "now think of an incident of physical pain." I called to mind a recent medical checkup that had involved taking several blood samples. The needle kicked fitfully, like a man whose sleep has been disturbed. He had me remember a moment of profound embarrassment (I'm not telling), and again, the needle twitched abruptly as if in response. What was being revealed here, he claimed, was that all living creatures, from microorganisms to pets to people, resonate to the field effect of the human heart.

Yikes! Just as an empathic person feels the pain of another, do other living things respond invisibly to the suffering and joy, hatred and love, that surround them? Is it possible we live in a universe that is not only sentient, but deeply feeling? Just try to hide your heart away; even your afternoon snack can read you like an open book.*

Starting with Descartes in the eighteenth century, ascribing an affective life to our fellow creatures has been considered scientifically disreputable. Mr. Think-Therefore-I-Am, though he had an expansive

---

* Though McCraty attributes the effects he is measuring to the proximate electromagnetic field of the heart itself, William G. Braud, Ph.D., senior research associate at San Antonio's Mind Science Foundation, believes them to be related to "nonlocal mind," postulated as a sort of omnipresent field of consciousness. In one of Braud's studies, red cells drawn from volunteers were placed in a solution with low salt content, which normally would cause them to rupture. The volunteers were told to try to mentally "protect" their own distant blood cells. Measurements made with a computer-linked spectrophotometer revealed that nearly a third of the participants had succeeded, seemingly, in mentally slowing their cells' destruction. The odds, gleaned from sixty-four separate sessions, were nearly 200,000 to 1 against chance. Overall, Braud has performed more than five hundred such experiments, all aimed at detecting the nonlocal influence of human consciousness on biological processes as diverse as the spatial orientation of fish, the locomotor activity of small rodents, and the brain rhythms of people. Consciousness, he has concluded, produces verifiable biological effects in bacteria, neurons, cancer cells, enzymes, fungi, mobile algae, plants, protozoa, larvae, insects, chicks, gerbils, cats, and dogs.

brain, seems to have had a constricted heart. He once remarked that animals had no feelings whatever: If a cat being vivisected yowled in pain, it was only the "mechanical noises of an earthen machine." If this sounds archaic, bear in mind it wasn't until 2003 that scientists announced they had "discovered" that a hooked fish feels pain (*so that's what all that agonized thrashing was about*).

Acknowledging a sentient world might make us kinder, gentler citizens of a planet that has already had to endure more than its share of our cruelties. Besides, a world filled to the brim with awareness is a more *lively* place, since it warrants making some kind of relationship. Who knows? As I was sitting here writing these words on a hot summer day, a fly began buzzing around the room. It was the noxious kind—a metallic iridescent bluebottle—that always sparks a jolt of irrational hatred. My official policy is swat-on-sight, but it had set right down upon, as it were, the topic at hand: a manuscript page with "All My Relations" in the bottom margin. I just couldn't. Instead I thought: *What if I* didn't *loathe it? What if my first thought* wasn't *to kill it dead?*

Just then, it landed on my forearm.

I looked down at it in the light of my desk lamp, trying hard to overcome my distaste. I admired its glittering carapace, which was, I had to admit, a marvel of nature's design shop. I did *tonglen,* contemplating the poignancy of its—his?—too-short, flit-about life. I breathed out love and appreciation for his job as nature's sanitation engineer. I pondered that he and I shared some 85 percent of our DNA.

Then a ridiculous idea occurred. I *talked* to him. "Why don't you just keep sitting there," I said reasonably, "and instead of trying to kill you, I'll put you back outside." I got up, keeping my arm level. I looked down. He hadn't budged. Moreover, he seemed to be hanging on, even when my office fan's full-tilt breeze hit his wings with enough gust to make them ruffle. He clung there as I ambled down the hall. Stayed put as I reached for the doorknob. Was still there when I opened the front door and stuck my arm outside. Okay, *shoo-fly!* I said. And he did.

Okay, he'd probably just dozed off on his union-mandated break. But I felt good about this exercise in what Hindus call *ahimsa*, non-harming. It could now be truly said of me, "He wouldn't hurt a fly." Besides, not hating him was better for my blood pressure.

This is not to say I've become the Fly-Whisperer. I tried my trick a few nights later when his big fat brother wriggled through the hole in the screen and began dive-bombing me like a kamikaze. The closest I got to a kindly attitude was to recognize that he was buzzing frantically through his life trying to get his needs met like the rest of us and to acknowledge that we were both foodies, despite differing notions of four-star dining. I can't say I didn't long for a sturdy yet flexible swatter.

S till, I confess: I'm going soft and gooey on all creatures great and small. It's been getting a little out of hand. The other day, shopping for a houseplant, I felt a wave of affection for every living thing in the store, from clerks to customers to the store's pet parrot, who, when I approached him, gave me a cheerful hello.

Hello, I said.

Hel-lo! he said.

Hel-*lo!* I said.

Hell*ooo!* he said.

This seemed to be, with varying inflections, his only conversational gambit (though maybe he concluded the same about me). Every time I tried to walk away, he'd shout his greeting, and I found it hard to leave him there famishing for small talk. Finally, I said goodbye and he said hello, though I felt a little guilty leaving him in the lurch.

So imagine how Aimee Morgana must feel. She's raised her captive-bred Congo African gray parrot, N'kisi, in her Harlem apartment across from the old National Geographic Explorers Club since he was a fuzzy little chick. Now, at age seven, he's as unalterably attached to her as a toddler. He loves her, and as the world's most verbose parrot—twelve hundred words thus far—he *can* count the ways.

I ask her how she trained him. She didn't, she insists. "He learned to speak like any child," Aimee explains. "I talked to him—a lot—just using language creatively, and he picked up on it." Like her friend Jane Goodall, who first approached her chimps with hand outstretched in a gesture of submission, Aimee, in her experiments to "explore avian language," decided to give N'kisi dominance in their social relationship, figuring it might facilitate learning. Whatever she did, it worked beyond her wildest dreams. "He was actually ahead of human children for the first few years," she says with parental pride. "He'd be using ten-word sentences versus their two-worders. Now we have actual conversations."

Is that so? The fact African grays can sensibly "talk" rather than randomly mimic was first demonstrated by MIT professor Irene Pepperberg, who trained a bird named Alex to identify ordinary objects and classify them by color and shape. "Alex proved parrots know what they're saying," says Aimee, "but it's pretty dry stuff—linguistics tests by behaviorists, using rewards. I don't give N'kisi any rewards, so he won't perform on cue." Her role was more playing Annie Sullivan to Helen Keller. "I'd show him water and say 'water.' Then if he said the word 'water,' I'd just give him a drink.

"Basically, we just live here together. I'm home-schooling a parrot," she says with self-amused irony. But then she gets closer to the truth: "I live in a magical world with a talking animal." Her apartment decor suggests a faculty lounge at the Hogwarts Academy. Aimee, who makes her living as a TV production designer, has turned her place into a cabinet of curiosities, filling it with a bricolage of animal skulls, giant crystals, and cases of luminous blue Morpho butterflies. Two life-sized, gold-painted skeletons twine in an embrace at the foot of her bed like an elaborate *memento mori.*

N'kisi doesn't just talk, Aimee insists. He has revealed a mind of his own, an interiority, a feeling-life. "I've discovered compassion, humor, altruism—the philosophy of an animal mind."

Hmm-mmm, oh-*kay* . . .

"I wanna fly over there now," N'kisi suddenly announces. African parrots are big birds. When he flaps over, the downdraft fans my face. He perches on the arm of the couch, his foot-long, bright crimson tail-feather hanging off the edge, peering sidelong into my eyes. His normal speaking voice is a digital recording of hers, but he says "Hel-*lo!*" to me in a hearty male voice, like a conventioneer doing a grip-and-grin at a regional sales conference. "That's his 'guy voice,'" Aimee informs me, "the one he uses for male visitors. He thinks it sounds tough."

When she tells him that I've written books, he says distinctly, equably, "Jane wrote a book."

"He's friends with Jane Goodall," she explains. N'kisi hoots like a chimp. "Jane taught him the chimpanzee greeting." She tells N'kisi I've written books about medicine and healing.

"You had to go to the hospital," he says to her.

I don't see any secret hand signals. This *is* getting a little weird. Aimee explains N'kisi's been very concerned about her health: She has been struggling with breast cancer. Once, when she nearly died of a chemotherapy overdose, she claims he said, "I worry about the chemo. Too much medicine." He sometimes seems as concerned about her as a child, as a parent, as a friend. Once when she was lying down on the couch trying to rest, he said in gentle tones, "Hey, baby, are you tired? Want me to put the light out?"

Normally, she says, he uses the pronouns "I" and "me" for himself and "you" and "your" when referring to others. But when he is dis-tressed about something unpleasant that is happening to her, he tends to use "I" or "we," as if it were happening to him as well. (I wonder if I'm hearing what puppies who lick their owners' faces to comfort them would say if *they* could talk.)

When Aimee had to go in for breast surgery, she explained to N'kisi a doctor would cut her body to take out the sick part, and then she was going to get better. N'kisi said on one occasion, "I wanna take you better. We'll cut my body there. It's okay. We're gonna cut my body, and we're gonna take it better, okay?" It could be argued he's imitating her own first-person remarks. Or, unless she's somehow made the whole outlandish thing up, Aimee's painted a persuasive portrait of a tenderhearted creature capable of empathy, sympathy, and even compassion.

But when she then claims that N'kisi does a little mind reading on the side, even I, Cedric the Gullible, arch an eyebrow. Then she pulls out a video of a recent experiment that I'm not sure I know how to argue with.

In the experiment, photos illustrating words from N'kisi's vocabulary were sealed in opaque envelopes and randomized by an outside party so that no one knew which image each envelope contained. Then, in a series of trial runs, Aimee was independently videotaped as she opened the envelopes behind closed doors in a room on the next floor. N'kisi, who remained in his cage downstairs, was taped by a second synchronized camera.

During one of the time-coded, two-minute sequences, Aimee can be seen sitting in her room looking at a picture of small, purple-pink flowers. N'kisi in his cage says, "We gotta go get the pictures of flowers. I gotta put pictures of flowers. Little flowers." She opens a picture of two men walking on the beach in skimpy, Speedo-style bathing suits. "Look at my pretty naked body!" N'kisi exclaims. She looks at a picture of a man talking on the phone—"Whatcha doin' on the phone?" N'kisi asks—and then a photo of two people hugging: "Can I give you a hug?" A panel of outside scorers determined that N'kisi had made twenty-three "hits" out of seventy-one sessions, far above chance.

Aimee says the strong results are due to the fact that, not to mince words, they love each other. I hear him call out to her: "I love you, weirdo, don't worry!" Is N'kisi compassionate? He talks the talk, and I imagine he'd walk the walk if he had proper feet. N'kisi means the "spirit of the thing": the soul, the mystery of the subjective (or *inter*subjective) life. Koko the gorilla signs "hug" by clasping herself around the shoulders with a rocking motion; Washoe the chimp gestures "please person hug" in American Sign Language; Kanzi the bonobo pokes at his "Hug" lexigram and grins. N'kisi says, "Can I have a kiss? Hurry up, I can't reach you!"

*I*f nature has a feeling-life, and we are part of its vast webbing, are there subtler ways in which we, too, reach out to each other? Could it be that, though we think ourselves sovereign individuals, we are swimming in an unsuspected sea of empathy? I pay a visit to Dean Radin, a former Bell Labs scientist and the author of *The Conscious Universe,* to see for myself. A diminutive man with a balding pate, his face framed by small wire-rims and a big moustache, wearing a gaudy T-shirt of a wildly colored tropical tree frog, Radin cuts a distinctly hobbity figure as we amble down to his laboratory at the rural Institute of Noetic Sciences (IONS) in Petaluma, California.

"Watch out for critters," he cautions as he unlocks the sliding glass door and a small lizard tries to skitter inside. His lab, a modest affair ("held together with spit and sealing wax," he jokes) consisting of a few computers, has one impressive central feature: a real Faraday Cage, a gleaming steel vault lined with copper shielding against any magnetic, electrical, or radio interference. Radin plans to wire me up, shut me in, and test whether, isolated from another experimental subject in a separate building, I can dive deep into their distant pool of emotion and somehow feel what they feel.

Radin points out that though the term *telepathy* became popularly known in the nineteenth century as "thought transference," the coinage literally means "far-feeling" or "feeling at a distance." Our experiment, he explains, will be literally testing for a transfer of "gut feelings": I and the other test subject will have electrodes attached to our abdomens to pick up electrical impulses from the dense concentration of neurons of the "enteric nervous system" (often called the "belly-brain"). The person I'll be distantly feeling, if all goes well, is Rose, a jolly, red-haired, matronly IONS staffer who's volunteered to act as the "sender." Radin asks us to exchange a personal object to help us tune in. I give her my watch; she takes a Celtic cross from around her neck and folds it into my hand. We hug and head off, like 1950s quiz show contestants, to our separate isolation booths.

Radin hands me a blue plastic Bic razor to rasp off some abdominal hair, leaving me not only feeling like a lab animal but, with a neat bald patch in my fur, looking like one. He attaches electrodes to my skin, their wires leading to a computer that will record my electrogastrogram, or EGG. The theory is that my unconscious "visceral perception" of Rose's feelings as she is shown a series of emotionally charged images may influence my readings. I recline comfortably in a chair, a set of earphones playing a soothing neutral tone stuck on my head, jacked in like Neo in *The Matrix*. "Close the pod bay door, Dean," I intone. He laughs politely.

I haven't been told how many images Rose will be seeing or at what intervals they will be presented to her. Holding her talisman, I try to "feel into" her feelings—"get a gut hunch" as Radin suggested. I do a little meditation: *Einfuhlung*, I repeat to myself as a mantra. *Einfuhlung mit Rose.* It's cozy in here. I sink into my padded chair. I get a fleeting image of a soldier with a gun; a little later, a clear, pacific sensation washes over me. I have no idea how much time passes

318

until the door abruptly swings open and Radin pops his head in to tell me it's over, setting about freeing me from the Laocoonian tangle of wires.

We cluster around the monitors as he examines our graphs, which compare, second by second, our patterns of physiological arousal. I'm surprised that during a series of violent images—a soldier with a gun (a standard image, after all), photos of starving Africans, bloody boxers, and killer sharks, all accompanied by a screeching soundtrack from the death-metal band Ramstein, neither I nor Rose show much agitation. Radin says this is common. "For sections that are negative or sad, volunteers' physiology typically becomes really quiet, as if they're holding their breath waiting for it to be over. Maybe it's like animals whose nervous systems 'play dead' under threat."

I'm embarrassed when Radin points out that toward the end of the session, according to the lines on my chart, I'd not only attained meditative equipoise but had fallen fast asleep. "But look here," he says, sounding, in his imperturbable way, excited. "There's a *huge* rise. Something fished you out in a hurry." Sure enough, at the very second that Rose was flashed a final image-and-sound stimulus, both her physiology *and* mine suddenly shot straight up, our graph lines nearly whanging off the chart in tandem.

"So what was *that*?" I ask.

He goes to his laptop, punches in the sequence, and the Beatles' "Twist and Shout" blasts out, accompanying a montage of smiling babies, bunnies, puppies, and kittens. I've been mad for the Beatles since my first high school cover band. And I do have a secret weakness, for which my friends roundly mock me, for baby animal pictures.

Statistically speaking, I've done better than chance, but I'm no star empath. When I ask Radin if he's had any real prodigies, he tells me about Steven and David, two medical students from the University of Florida who met for the first time in his lab. They were put in

319

separate rooms, wired up to brain EEGs, and instructed only to "tune into the presence of the other person." Radin pulls up the resultant charts for me on his computer. They're uncanny: The two students' tracings mirror each other with precision *every single time.* Peak for peak, trough for trough, the "receiver's" graph line maneuvers along the "sender's" flight path like a heat-seeking missile.

I am getting the feeling we are more than just connected; maybe we are *saturated* with each other, soaked through to the skin (and under it), brain, heart, guts—*you in me, me in you,* for real. Radin's experiments certainly raise some intriguing questions. Might a compassionate doctor be directly affecting the physiology of the patients he treats? (One HeartMath experiment demonstrated how a person's "coherent" heart rate variability could entrain another's EEG in a similar pattern—from several feet away.) Is this why Tibetan doctors are constantly reciting mantras for compassion and healing under their breath? Could a loving teacher be invisibly augmenting her students' attention spans? Is there a baseline scientific truth to "I'm picking up good vibrations"? What if our empathic sensing of another's feelings is not elicited solely by subtle facial cues, tone of voice, and body language, as social scientists believe, but by some emotional *emanation*? (Perhaps this was the mystery Edith Stein had wrestled with back in the 1920s when she posited that "true" empathy was distinguished by "immediately . . . reach[ing] its object directly without representation.")

If such emanations could be said to exist, Radin maintains they would be relatively weak. His instrumentation reveals that the amplitude of the receiver's response is far less than that of the sender: If the sender is engulfed by a crashing emotional wave, the receiver may only be moistened by the spray. It appears, too, that most people must work at staying tuned in, since we all seem to have an unconscious self-protective function (some psychologists call it an "empathic wall") that screens out others' unwanted feelings.*

My girlfriend, knowing I'm interested in this sort of thing, occasionally springs her own pop-quiz experiments on me. Driving around in her car one mid-December day, she playfully told me, "Okay, one of your really big Christmas presents is in the trunk. If you can guess what it is, I'll give it to you right now." I tried to clear my thoughts and get into a receptive state so as not to prejudge any images that might come to mind. (Parapsychologists theorize that psi is "primary process" cognition—a form of perception that is mostly pre-conscious.)

A picture immediately rose in my mind: a dead, gutted, still bloody sheep carcass lying crossways in the car's trunk. I was baffled.

"You got me, uh . . . a year's supply of *mutton*?"

She pulled the car over, opened the trunk. In it lay a nylon garment bag. She unzipped it to reveal an ankle-length, fleece-lined coat.

"Sheepskin," she said. "Do you *love* it?"

It was hard to say. I couldn't get the emotionally charged image out of my mind. I didn't want to hurt her feelings—it was a luxurious present. But now I was thinking (oh, *please* don't laugh) of a childhood encounter with a lamb at a petting zoo, recalling that eyes-wide feeling when, flush with some camaraderie of littleness, I reached out to stroke the sweet-faced creature's warm, soft fur. I asked apologetically if she could return the coat; I just couldn't strut around wrapped in a dead sheep. Though it had never bothered me before, the idea of turning living beings into fashion statements now seemed

---

* There may be an all-too-prosaic reason we find it hard to remain empathically tuned in: our tendencies toward self-centeredness. As Alfie Kohn explains in his book, *The Brighter Side of Human Nature:* "What often seems to happen is that genuine, other-oriented empathy gives way after a moment to dwelling on one's own experiences. One starts by feeling *her* joy, but this calls up a memory of the last time something unexpected and delightful happened to oneself, and soon the other's reality has slid away. Hoffman calls this 'egoistic drift,' and the impact is that one's capacity for empathy is a function not only of whether one can respond to others, but whether one can continue responding to others, *persisting* in the other-orientation."

a little barbarous. It was as if my vision had been received via some other organ of perception, the heart itself, which knows better than the intellect our true relationship to the things in this world.

One translation of the Buddhist term for compassion is "resonating concern." We say, "You touched a chord in me." A cello is bowed, and a string on an instrument across the room thrums. And not just across the room. The profoundly illogical phenomenon in quantum physics known as *nonlocality* implies that it could be across the galaxy. It has been shown that when light particles are shot from the same source in opposite directions, each tiny photon is instantaneously affected by what happens to its twin, even if the distance that separates them is light years. This interconnection, called *quantum entanglement,* has startling implications. Says a recent article in *New Scientist:* "When two electrons are entangled, it is impossible even in principle to describe one without the other. They have no independent existence."

Writing about this nonlocal coherence between separate entities, physicist Henry Stapp labels it the "most profound discovery in all of science." Profound, he says, because it suggests the truth of an ancient mystical formula: "We are all one; what I do to you, I do unto myself." Can it be that *you in me, me in you* is woven with infinitesimal care into the very fabric of the cosmos? The late systems engineer R. Buckminster Fuller, who designed the first geodesic dome and christened our planet Spaceship Earth, was once asked where a proper investigation of human nature should begin. He answered, as if it were plain as the nose on your face, "Why, you start with the *universe.*"

Which is where the organization known as SETI (Search for Extraterrestrial Intelligence) comes in. Based in Mountain

View, California, in the fertile delta of dot-com civilization, SETI has been deploying the world's largest radio telescope to scan a thousand sunlike stars—a quest that, thanks to vast increases in computational power, is trillions of times more effective than SETI's first hesitant census-taker's knock on heaven's door back in 1960.

SETI has now turned its attention to an overlooked contingency in the alien contact scenario—not just what message they might be trying to send us, but how we should reply. Years ago, when Pioneer 10 took its baby steps into the cosmos, we sent out an invitation of sorts: an embossed golden map of our solar system (along with a sort of Earth's Greatest Hits compilation that included that rocket-in-my-pocket rave-up, "Johnny B. Goode"). Carl Sagan, who designed the messages, later mused that any civilization advanced enough to pro-duce detectable signals must be cooperative enough to produce large-scale technology—and, if they were still out there, to have survived its Faustian consequences. They would therefore, he surmised, also prize altruism—something he'd neglected to stress in his cosmic care package.

Taking his cue, the Mountain View scientists are crafting what amounts to a new Human Manifesto. Our message to the stars, they've decided, should not just be that we're such almighty big-brains (the cosmic equivalent of cocktail party bores), but that we have hearts of gold. SETI hopes to encode, in the universal language of math and science, that humankind is, well . . . *kind*. If we can pass along that much—fold a love note and loft it like a paper airplane to a neighbor across the starry gulf—maybe they'd be persuaded we're worth getting to know.

The idea that there could be intelligent beings on other worlds is no longer far-fetched. Almost every other week, astronomers an-nounce the discovery of a new extrasolar planet (over a hundred out of potential billions). Our earliest TV broadcasts could already be showing at some multi-screen galactic googolplex. How must we look to them: like belligerent, thin-skinned anthropoids who traded up from aboriginal throwing sticks to ICBMs? greedy hominids recklessly fouling our nest? Or as sparks of light, long slumbering in dense matter, now finally waking up?

For years now, the thousand-foot dish antenna at Arecibo had sat receptive, its petals opened heavenward, awaiting a precious drop of intelligent communication amid the random patter of galactic rainfall. SETI had outsourced processing the enormous data stream via a computer program called SETI@Home, which had sat as a screensaver in the computers of four million volunteers in over two hundred countries, quietly crunching numbers in the machines' downtime, scanning for pattern. SETI had managed to cull 166 candidate stars that *could* be sending out signals, to which they'd added five observed extrasolar planetary systems, thirty-five proximate sunlike stars, and fifteen nearby galaxies.

Now, at last, in March 2003, SETI had scheduled a rare block of fifteen hours of precious radio-telescope time to reexamine the most promising sectors of the sky in hopes of finally making contact. That same week, a small group of scientists gathered in Paris to discuss what could quickly become a pressing question: If someone *had* sent us a message, what should we say back?

It was a muted, murky springtime in the City of Lights. Though ranks of young lovers billed on benches along the Seine and strollers admired the parks' new yellow and white crocuses, the boulevards felt less crowded than usual. The tourists had stayed home. The first laser-guided smart bomb had just ploughed headfirst into a Baghdad bunker. The French president had reiterated his opposition to the war, and in Washington's congressional kitchens, Earth's first Freedom Fries received their baptism by hot grease. Even as we inclined an ear toward the heavens, we had ceased listening to each other. The planet's airwaves were thick with discussions of acceptable collateral damage, not an auspicious time to persuade alien ham radio enthusiasts to be humankind's new best friend.

None of this fazed the hardy band of international scientists scattered on antique floral print couches in a grand *maison,* its stucco walls decorated with modern art and Hubble blow-ups. If anything, it made their mission more urgent. The meeting had been convened by SETI's "Interstellar Message Group Leader," Douglas Vakoch. A calm, alert man with a modified pageboy, a trim beard (nearly all the wisemen at this gathering favored facial hair), and an endearing air of humility, he opened by summarizing the protocols of the International Academy of Astronautics: If a strong candidate signal were identified (as it could be at any moment), the policy would be to immediately announce first contact to the world.

The gravitas of the meeting duly noted, he shifted to the task at hand, posing a pointed question: "Why should we think we have an ultimate understanding of compassion, given how poorly we act upon it? Maybe we'd best imagine we're speaking to a slightly older civilization than our own, one that's gotten through this phase and come out the other side."

What *would* we say to them? I ask Vakoch over tea. "Maybe we'd first talk about relationships between creatures in the language of biology, of kin selection and DNA transmission," he suggests, sipping his Darjeeling. "Based on that, we could try to convey something about reciprocal altruism: 'We'll be nice to you if you're nice to us.' "

But what if, I wonder, they find mere conditional niceness hopelessly primitive? Shouldn't we show we can be generous to someone even if they don't deserve it? That we can be kind beyond calculation, forgive when we've been wronged?

When Vakoch replies they are devising computer algorithms to express that very thing, I catch some of the excitement of this project: to lift ourselves for a moment above the muck of earthly affairs and put our best foot forward to the stars; to announce, officially, that we're not just a species mired in quotidian callousness and endless tribal squabbles; to tell Someone Out There that we're becoming what we aspire to be—Really Good People—and maybe convince ourselves in the process.

It's an exercise in perspective-taking. By reimagining altruism through ET's eyes, can we find new ways of thinking about compassion itself? It is less a question about deep space than the deeper recesses of the human heart. Would discovering some alien Other, as the old sci-fi premise has it, render trivial the differences among us, so that we would finally regard each other as fellow earthlings, worthy of each other's terrestrial mercies?

Vakoch has been seeing the world through this exotic lens all his life. He decided early in sixth grade that it was only rational to assume ET was out there somewhere. His high school science fair project was entitled "Encoding Interstellar Messages," and he has never strayed far from his original path, though his ideas of how to get where he's going have diverged. At first, he thought we should trumpet our scientific strengths to the stars. Now, he muses, if we want to get a compassionate response from a more mature civilization, we might tell them how fragile we are.

"When we think of representing ourselves in interstellar messages," he says, "we usually think of how we can show we're great and powerful. But what makes us potentially unique in this galaxy is that we're so *young*. Maybe our most interesting characteristic to a civilization that's thousands or even millions of years more advanced is that we're still frail and mortal creatures. We can't download our consciousness or continually back ourselves up. Death *means* something to us. The sense of personal finitude, that we each will end, tends to overcome egotism. It can be an opening to care for the other." I'm moved: If this is the applause line for our galactic debut, it could be a big opening night.

But how do we know how advanced *their* compassion is? Should we broadcast our vulnerabilities willy-nilly to the whole universe, let everyone in hailing range know what a wussy little orb we really are?

Although a predisposition to cooperate is genetically encoded in our species—and is probably a trait of civilized creatures anywhere— there could be crucial differences in degree. "Maybe *they've* only gotten as far as kin-selected altruism. Then they may be ethnocentric like we are," says one scientist whose fringe of white beard reminds me—I can't help it—of old Professor Zaius in the original *Planet of the Apes*. But here on Earth, he adds, "the definition of the in-group is malleable—sometimes it's your immediate family, sometimes it's all your uncles and cousins, sometimes your whole village, or everyone who speaks your language. We'd better find a way to convince them, 'Hey, we're your relatives, we're like you.'"

Or maybe out there in the galaxy, he posits, the in-group consists of any intelligent species. That could be good; or maybe not. What if the intergalactic smart set didn't agree we make the cut?

Or what if, as another scientist queries, they'd want to see "a moral imperative, something we strive to attain, rather than possess automatically as a species"? How to convey the sincerity of our striving was the subject of intense discussion. Religious imagery, it was suggested, embodies the human aspiration toward compassion and virtue. On the other hand, religions' centuries of sectarian strife show that one group's standard of virtue is another's definition of moral turpitude. There seems to be no limit on how badly "universal truths" can be mishandled.

To say nothing of visual imagery, another messaging strategy. I've wondered how Sagan's image of the man with the upraised hand, our classic we-come-in-peace gesture, has been received across the parsecs (after all, the V-for-Victory sign in some cultures is a crude sexual insult). One message designer shows an animation of a spindly biped carrying a similarly shaped but differently colored creature in its arms. The idea, he says, is to signal that we care for our injured, a compassionate human trait going back to the fossil evidence. But it occurs to me an alien might think, *It's only protecting its mate, its kin, its tribesman;* or worse: *It's bringing home the groceries.*

It's proposed that a Madonna and Child image would be the most universal way of conveying the value we place on parental care of infants. "This is almost surely a trait of all intelligent species," notes a scientist. "At the very least, some transgenerational bonding necessary for the emergence of culture." But is this enough to demonstrate compassion? We love our own children, and our brothers kids', and even the next-door neighbor's. But what about the stranger's children? What about the children of our enemies? There were uneasy jokes about hoping the aliens didn't get cable, so they wouldn't see any CNN images of child victims of famine and war (in which case, sending our message of peace and love might result in our being designated on all star charts as the Planet of the Big Fat Liars).

Decades ago, in this Parisian house built by a Portuguese sculptor, where pulleys that once hoisted the blank marble blocks still dangle from the ceiling, Soviet cosmonauts and American astronauts had met at the peak of the Cold War to seek commonality across what seemed an unbridgeable gulf. I can sense the same wistful hankering for human harmony beneath all this passion for galactic dialogue. If we can figure out how to describe lovingkindness to an alien, why can't we manifest it here on Earth, a place where, despite a bravura bit of celestial PR, we are increasingly alienated from one another? Are we really capable of becoming one people, one world? Can we create a global civilization based on compassion and stewardship—the kind we'd like to imagine might be Out There among the stars—here on the home planet, before it really is too late?

A few days into the event, the question (at least the Out There part of it) was mooted, at least for now. There had been no gush of eager cosmic chatter at Arecibo. The search, at least this phase of it, had drilled another dry hole. Humanity would have a little more alone time to get its act together, though who knows for how long. Vakoch points out that SETI will be ramping up its search to include a hundred thousand stars in the Milky Way, a locale where, as another SETI-ite put it, "planets are as common as phone poles."

"If there is life out there, we'll have a reasonable chance of detecting it," says Vakoch modestly. Contact within twenty-five or at most fifty years is the number commonly bandied about. Then he tells me something that brings me up short. "If we hear from another civilization tomorrow or next week, there's nothing to stop anybody on Earth from transmitting back. My concern is that the first response they receive will set the tone for dialogue over centuries and millennia."

Oh, that's just great, I think. I strive for tolerance, but the notion that the first voice they hear could be the Grand Cuckoo of the Aryan Brotherhood, or the Vizier of the Final Jihad, or the President of the East Rutherford Rotarians . . . I must look appalled, because Vakoch hastens to add, "Some of us are adamant we should have a very coherent message all ready to go, so immediately upon detection, a strong signal will get sent out that says, somehow, this is the official one."

Somehow? As soon as word of First Contact leaks out, everyone and his brother will be elbowing each other in the eyeball to set himself up as Proconsul of Terra.

This won't do. While we have a little breathing room, before they send the Space Patrol or the little green men in white coats, I've decided to send my own message in a bottle, see if I can make a few ripples in the cosmic pond; you know, just to set the right tone. (Besides, I have to admit: Acting Plenipotentiary of Gaia has kind of a nice ring to it.)

I can't tell you how I transmitted the message below (let's just say it involved a strategic partnership between UPS Air and the Susquehanna Bottling Company). By the time you read this, it will be caroming off the constellations:

TO: OCCUPANT (Please Forward if Necessary)
LIMITED-TIME OFFER—SEE INSIDE FOR DETAILS!

Dear Alpha,

I hope you won't mind if I call you that, after Alpha Centauri, one of our regular-yellow-star neighbors. I could call you Zeta, after Zeta Reticuli, to cover the bases, but I like Alpha, Aleph, the beginning: This could be the start of a beautiful relationship.

First off, I *know* we're the new kid on the block. The Hubble might as well be the Humble for what it's shown us about where we fit in the big picture: a miniscule pin stuck into a map of infinity *(You Are Here);* a pale blue-green speck in a vertiginous, star-spackled Vast. It's been a corrective lens for human astigmatism.

Our astronomers say we're just one of hundreds of millions of habitable planets. And that 75 percent of the stars in our galaxy's temperate zone are older than our sun, meaning you could be our big brother ten *million* years ahead in birth order (so much for sibling rivalry). I bet we remind you of yourselves back when you were young and full of mischief; didn't *you* once go around stockpiling weapons of mass destruction, extinguishing your fellow creatures, soiling land, water, and air like there's no tomorrow? (If you're reading this, you've *had* a tomorrow, and I can't tell you how encouraging I find that.)

If we can nearly see you now, you've already spotted us. Maybe you've homed in our planet's most visible artificial landmark, the Great Wall of China, leaving no doubt there's belligerent—I mean, *intell*igent!—life down here. Sort of: Our *really* largest man-made features are the clouds of smoke from burning rainforests, the bone-white of dying coral reefs, the leaching tan of encroaching deserts—ultralarge-scale public art installations whose theme, I suppose, is our lack of love for each other, for ourselves, and for our fellow beings.

I try to imagine what kind of beings you are. Maybe you'd appear to us as superevolved lizards or cerebral fish; as the magenta-winged offspring of clever birds or the brainy descendants of great cats. Some of the creatures we're carelessly extinguishing might remind you of your next of kin. Seeing how we treat the nonhuman species here at home probably doesn't give you much confidence about inviting us to dinner. (I'll assume you're too evolved to want us *for* dinner.)

On the off-chance you've snagged our Pioneer's golden tablet, you know what *we* look like. (Hint: We're the bipeds on the right, not that rectangle-thing in the middle.) I hope you enjoyed the Solomon Island panpipe music and the solar calibration charts and those intimate diagrams of our anatomy (*we'll show you ours if you'll show us yours*). But we forgot to put our best foot forward. The geniuses who put that parsec-traipsing *piñata* together left out the good stuff, like something called the Sermon on the Mount ("Do good to them that hate you"—how's that for a starter?); to say nothing of the Dhammapada, the Mishnah, the Mathnawi of Rumi, the Tao Te Ching, the Upanishads, and lots more where those came from.

I could just summarize them by saying *we get it:* each of us a thread, woven by universal affinity, in the tapestry of the Great Whole. We could ace the written portion of the galactic entrance exam; it's the practicum we'd flunk. We can sense there comes a point when an intelligent species gets *so* smart it's too clever by half, and the only possible way through the evolutionary bottleneck—what I expect you did—is just to pop the cork of universal love. Love each other, love the planet; love madly, with no fear, without restraint. Our sci-fi writers always envision you with really big heads; but if you've made

331

it any further than we have, you must have gigantic hearts. I like to imagine you can feel the invisible waves and fluxes flowing between creatures as directly as we feel each other's warmth and breath and pulse. (Our nonverbal signals to each other are relatively crude— even an octopus blushes more expressively, in more colors. Too often we're left guessing at each other's feelings, getting it all wrong.)

Speaking of feelings, as I write these words, I feel far away not just from your world, wherever that is, but from my own. It steals over all six billion of us from time to time; a moment we say silently to ourselves, how *can* we? How can we let each other suffer so; how can we trash our Garden; how can we not take care of *every*one's children? We're going through a terribly awkward phase, that's for sure, and taking our own sweet time coming out of it. We're just figuring out how to talk to each other and, more importantly, how to listen. (That's what that great dish at Arecibo really symbolizes—a big human eardrum.)

Now we're all abuzz that mass communications have created some kind of planetary nervous system, an awakening bud of self-consciousness—the Global Brain. But you're probably awaiting a bigger development—the Global Heart. Maybe you're already scanning the heavens with your intergalactic stethoscopes, listening for coherent heart murmurs among the pulsars; for what the Little Prince (was he one of your guys?) said was essential but invisible to the eye. If your instruments can detect *that* spectrum, then you've seen more than our great walls—you've seen through the cracks to all our small kindnesses. You know us not as the Planet of the Super-Clever Apes, but the Planet of the Angels-in-Training.

We are growing beyond our Big Blue Marble phase, when we first looked in the mirror and recognized an *Us*. Now we're ready for relationship: We're looking for an Other, someone to start an I-Thou relationship. At the same, we're realizing maybe there *is* no Other. We know that, strictly speaking, everything started out as a dot of quantum fuzz, expanding into a universe in a fraction of a second (1/10 to the 25th power, we figure). Way Back When, it was all stuck together, a single agglomerated substance of One. So if nonlocality is true—if each mote that's been in contact with another stays so forever, then the stardust we are and you are and everything is remains in some state of unbreakable entanglement. Call it the Cosmic Mirror Neuron. Or as one of our great Earth poets, William Blake, put it: *Thou canst not stir a flower without disturbing a star.*

Not that we mean to (disturb you, that is, with all our flower-stirring). It's just that for so long, we've been the frog at the bottom of the well, thinking our little round patch of sky was the universe. Six hundred years ago, our religions were still telling us the Earth was the center of Creation; and now the Hubble vistas are our stained-glass windows.

We know you're out there, somewhere. But until we hear from you, the stars look lovely, bright, and cold. A famous biologist—a winner of our great Peace Prize, no less—once looked through a telescope and pronounced: "Man at last knows he is alone in the unfeeling immensity of the universe." You'd probably have a good laugh over that one. Not just the alone part—the *unfeeling* part. The universe must be *agog* with feeling: How else could it have given birth to such deeply feeling progeny? This irresistible urge to reach out to you is a sign of our gregariousness; of our desire—our profligacy—to make relatives. We're ready to dive into the cosmos heart-first.

We've seen the nurseries of light where suns are spawned in searing fire. We've trembled at the roiling black hole at the center of the Milky Way, gobbling up stars like TicTacs. We know that life's job is coherence, attraction; that entropy already has all the help it needs.

The point is, dear Alpha, dear cipher in the inky void: We'll get there. We're a last-minute, dog-ate-my-homework kind of species—impulsive, shortsighted, just down from the treetops. We'll make it through, just in the nick of time.

By the time this reaches you, millenia will have passed. But if we're still here to receive your reply, we'll be home free. Heck, if we manage to find a steady source of dilithium crystal, we may land on your doorstep to accept it in person—all spruced up, hair slicked back, nice smile (not showing too many teeth), with a little gift for the Missus or the Mister or the Little Spores. We may even have a thing or two to teach *you*.

Maybe we already do. I've enclosed an attachment, the diamond words of ancient seers (and not incidentally, the newest findings of our scientists), translated into the universal harmonic language by some galactic goodwill ambassadors called the Beatles:

All You Need Is Love. (You can trust me on this.)

Very Truly Yours,

A Friend

P.S. Please send a formula for neutralizing spent plutonium, the schematics for superluminal drive, and a design for a cellophane-free CD case? Thanks!

CONCLUSION

And the day came when the risk it took
to remain closed in a bud became more painful
than the risk it took to blossom.

—Anais Nin

*M*eanwhile, back on Earth, what began as a project feels more like a life. I mean, is there anywhere compassion is contraindicated? It's good for body, mind, and spirit; good for loved ones and total strangers; good for all this world. No reason not to have some with my orange juice each morning.

I know for a plausible fact that people do change for the better, and incrementally change others. I know that compassion's a grace of sorts, inhering in the nature of things, but is brought forth by a certain exertion, as butter emerges from milk by the labor of the churn.

So I labor, little by little. I've started volunteering at a home for mentally disabled adults. A few of them are functional enough to hold down a janitor's job, while others, heartbreakingly, are too impaired to talk. When we go on field trips to the bowling alley, half the balls roll into the gutter. When we play laser tag, the beams bounce everywhere but the target. We win some, lose most, but who cares? I like making my way in the world with them. Their need draws out, as if by capillary action, a more generous flow of affection. It makes so-called charity mutual.

Sometimes I help out at a local family assistance center, stacking the cans, doing intake; or fill in a shift here and there at the homeless shelter. Compassion is one job that's always hiring, with nil chance of getting downsized. I don't do all that much, dear reader; probably less than *you* do. But I've noted that simple kindness never fails to live up to its billing. That trick that's no trick at all works as advertised: Amaze Your Friends and Confound Your Enemies. The instructions are basic. When your heart feels empty, try filling up somebody else's. What's in it for you? Nothing but love's infinite debt.

Teilhard de Chardin took the infinite part seriously. He insisted that compassion is—must be—endlessly extensible. "We are often inclined to think," he wrote, "that we have exhausted the various natural forms of love with a man's love for his wife, his children, his friends, and to a certain extent for his country. Yet precisely the most fundamental form of passion is missing from this list . . . A universal love is possible; it is the only complete and final way in which we are able to love."

Looking at the mess that, despite our best intentions, our normal, incomplete love has made of things, it's hard to argue. Sometimes, just when it feels like the tide is turning, our planet seems to plunge—absurdly, tragically—back into strife and plunder. Yet even a cursory reading of the paper suggests that we're living through a Great Transition (though it may seem like a Great Contradiction). The other day came the news that dozens of nations have agreed to create a shared observation system for our atmosphere, oceans, and land masses. Even the American commerce secretary was moved to poesy, calling it "the heartbeat of Mother Earth." But the adjacent headline would give Mom a heart attack: "Faster 2nd Quarter Growth Fuels Optimism," it trumpeted, exulting over a resource-gobbling economy turbocharged by "rising military and consumer spending." It was accompanied by photos of SUVs and an Abrams tank.

Polls show that most people in the world favor humbler, more compassionate solutions to our common problems. Not only favor them but, resolving to love in a more complete and final way, try to put them into action. A society based on universal compassion is not just our only hope; it is an evolutionary imperative.

D e Chardin, for one, believed that our entire species is heading toward some new and improved version—and why not? Evolution
reveals that we've *come from* somewhere; we must be *going* somewhere. Some of our woes seem to stem from quirks of our brain's evolutionary history: We are wired, neurobiologist Joseph LeDoux points
out, for "emotional arousal to dominate and control thinking." But
that story's far from over. LeDoux also notes that in higher primates,
the neural connections between cognitive and emotional areas have
grown so extensively in a mere eyeblink of eons it could be said our
species is fairly racing toward "a more harmonious integration of
reason and passion."

Darwin himself was certain of it. "Looking to future generations,"
he wrote in an uncharacteristic burst of optimism, "the struggle between our higher and our lower impulses will be less severe, and
virtue will be triumphant." I spoke to one leading evolutionary biologist who affirmed it (though he cautiously refused to elaborate): "Recent evidence for directional trends in evolution involve increases in
empathy, affectionate attachment, and intersubjective awareness."
Maybe, just maybe, after three and a half billion years of scrambling,
clambering ascent, it's survival of the kindest from here on out.

In 2003, it was discovered that humans and African apes, alone
among the mammals, have large, specialized neurons called spindle
cells. (Bonobos have two thousand of them, an adult human over
eighty thousand.) These cells, which have been called the "air traffic
controllers for emotion," show up in the frontoinsular cortex, an area
that in human brain imaging lights up on quintessentially human occasions: when we gaze lovingly at a romantic partner; feel embarrassment; perceive unfairness or deception; or respond to an infant's
cry. It has been speculated that it might be the biological seat of the
moral sense.

It is located within a brain region that began an explosive growth
spurt a mere hundred thousand years ago. It means that fully fledged

Homo sapiens sapiens—noble not only in form, but in sensibility—may have popped onto the stage in what is very nearly historical time. What we think of as our most human characteristics are so brand spanking new, it's hard to imagine they won't be subject to future upgrades.

There are already murmurs among geneticists that we should consider doing the work ourselves. With the sequencing of the three billion basepairs of the genome, the audacity of tinkering with our own nature is no longer just a sci-fi premise. Scientists like DNA codiscoverer James Watson are already chafing at the restraints: "Sure, we talk about making better plants and making better animals," he fumed recently, "but you're not allowed to talk about making *better humans.*"

But what *is* a better human? In Watson's estimation, smarter, to be sure, but not necessarily kinder. He has opined that the "two stupidest sentences" in the English language are "love thine enemy" and "the meek shall inherit the earth." (Bibical scholars translate "the meek" as "the humble-minded" or "the peacemakers." The dictionary defines meek as "not inclined to anger or resentment." For my money, the meek can't inherit the Earth soon enough.)

So flash forward, if you will, to the not-too-distant future. You're shopping for your kid, literally: perusing the aisles for those genes that will best enhance your progeny. You've scrimped and saved for those premium genes for brilliance, good looks, disease resistance, and athleticism. You can afford one more selection: either that ambition gene everyone's been talking about or an altruism gene. Which are you going to pick? Do you want your kid to have Mengzi's mind that is unable to bear the suffering of others? How will he fare on the playground of the future, surrounded by genetically turbocharged kids whose parents didn't prioritize tenderheartedness? Will genes for empathy and altruism wind up as K-Mart Blue Light Specials, right next to the Martha Stewart Laser Pruning Shears?

In his novel *Brave New World,* Aldous Huxley, intellectual godfather of human genetic engineering, conceived of a society dominated by specimens factory-bred for dazzling intellectual gifts and cold, calculating hearts. But this common portrait of the superbrainy is completely at odds with contemporary studies of gifted children. Educators have observed acute moral sensitivities; a tendency to forgive easily when offended; precocious concerns about peace and justice. They have also noted the difficulties these children have in, as one researcher put it, "continuing with the generous, compassionate, and altruistic responses of early childhood." (Emotionally sensitive boys may become extra-aggressive to avoid "the considerable risk for peer rejection and ridicule"; their empathic "overexcitability" makes them vulnerable.)

But also chronicled is what happens when such children are nurtured and encouraged: The world becomes a kinder place. One boy conceived a personal mission to protect the rights of children at the age of five, and began speaking at public events. By the time he was ten, he had formed his own national organization. A four-year-old, upset at seeing a flood on the news, packed up his toys to send to the disaster zone, then persuaded other kids to do the same, until the town's children (and some inspired adults) filled a semi-trailer for the victims.

I recently met a seven-year-old girl, call her Cicely, with an off-the-charts IQ. She ran into the room like a ray of light. She had large, bright blue eyes, like a Keane painting. Her mother, a former barmaid, remembers her as "this talking infant who startled people: Did that *baby* just say that?"

To make me feel at home, Cicely proposed a tea party, serving me on a little tray she'd set with her miniature cups and saucers. "To put a fish in a pond to be caught for sport," she observed, making rather pointed teatime chitchat, "that's rather cruel, don't you think?" Most certainly is, I agreed, pretend-sipping as she regarded me gravely.

Cicely is ferociously articulate, but her mother told me she has been most astonished by her acute empathy. "When she was little, she'd bring in leaves at the end of fall 'so they won't be cold all winter.' If even a cartoon character gets into trouble, she can't stand it. She'll chant, 'Oh, no, oh, no,' and breathe real fast." When someone in Cicely's class refused to sit down next to the most unpopular kid, she ran over and threw an arm over the rejected girl's shoulder, repeating with great feeling, "I really, *really* like you." One Halloween, said her mother, "We ran out of candy and she told me, 'Mom, just put all the stuff I got in *their* bags.' I would never have given away my Halloween goodies when I was kid—*never.*"

For all that, Cicely's a well-balanced, even merry child. When I discovered a tiny hair in my little cup, we sleuthed from its blonde color it was her eyelash. "Eyelash Tea!" she exclaimed, grinning at me delightedly, miming another pour.

I often wonder if those most gifted with "caring thinking" aren't some sort of harbingers. But we don't need a new set of genes or extra smarts to share our candy. Something within us already conduces toward heartfulness, and its nature is to grow with the merest effort. Aldous Huxley, asked on his deathbed to sum up what he had learned in his eventful life, said, "It's embarrassing to tell you this, but it seems to come down mostly to just learning to be kinder." And though I set out to write a more hardheaded, less softhearted (and perhaps less soft*headed*) book, I can only conclude the same.

People living in arid countries have found a simple method of collecting water. They spread out sheets of fabric at night and siphon off the dew that condenses on them each morning. Like moisture, love really *is* in the air. It will settle upon the thinnest reed, scintillate on a bare tip of grass, free for the taking. It is an elixir that can heal, drop by drop, all the sorrow and separation in the world. It changes pretty much everything.

NOTES

1. THE CIRCLE OF COMPASSION

page 10 *"extend how you relate to yourself toward others"* Richard J. Davidson and Anne Harrington, *Visions of Compassion: Western Scientists and Tibetan Buddhists Examine Human Nature* (New York: Oxford University Press, 2002).

page 10 *"open the lock of self-love and wrest it away from a person"* Søren Kierkegaard, *Works of Love,* ed. and trans. Howard V. Hong and Edna H. Hong (Princeton, NJ: Princeton University Press, 1995).

page 11 *"openness to mutual influence"* Janet L. Surrey, "The Self-in-Relation," in *Women's Growth in Connection,* eds. J. V. Jordan, A. Kaplan, J. B. Miller, I. Stiver, & J. Surrey, 51–66. (New York: The Guilford Press, 1991). Surrey critiques Winnicott's model of "object relations," citing its "basic assumption of narcissism and human separateness."

page 16 *"[T]his united I selfishly cuts itself off from everyone else"* Søren Kierkegaard, op. cit., 56.

page 17 *"[O]ur brains are physically wired to develop in tandem with another's"* Allan N. Schore, *Affect Dysregulation and Disorders of the Self* (New York: W. W. Norton & Co., 2003), xv.

2. ROOTS, BRANCHES, AND THE CLEAR BLUE SKY

page 28 *only two entries for "survival of the fittest"* David Loye, *Darwin's Lost Theory of Love: A Healthy Vision for the New Century* (San Jose: toExcel/iUniverse, 2000).

page 30 *"hard to believe a banana is 30 percent as conscious as I am"* Kate Prendergast, "Updating Our Origins; Biology, Genetics and Evolution: An Interview with Steve Jones," *Science and Spirit* 10, no. 5 (2000): 24.

page 36 *a group of psychiatrists at Northwestern University trained rhesus monkeys to pull a chain* Stanley Wechkin, Jules H. Masserman, and William Terris, Jr. "Shock to a Conspecific as an Aversive Stimulus," *Psychonomic Science,* 1 (1964): 47–48; and "'Altruistic' Behavior in Rhesus Monkeys," *The American Journal of Psychiatry,* 121 (1964): 584–85.

page 36 *Italian neuroscientists pinpointed a mechanism in the primate brain* V. Gallese and A. Goldman, "Mirror Neurons and the Simulation Theory of Mind-Reading," *Trends in Cognitive Sciences,* 12 (1998): 493–501.

page 37 *"archaic kind of sociality, one which does not distinguish between self and other"* Leslie Brothers, "A Biological Perspective on Empathy," *American Journal of Psychiatry* 146, no. 1 (1989): 10–19.

page 39 *giving her a hug while making "consoling sounds"* Carolyn Zahn-Wexler and Marian Radke-Yarrow, "The Origins of Empathic Concern," *Motivation and Emotion* 14, no. 2 (1990): 107–30.

page 41 *Kanzi tried to wash her wound* Sue Savage-Rumbaugh, Stuart G. Shanker, and Talbot J. Taylor, *Apes, Language and the Human Mind* (New York: Oxford University Press, 1998).

page 48n *social modification of what are usually considered hardwired traits among baboons* Natalie Angier, "No Time for Bullies: Baboons Retool Their Culture," *New York Times,* (April 13, 2004): F1.

page 51 *"we just pay less attention to compassion"* His Holiness the Dalai Lama, "Understanding our Fundamental Nature," in Richard Davidson and Anne Harrington, op. cit., 90.

3. EMPATHY: YOU IN ME, ME IN YOU

page 55 *"they think everybody's always thinking the same things"* Dennis Krebs and Christine Russell, "Role-Taking and Altruism: When You Put Yourself in the Shoes of Another, Will They Take You to Their Owner's Aid?" in *Altruism and Helping Behavior,* eds. J. Philippe Rushton and Richard M. Sorrentino, 137. (Hillsdale, NJ: Lawrence Erlbaum Associates, 1981).

page 57 *"Confucian self-development lies in how we treat this spontaneous feeling of compassion"* Franklin Perkins, "To Be Human Is to Be Humane," *Parabola* 28, no. 1 (2003): 14–15.

page 57 *Some research even links "guilt-proneness" to the ability to take another's perspective* Karen Leith and Roy F. Baumeister, "Empathy, Shame, Guilt, and Narratives of Interpersonal Conflicts," *Journal of Personality* (1998): 66: 1–37.

page 59 *other-directed empathy shows "somatic quieting"* Elliott Sober and David Sloan Wilson, *Unto Others: The Evolution and Psychology of Unselfish Behavior* (Cambridge, MA: Harvard University Press, 1998), 235–36.

page 61 *"in order to know the mystery of the* Thou *in its whole truth"* Martin Buber in Alfie Kohn, *The Brighter Side of Human Nature: Altruism and Empathy in Everyday Life* (New York: Basic Books, 1990), 153.

page 64n *"Sherman would become fearful and allow himself to be comforted by Austin."* Sanjida M. O'Connell, "Empathy in Chimpanzees: Evidence for Theory of Mind?" *Primates* 36, no. 3 (July 1995): 401.

page 64 *the Chameleon Effect in just about everybody* T. L. Chartrand and J. A. Bargh, "The Chameleon Effect: The Perception-Behavior Link and Social Interaction," *Journal of Personal and Social Psychology* 76(6): 893–910. See also M. Iacoboni, et al., "Cortical Mechanisms of Human Imitation," *Science*, 286 (1999): 2526–8.

page 64 *rate highest on the empathy scale* Tanya L. Chartrand and John A. Bargh, "The Chameleon Effect: The Perception-Behavior Link and Social Interaction," *Journal of Personality and Social Psychology* 76 (1999): 893–910.

page 71n *consciousness might not be our vaunted "sense of self"* V. Gallese, "The 'Shared Manifold' Hypothesis: From Mirror Neurons to Empathy," *Journal of Consciousness Studies,* 8, no. 5–7 (2001): 33–50.

page 72 *"You need to love all persons as yourself"* Matthew Fox, *A Spirituality Named Compassion* (New York: Harper San Francisco/HarperCollins, 1990).

page 72 *just as impossible as "to cut the sky in two with a knife"* Shantideva, *The Way of the Bodhisattva,* trans. Padmakara Translation Group (Boston: Shambhala Press, 1997).

page 73 *exercise proposed by a Buddhist scholar* Ruben L. F. Habito, "Being and Emptiness: Buddhist Perspectives on Compassion," *Science & Spirit,* 11, no. 1 (2000): 46.

4. STREET RETREAT: THE DEBT OF LOVE

page 79 *"the most dangerous acquaintance love can make"* Søren Kierkegaard, op. cit., 186.

page 83 *"or picking up a child who has fallen on the floor"* Bernie Glassman, *Bearing Witness* (New York: Bell Tower-Random House, 1999).

page 84 *argued against harboring any delusions* Søren Kierkegaard, op. cit., 62.

page 94 *"When we fear rejection, we don't let generosity arise"* Bernie Glassman, op. cit., 201–2.

5. THE GOOD EYE

page 101   *"to see their highest and holiest potential"*   Estelle Frankel, "Sweetening the Judgements: The Kabbalah of Compassion," *Parabola* 28, no. 1 (2003): 14–15.

page 105   *"the Activity of Being in Crowds"*   9th Karmapa Wang-ch'ug Dorje, *The Mahamudra: Eliminating the Darkness of Ignorance,* trans. Alexander Berzin (Dharmsala, India: Library of Tibetan Works and Archives, 1978), 101.

page 116   *"The moment you start hearing what you yourself are saying, you must stop"*   Martin Buber, *Tales of Hassidim: The Early Masters,* trans. Olga Marx (New York: Schocken Books, 1947), 107.

6. HEART SCIENCE, HEART'S MYSTERY

page 124   *a widely reported 1986 experiment*   David C. McClelland, "Some Reflections on the Two Psychologies of Love," *Journal of Personality* 54, no. 2 (June 1986): 344–49.

page 133   *"The heart is a tomb, and there our thoughts and intellect are buried"*   St. Markarios of Egypt, *The Philokalia* 3, in *Parabola* 26, no. 4 (Winter 2001): 70.

page 135   *"I don't see how . . . a few repetitions of the 'Hail Mary' are going to solve any problems"*   Frank Bruni, "Faith Fades Where It Once Burned Strong," *New York Times,* October 13, 2003, A1.

page 137   *"there's going to be something in your brain that's different from someone who didn't do that"*   Harvard neuroscientist Stephen Kosslyn quoted in Stephen S. Hall, "Is Buddhism Good for Your Health?" *New York Times,* September 14, 2003, sec. 6, p. 46.

page 137   *"You generate this quality of loving, and let it soak the mind"*   Daniel Goleman, *Destructive Emotions: How Can We Overcome Them?* (New York: Bantam Books, 2003), 6.

page 138   *"caring and concern, mixed with a not unpleasant strong, poignant sadness"*   Daniel Goleman, op. cit., 11–27.

8. THE ALTRUIST

page 175 *[Oliner's studies] found that rescuers had a particular character-istic* Samuel and Pearl Oliner, *The Altruistic Personality: Rescuers of Jews in Nazi Europe* (New York: The Free Press, 1988), 174. The Oliners add, "Rescuers thus did not differ from others with relation to the type of empathy called 'emotional contagion'—that is, a general susceptibility to others' moods. Rescuers did not any more than non-rescuers become worried just because others were worried or get upset just because a friend was upset. Nor did they differ from non-rescuers with respect to being moved by others' positive emotional experiences."

page 177 *August Comte, the eccentric nineteenth-century French visionary* Mary Pickering, *Auguste Comte: An Intellectual Biography vol. 1.* (Cambridge, MA: Cambridge University Press, 1993), 315.

page 179 *"The Nazis thus attempted to use biology to deter rescuers, but did not succeed"* Kristin Renwick Monroe, *The Heart of Altruism: Perceptions of a Common Humanity* (Princeton, NJ: Princeton University Press, 1996), 165.

page 186 *"unconscious recognition . . . of the close dependency of everyone's happiness upon the happiness of all"* Peter Kropotkin, *Mutual Aid: A Factor of Evolution* (Boston, MA: Porter Sargent Publishers, 1976), 21–22.

page 186 *"feeling or instinct of human solidarity and sociability which moves me"* Kropotkin cited in Daniel Batson, *The Altruism Question: Toward a Social Psychological Answer* (Hillsdale, NJ: L. Erlbaum, 1991), 40.

page 188 *children who are shown TV programs with positive messages* Alfie Kohn, op. cit., quotes George Gerbner and his colleagues at the Annenberg School of Communication at the University of Pennsylvania. George Gerbner, "The Politics of Media Violence: Some Reflections" in *Mass Communication Research: On Problems and Policies: The Art of Asking the Right Questions,* eds. Olga Linné and Cees J. Hamelink (Norwood, NJ: Ablex Publishing, 1994).

page 188 *In a small town, three-quarters of passersby stopped to help; in a city, only half* Alfie Kohn, "Beyond Selfishness," *Psychology Today* (October 1998): 34–38.

page 191 *"qualitatively different new intelligence . . . caring thinking"* Caring Thinking was introduced by Matthew Lipman at the 6th International Conference on Thinking in Boston in 1994.

page 191 *"motivated by an intense social and moral conscience"* Lipman, op. cit.

page 192 *"if men suddenly see a child about to fall into a well"* Mencius (Mengzhi) quoted in Frans de Waal, *The Ape and the Sushi Master: Cultural Reflections by a Primatologist* (New York: Basic Books-Perseus Publishing, 2001), 255.

page 194 *small number of Holocaust rescuers credited religion* Samuel P. Oliner, *Do Unto Others* (Boulder, CO: Westview Press, 2004), 108.

page 196 *joked that his morals were "only slightly better than those of an average American congressman"* Monroe, op. cit., xi.

9. THE ELIXIR OF FORGIVENESS

page 206 *"fantasies about killing people they don't like"* Douglas Kenrick and David Buss in Steven Pinker, *The Blank Slate: The Modern Denial of Human Nature* (Viking/Penguin Putnam, 2002), 316–17.

page 214 *cardiac patients who blame others for their initial heart attack* Carl E. Thoreson, Alex H. S. Harris, and Frederic Luskin, "Forgiveness and Health: An Unanswered Question," in *Forgiveness: Theory, Research, and Practice,* eds. Michael E. McCullough, Kenneth I. Pargament, and Carle E. Thorsen (New York: The Guilford Press, 2000), 257.

page 215 *"To forgive, one must have the capacity"* Robert A. Emmons, "Personality and Forgiveness," in Michael E. McCullough, op. cit., 166.

page 215 *a person who is too self-centered may be incapable of forgiving* John Patton, "Forgiveness: Pastoral Care and Counseling," in Michael E. McCullough, op. cit., 289.

page 216 *"end up replacing resentment with alienation"* Robert Enright, *Forgiveness Is a Choice* (Washington, DC: American Psychological Association, 2001), 36.

page 216 *"resulting in not only failure to treat the addiction, but, in some cases, the murder of the 'forgiver'"* Sharon Lamb and Jeffrie G. Murphy, eds. *Before Forgiving: Cautionary Views of Forgiveness in Psychotherapy* (New York: Oxford University Press, 2002), 89.

10. LOVING THE MONSTER

page 231 *"I felt pity to see this man destroyed"* Jason Horowitz, "Pity for Hussein at the Vatican," *New York Times,* December 17, 2003, A20.

11. ANOTHER LITTLE PEACE OF THE HEART

page 247   *"Revengefulness is that passion which ariseth . . ."*   Thomas Hobbes, *The Elements of Law Natural and Politic: Part I, Human Nature, Part II, De corpore politico; with Three Lives,* ed. with an introduction by J. C. A. Gaskin (New York: Oxford University Press, 1994), 52.

page 256   *"Self-esteem is in large measure a function of the esteem accorded"*   D. L. Horowitz, *Ethnic Groups in Conflict* (Berkeley: University of California Press, 1985).

page 261   *"People would often rather die than live with such a sense of shame"*   Neil Altman, "Humiliation, Retaliation, and Violence," *Tikkun* 19, no. 1 (January-February 2004): 17.

page 261   *"'never again' to be subject to such humiliation as to be helpless prey to a ruthless predator"*   Neil Altman, Ibid.

pages 262–263   *"Each group nourishes its own pride and vanity"*   William G. Sumner and Albert G. Keller, *Folkways: A Study of the Sociological Importance of Usages, Manners, Customs, Mores and Morals* (Boston: Ginn, 1906).

page 263   *" 'We are men, the rest are something else' "*   William G. Sumner, *War and Other Essays* (New Haven: Yale University Press, 1911).

page 263   *"all other peoples are a degeneration from their pure stock"*   Johan M. G. Van der Dennen, "Of Badges, Bonds and Boundaries: Ingroup/Outgroup Differentiation and Ethnocentrism Revisited," Proceedings of Fifth Annual Meeting of the European Sociobiological Society, St. John's College, Oxford, UK, January 5–6, 1995, 97.

page 263   *rival tribes were linguistically lumped with game animals*   R. F. Murphy, "Intergroup Hostility and Social Cohesion," *American Anthropologist* 59 (1957): 1018–35. Also see R. F. Murphy, *Headhunter's Heritage* (Berkeley: University of California Press, 1960).

page 266   *"The injury cannot be healed"*   Primo Levi, *The Drowned and the Saved,* ed. Erroll McDonald, trans. Raymond Rosenthal (New York: Random House, 1988), 12.

page 273   *"Irrational beliefs serve the purpose far better than rational ones"*   Robert Bigelow, *The Dawn Warriors: Man's Evolution towards Peace* (Boston: Little Brown, 1969).

12. THE BELOVED COMMUNITY

pages 282–290 The author wishes to thank Courtney Cowart for granting generous access to her unpublished interview transcripts, from which some quotes are drawn.

page 289 *"As I stood with them and saw white and Negro . . ."* Martin Luther King, *Where Do We Go from Here: Chaos or Community?* (New York: Harper & Row, 1967), 284.

page 291 *"The economy of nature is competitive from beginning to end"* Michael Ghiselin, *The Economy of Nature and the Evolution of Sex* (Berkeley: University of California Press, 1974).

page 293 *"The heart brightens up [akarui]"* Jonathan Haidt, "Elevation and the Positive Psychology of Morality," in *Flourishing: Positive Psychology and the Life Well-Lived,* eds. Corey L. Mikeyes and Jonathan Haidt (Washington, D.C.: American Psychological Association, 2003), 283.

page 294 *"elevated sentiments" upon seeing "an act of charity"* Ibid., 284.

page 294 *"there is good in people, love is real, it's in our nature"* Ibid., 287.

13. ALL MY RELATIONS

page 308 *the snails dying off in large numbers* U.S. Fish & Wildlife Service Region 3 Endangered Species Press Release, http://midwest.fws.gov/endangered/Snails/tcca-8-02-nr.html.

page 309 *"Life itself was something to be valued for these altruists"* Kristin Renwick Monroe, op. cit., 206–7.

SELECT BIBLIOGRAPHY

BOOKS

Aczel, Amir D. *"Entanglement" The Greatest Mystery in Physics.* New York: Four Walls Eight Windows, 2002.

Batson, C. Daniel. *The Altruism Question: Toward a Social Psychological Answer.* Hillsdale, NJ: L. Erlbaum, 1991.

Bigelow, Robert. *The Dawn Warriors: Man's Evolution towards Peace.* Boston: Little Brown, 1969.

Buber, Martin. *Tales of Hassidim: The Early Masters.* Translated by Olga Marx. New York: Schocken Books, 1947.

Cory, Gerald A., and Russell Gardner Jr., eds. *Evolutionary Neuroethology of Paul MacLean: Convergences and Frontiers.* Foreword by Jaak Panksepp. Westport, CT: Praeger Publishers, 2002.

Damasio, Antonio. *Looking for Spinoza: Joy, Sorrow, and the Feeling Brain.* Orlando, FL: Harcourt, 2003.

Davidson, Richard J., and Anne Harrington. *Visions of Compassion: Western Scientists and Tibetan Buddhists Examine Human Nature.* New York: Oxford University Press, 2002.

De Waal, Frans, and Frans Lanting. *Bonobo: The Forgotten Ape.* Berkeley: University of California Press, 1997.

De Waal, Frans. *The Ape and the Sushi Master: Cultural Reflections by a Primatologist.* New York: Basic Books-Perseus Publishing, 2001.

Dorje, Wang-ch'ug. *The Mahamudra: Eliminating the Darkness of Ignorance.* Translated by Alexander Berzin. Dharmsala, India: Library of Tibetan Works and Archives, 1978.

Dresner, Samuel H. *Levi Yitzhak of Berditchev: Portrait of a Hasidic Master.* New York: Shapolsky Publishers, 1986.

Emmons, Robert A. "Personality and Forgiveness." In *Forgiveness: Theory, Research and Practice,* edited by Michael E. McCullough, Carl E. Thoresen, Kenneth I. Pargament. New York: Guilford Press, 2001.

Enright, Robert. *Forgiveness Is a Choice.* Washington, DC: American Psychological Association, 2001.

Fuller, Robert W. *Sombodies and Nobodies: Overcoming the Abuse of Rank.* Robert W. Fuller. Gabriola Island, B.C., Canada: New Society Publishers, 2003.

Ghiselin, Michael. *The Economy of Nature and the Evolution of Sex.* Berkeley: University of California Press, 1974.

Glassman, Bernie. *Bearing Witness.* New York: Bell Tower-Random House, 1999.

Gobodo-Madikizela, Pumla. *A Human Being Died That Night: A South African Story of Forgiveness.* Boston: Houghton Mifflin, 2003.

Goleman, Daniel. *Destructive Emotions: How Can We Overcome Them?* New York: Bantam Books, 2003.

Haidt, Jonathan. "Elevation and the Positive Psychology of Morality. In *"Flourishing: Positive Psychology and the Life Well-Lived,* edited by Corey L. Mikeyes and Jonathan Haidt. Washington, DC: American Psychological Association, 2003.

Hobbes, Thomas. *The Elements of Law Natural and Politic: Part I, Human Nature, Part II, De corpore politico; with Three Lives.* Edited with an introduction by J. C. A. Gaskin. New York: Oxford University Press, 1994.

Horowitz, D. L. *Ethnic Groups in Conflict.* Berkeley: University of California Press, 1985.

Kierkegaard, Søren. *Works of Love.* Edited and translated by Howard V. Hong and Edna H. Hong. Princeton, NJ: Princeton University Press, 1995.

King, Martin Luther. *Where Do We Go from Here: Chaos or Community?* New York: Harper & Row, 1967.

King, Rachel. *Don't Kill in Our Names.* New Brunswick, NJ: Rutgers University Press, 2003.

Kohn, Alfie. *The Brighter Side of Human Nature: Altruism and Empathy in Everyday Life.* New York: Basic Books, 1990.

Krebs, Dennis, and Christine Russell. "Role-Taking and Altruism: When You Put Yourself in the Shoes of Another, Will They Take You to Their Owner's Aid?" In *Altruism and Helping Behavior,* edited by J. Philippe Rushton and Richard M. Sorrentino. Hillsdale, NJ: Lawrence Erlbaum Associates, 1981.

Kropotkin, Peter. *Mutual Aid: A Factor of Evolution.* Boston, MA: Porter Sargent Publishers, 1976.

Lamb, Sharon, and Jeffrie G. Murphy, eds. *Before Forgiving: Cautionary Views of Forgiveness in Psychotherapy.* New York: Oxford University Press, 2002.

Levi, Primo. *The Drowned and the Saved.* Edited by Erroll McDonald. Translated by Raymond Rosenthal. New York: Random House, 1988.

Loye, David. *Darwin's Lost Theory of Love: A Healing Vision for the New Century.* Lincoln, NE: iUniverse.com, 1998.

McCullough, Michael E., Kenneth I. Pargament, and Carle E. Thorsen, eds. *Forgiveness: Theory, Research, and Practice.* New York: The Guilford Press, 2000.

Monroe, Kristin Renwick. *The Heart of Altruism: Perceptions of a Common Humanity.* Princeton, NJ: Princeton University Press, 1996.

Oliner, Samuel P. *Do Unto Others.* Boulder, CO: Westview Press, 2004.

Oliner, Samuel, and Pearl Oliner. *The Altruistic Personality: Rescuers of Jews in Nazi Europe.* New York: The Free Press, 1988.

Peterson, Dale, and Richard Wrangham. *Demonic Males: Apes and the Origins of Human Violence.* Boston: Mariner Books-Houghton Mifflin, 1997.

Pickering, Mary. *Auguste Comte: An Intellectual Biography vol. 1.* Cambridge, MA: Cambridge University Press, 1993.

Piechowski, M. M. "Emotional Giftedness: The Measure of Interpersonal Intelligence." In *Handbook of Gifted Education,* edited by Nicholas Colangelo and Gary A. Davis. 2nd ed. Needham Heights, MA: Allyn and Bacon, 1997.

Pinker, Steven. *The Blank Slate: The Modern Denial of Human Nature.* New York: Viking, 2002.

Post, Stephen G., and Lynne G. Underwood, et al. *Altruism and Altruistic Love: Science, Philosophy, and Religion in Dialogue.* New York: Oxford University Press, 2002.

Rose, Hilary, and Steven Rose. *Alas Poor Darwin: Arguments Against Evolutionary Psychology.* New York: Harmony Books-Random House, 2000.

Rushton, J. Philippe, and Richard M. Sorrentino, eds. *Altruism and Helping Behavior.* Hillsdale, NJ: Lawrence Erlbaum Associates, 1981.

Savage-Rumbaugh, Sue, and Roger Lewin. *Kanzi, The Ape at the Brink of a Human Mind.* New York: John Wiley and Sons, 1994.

Schwartz, Jeffrey M., and Sharon Begley. *The Mind and the Brain: Neuroplasticity and the Power of Mental Force.* New York: Regan Books-Harper Collins, 2003.

Shantideva. *The Way of the Bodhisattva.* Translated by Padmakara Translation Group. Boston: Shambhala Press, 1997.

Smith, Adam. *The Theory of Moral Sentiments.* Cambridge, UK: Cambridge University Press, 2002.

Sober, Elliott, and David Sloan Wilson. *Unto Others: The Evolution and Psychology of Unselfish Behavior.* Cambridge, MA: Harvard University Press, 1998.

Stein, Edith. *On the Problem of Empathy.* Translated by Waltraut Stein. The Hague: Martinus Nijhoff, 1964.

Sumner, William G. *War and Other Essays.* New Haven, CT: Yale University Press, 1911.

Surrey, Janet L. "The Self-in-Relation." *In Women's Growth in Connection,* edited by Janet L. Surrey, Judith V. Jordan, et al., New York: The Guilford Press, 1991.

Teilhard, de Chardin Pier. *The Phenomenon of Man.* New York: Harper and Brothers Publishers, 1959.

Thoreson, Carl E., Alex H. S. Harris, and Frederic Luskin. "Forgiveness and Health: An Unanswered Question." In *Forgiveness: Theory, Research, and Practice,* edited by Michael E. McCullough, et al. New York: The Guilford Press, 2000.

Ury, William. *The Third Side: Why We Fight and How We Can Stop.* New York: Penguin, 2003.

Von Kreisler, Kristin. *Beauty in the Beasts: True Stories of Animals Who Choose to Do Good.* New York: Jeremy P. Tarcher-Penguin Group, 2002.

Wright, Robert. *The Moral Animal: The New Science of Evolutionary Psychology.* New York: Pantheon Books-Random House, 1994.

ARTICLES/PAPERS

Altman, Neil. "Humiliation, Retaliation, and Violence." *Tikkun* 19, no. 1 (January-February 2004): 17.

Brothers, Leslie. "A Biological Perspective on Empathy." *American Journal of Psychiatry* 146, no. 1 (1989): 10–19.

Campbell, W. K., E. Rudich, and C. Sedikides. "Narcissism, Self-Esteem, and the Positivity of Self-Views: Two Portraits of Self-Love." *Personality and Social Psychology Bulletin* 28 (2002): 358–68.

Darren, G., Patrice Carroll, et al. "Gender-Related Patterns of Helping Among Friends." *Psychology of Women Quarterly* 22 (1998): 685–704.

Frankel, Estelle. "Sweetening the Judgements: The Kabbalah of Compassion." *Parabola* 28, no. 1 (2003): 14–15.

Haidt, Jonathan. "The Emotional Dog and Its Rational Tail: A Social Intuitionist Approach to Moral Judgment." *Psychological Review* 108 (2001): 814–34.

Hall, Stephen S. "Is Buddhism Good for Your Health?" *New York Times,* September 14, 2003, sec. 6: 46+.

Kohn, Alfie. "Beyond Selfishness." *Psychology Today* (October 1998): 34–38.

Levin, Jeff. "A Prolegomenon to an Epidemiology of Love: Theory, Measurement, and Health Outcomes." *Journal of Social and Clinical Psychology* 19 (2000):117–36.

Lipman, M. "Caring Thinking." Proceedings of the Sixth International Conference on Thinking, Massachusetts Institute of Technology, Boston, MA, July 17–22, 1994.

McClelland, David C. "Some Reflections on the Two Psychologies of Love." *Journal of Personality* 54, no. 2 (June 1986): 344–49.

McDonald, Michael F., Antonia J. Z. Henderson, Monica A. Landolt, et al. "The Living Anonymous Kidney Donor: Lunatic or Saint?" *American Journal of Transplantation* 3 (2003): 203–213.

Murphy, R. F. "Intergroup Hostility and Social Cohesion." *American Anthropologist* 59 (1957): 1018–35.

O'Connell, Sanjida M. "Empathy in Chimpanzees: Evidence for Theory of Mind?" *Primates* 36, no. 3 (July 1995): 401.

Pinker, S. "Is There a Gene for Compassion?" Review of *The Moral Animal,* by Robert Wright. *New York Times* (September 25, 1994): BR3+.

Preston, S. D., and Frans B. M. de Waal. "Empathy: Its Ultimate and Proximate Bases." *Behavioral and Brain Sciences.* August 2001. http://www.bbsonline.org/Preprints/Preston/.

Silverman, L. K. "The Moral Sensitivity of Gifted Children and the Evolution of Society." *Roeper Review* 17, no. 2 (1994): 110–16.

Van der Dennen, Johan M.G. *"Of Badges, Bonds and Boundaries: Ingroup/Outgroup Differentiation and Ethnocentrism Revisited."* Proceedings of the Fifth Annual Meeting of the European Sociobiological Society, St. John's College, Oxford, UK, January 5–6, 1995.

Zahn-Wexler, Carolyn, and Marian Radke-Yarrow. "The Origins of Empathic Concern." *Motivation and Emotion* 14, no. 2 (1990): 107–30.

INDEX